Public Relations and Marketing for Archives

A How-To-Do-It Manual®

Edited by
Russell D. James
and Peter J. Wosh

HOW-TO-DO-IT MANUALS®

NUMBER 176

Society of American Archivists
Chicago

Neal-Schuman Publishers, Inc.
New York   London

Co-published by:

Society of American Archivists
17 North State St., Suite 1425
Chicago, IL 60602
http://www.archivists.org

Neal-Schuman Publishers, Inc.
100 William St., Suite 2004
New York, NY 10038
http://www.neal-schuman.com

Library of Congress Cataloging-in-Publication Data

Public relations and marketing for archives : a how-to-do-it manual / edited by Russell D. James and Peter J. Wosh.
  p. cm. — (How-to-do-it manuals ; no. 176)
  Includes bibliographical references and index.
  ISBN 978-1-55570-733-0 (alk. paper)
  1. Archives—Public relations—Handbooks, manuals, etc. I. James, Russell D. II. Wosh, Peter J.

CD971.P83 2011
021.7—dc23
                                                              2011026898

Contents

Contents

List of Figures

Preface

Successful archivists make their institutions vital in many ways, not the least of which is engaging in public relations and marketing activities. They publicize their exhibits and public programs, highlight significant materials on their websites, and give presentations to community and school groups. Many archivists receive minimal formal training on how to maximize public relations or marketing activities. Archives, especially in times of financial cutbacks and other worries, need to use public relations and marketing in order to increase awareness of their mission to safeguard the history of the communities they serve and to remain competitive in the race for continued funding. *Public Relations and Marketing for Archives: A How-To-Do-It Manual* is designed to help archivists plan and implement effective marketing and public relations that reach every segment of their potential audience, from users to donors.

Archivists must keep in mind that the concepts of public relations and marketing are vital to the operation of an archives. They are so important, in fact, that archivists should include some statement of the need for such programming in their mission statement, such as:

> *The archives shall collect, preserve, maintain, and make available to the public materials of an historical nature that express and evidence the history of the local community. Through marketing and public relations activities, the historical materials will be made accessible to the public.*

Although this statement expresses only a minimal conception of what archives can do in regard to marketing and public relations, it conveys the critical nature of marketing to the value of an archives. Rather than wait for researchers to visit the archives, prudent archivists will actively engage in public relations and marketing activities to the communities they serve, enticing them to become intellectual colleagues and perhaps even financial supporters.

Public Relations and Marketing for Archives: A How-To-Do-It Manual is designed to help answer such questions as:

- What specific presentation strategies should the archivist consider when speaking to groups ranging from middle-school student to seasoned genealogists?
- What are the best ways to use photographs in a public relations campaign?

- What are the critical elements to include in a press kit promoting an upcoming exhibit?
- How can a blog or other social media be used as a public relations vehicle?
- How can a website effectively promote an upcoming exhibit?

These, as well as a host of other practical questions, are addressed in the following chapters. Our contributors include a variety of experts who have managed marketing campaigns for their archives.

This book's 12 chapters are arranged in two major parts. "Part I: Approaches" contains seven chapters, each devoted to one critical public relations vehicle: websites, social media, blogging, media outlets, press kits and news releases, newsletters, and visual materials. "Part II: Audiences" concentrates on five important recipients of our public relations and marketing strategies: those who come to our educational programming events; those who attend our public presentations; historical societies, genealogists, and volunteers; donors; and college students.

In the pages that follow, you will find examples, forms, and/or checklists to help make implementation easier. References and Additional Resources point readers toward a broader outreach in the literature of the archives, museum studies, and the public relations fields. Each contributor focuses on practical approaches to public relations and marketing and encourages archivists to engage in careful evaluation activities. At the end of each chapter, "The Plan" relates the chapter contents to the marketing plan to help readers construct their own planning documents. A sample marketing plan, which can be adapted to a variety of institutional settings and environments, is included as an appendix. The best plans are developed as a holistic piece, with each strategy directed to help achieve a universal vision for reaching all segments of the audience.

Public Relations and Marketing for Archives provides a starting place for archivists who want to publicize and market their collections and services, showing how to begin the process through careful planning, execution, and evaluation of these activities to such audiences/communities as funders, donors, volunteers, students of all ages, and the community at large. It has been designed to offer concrete tools for novices and experts who want to make sure their plans and their execution are as effective as possible at raising the profile of their archives.

Introduction

Peter J. Wosh

American archivists have long lamented their seeming ineffectiveness at mounting successful public relations efforts. William David McCain (1907–1993), the ardent segregationist who helped both to found the Society of American Archivists (SAA) and to revitalize the Sons of the Confederate Veterans, first directed professional attention toward this problem in October 1939. At the time, McCain was serving as director of the Mississippi Department of Archives and History, and he viewed the third annual meeting of the recently established SAA as an ideal opportunity to discourse on "The Public Relations of Archival Depositories." McCain (1940) informed his archival colleagues that "I have listened to enough private discussions and complaints during the past three years to convince me that archival officials have devoted insufficient attention to the cultivations of friendly relations with the general public" (p. 235). The Mississippian outlined an ambitious outreach program that included cajoling newspapermen, making common cause with the genealogists, delivering humorous talks at Rotary Club meetings and Kiwanis luncheons, lecturing local college classes, and lobbying legislators. McCain admitted, however, that experiences in Mississippi did not always provide a positive blueprint for public relations action. He specifically recalled that "at one time relations between the department [of archives and history] and the legislature became so strained that one of its members, a former Populist candidate for governor, struck the director over the head with a heavy hickory cane"; in response, "the director carried a loaded pistol in anticipation of further altercations" (p. 240). Still, McCain concluded, the advantages of aggressive public relations activities outweighed the dangers: "the success or failure of an archivist depends largely upon the number of friends he makes for himself and his work" (p. 244).

Few subsequent archivists have advocated carrying concealed weapons as part of their outreach strategies, but the profession has taken great strides in recent years to craft new relationships with users and potential allies. Over the past 30 years, conference presenters, graduate educators, association consultants, and workshop leaders have urged archivists to pay greater attention to advocacy and outreach. Mary Jo Pugh has traced this transformation to the mid-1980s, arguing that archivists began eschewing their "materials-centered" biases and taking a more "user-centered" approach to archives administration (Pugh, 2005). As McCain's early paper indicates, however, such ideas and concepts actually had been percolating around archival circles for decades. Still, a growing literature that began to coalesce in the 1980s and 1990s clearly signaled some new professional priorities. Elsie Freeman Finch, who served a long and distinguished tenure as chief of the Education Branch of the National Archives, led this movement. In 1994 she edited an especially influential collection of essays, *Advocating Archives: An Introduction to Public Relations for Archivists.* Archival contributors to Finch's book related their experiences in working with media outlets, marketing to corporate audiences, raising funds, recruiting volunteers, organizing friends' groups, and managing anniversaries. The text quickly became required reading in graduate education programs, and it also spawned a lively monographic literature in such journals as the *American Archivist*, *Archivaria*, *Archival Issues*, *Provenance*, and similar publications (Finch, 1994).

Finch's work has endured as a useful and foundational public relations text in the archives community. Several factors make this an opportune moment to build on her foundational work. First and foremost, technology undeniably has transformed the North American communications infrastructure over the past 15 years. New media commentator Clay Shirky has argued that "everyone is a media outlet" in the Internet Age and that "our social tools remove older obstacles to public expression, and thus remove the bottlenecks that characterized mass media" (Shirky, 2008). Whether or not readers accept Shirky's view that such changes invariably lead to greater democratization and freedom, new media clearly offer enhanced opportunities for both creating and connecting with communities of interest. Archivists have only begun to explore the possibilities for reconfiguring their own outreach efforts. Kate Theimer has written extensively on the ways in which archivists and manuscript curators might appropriate social networking technologies to develop their programs (Theimer, 2010). Gordon Daines and Cory Nimer (2009) have edited a series of case studies highlighting actual archival implementations of web-based strategies to reach new audiences. *Public Relations and Marketing for Archives* contributes to this developing dialogue. Michele M. Lavoie, Lauren Oostveen, and Lisa Grimm discuss the ways in which websites, social media, and blogging constitute core components of any public relations program in 2011. This book, however, does not neglect more traditional ways of working with media, as evidenced by the contributions of Stephanie Gaub, Russell James, and William Jordan Patty. Still, new media take center stage here in a way that would have been unimaginable just 15 years ago.

Second, contemporary archivists have a much more nuanced and comprehensive approach toward their researchers. User studies have proliferated throughout the archival literature over the past decade, and the profession now enjoys a sophisticated understanding of its diverse clientele. Elizabeth Yakel and Deborah Torres have argued in another context that archivists need to learn how to increase their users' "archival intelligence," and *Public Relations and Marketing for Archives* contains several strategies for fostering more effective communication with all users (Yakel and Torres, 2003). The chapters in this book by Maria Mazzenga and Elizabeth A. Myers, who discuss educational programming and public speaking, respectively, offer particularly helpful advice in this regard. Archivists in recent years also have focused on the need to attract new audiences and communities. *Public Relations and Marketing for Archives* especially speaks to their concerns. If earlier generations of manuscript curators viewed their repositories primarily as resources for scholars and administrators, contemporary archivists articulate a more inclusive approach. One specific case illustrates the broader point. Gregory Jackson's chapter, "College Students," contributes to a literature that has exploded in the past five years. Magia Krause (2010), Janet Bunde and Deena Engel (2010), Peter Carini (2009), Doris Malkmus (2008), Wendy Duff and Joan Cherry (2008), Xiaomu Zhou (2008), and Peter J. Wosh et al. (2007) have all contributed case studies, survey research articles, and ethnographic treatments of this subject. This book thus reflects archivists' convictions that they need to attract and relate to broader audiences who bring different levels of knowledge and understanding to their collections. At the same time, traditional users receive their due. Suzanne Campbell's emphasis on heritage groups and genealogical societies, as well as Victoria Arel Lucas's focus on donors, would both have been very familiar topics for William David McCain to consider when he penned his public relations piece in 1939.

Third, advocacy has assumed a new prominence in archival thought. In recent years, SAA presidents have attempted to stake out professional positions on controversial topics, and the society itself has adopted advocacy as a key strategic planning objective. American Archives Month and similar programs have attempted to raise professional visibility, and individual repositories have made greater efforts to market their programs in a more creative fashion. *Public Relations and Marketing for Archives* clearly demonstrates the ways in which effective public relations programs can intersect with outreach endeavors to build support for archivists' agendas. Larry Hackman has defined advocacy as "activities consciously aimed to persuade individuals or organizations to act on behalf of a program or institution," and the following chapters in this book nicely complement his *Many Happy Returns: Advocacy for Archives and Archivists* (Hackman, 2011: vii). Successful program leadership involves building constituencies, nurturing supporters, and strengthening institutional infrastructures. Unless archives administrators cultivate the formal and informal relationships that allow them to grow their operations, they fundamentally fail. Positive public relations programs require sustained activity, committed professional staff, and hard work. Archivists should view pubic relations as a core component of their work rather than an added burden. Most critically, they need to create, in Hackman's words, an "opportunity agenda" that strategically pursues well-defined goals. Although public relations and outreach activities remain distinct

American Archives Month
For more information, visit:
http://www.archivists.org/initiatives/american-archives-month.

from advocacy, they form the building blocks on which strong archival advocacy programs rest.

Advocacy, user relations, and technology all figure prominently in the following chapters. Russell James assembled many of the authors in this book with the goal of creating a useful practitioner-based resource. The working archivists and curators who contributed to this volume possess extensive experience in managing public relations activities for their institutions. They present their suggestions in clear and understandable prose, making good use of examples, forms, checklists, and links to relevant resources throughout the volume. Bibliographic notes and web citations point readers toward a broader outreach literature in the archives, museum studies, and public relations fields. Each contributor focuses on practical guidelines and encourages archivists to engage in careful evaluation activities. At the end of each chapter, "The Plan" summarizes the contents and provides the necessary blueprint for readers to construct their own planning documents. A sample marketing plan, which can be adapted to a variety of institutional settings and environments, is included as an appendix.

Public Relations and Marketing for Archives does not claim to constitute the definitive work on this topic. Rather, it seeks to synthesize best practices and provide a useful toolkit for planning effective programs. All archivists engage in public relations and marketing activities. They often work in institutional isolation, however, and do not always have the time or opportunity to share their special insights with colleagues. This book demonstrates the value of working outward from particular programs to formulate general principles. It also illustrates the importance of archivists in smaller and medium-sized institutions contributing to the growing body of public relations and marketing literature within the profession. Finally, it confirms some of the prescient comments made by William David McCain more than 70 years ago. Archivists do indeed need to make friends with reporters, donors, users, and allied professionals. They should also adapt insights from the marketing, public relations, and communications industries to their own operations. If their current climate appears more congenial and less confrontational than the legislative halls of early twentieth-century Mississippi, archivists still face substantial programmatic challenges that require strategic approaches, careful planning, and perhaps an occasional hickory cane.

References

Bunde, Janet, and Deena Engel. 2010. "Computing in the Humanities: An Interdisciplinary Partnership in Undergraduate Education." *Journal of Archival Organization* 8, no. 2: 149–159.

Carini, Peter. 2009. "Archivists as Educators: Integrating Primary Sources into the Curriculum." *Journal of Archival Organization* 7, no. 1: 41–50.

Daines, J. Gordon III, and Corey L. Nimer, eds. 2009. "Web 2.0 and Archives." *The Interactive Archivist: Case Studies in Utilizing Web 2.0 to Improve the Archival Experience.* Chicago: Society of American Archivists. http://lib.byu.edu/sites/interactivearchivist.

Duff, Wendy, and Joan Cherry. 2008. "Archival Orientation for Undergraduate Students: An Exploratory Study of Impact." *American Archivist* 71, no. 2: 499–529.

Finch, Elsie Freeman. 1994. *Advocating Archives: An Introduction to Public Relations for Archivists.* Metuchen, NJ: Society of American Archivists and Scarecrow Press.

Hackman, Larry. 2011. *Many Happy Returns: Advocacy for Archives and Archivists.* Chicago: Society of American Archivists.

Krause, Magia G. 2010. "Undergraduates in the Archives: Using an Assessment Rubric to Measure Learning." *American Archivist* 73 (Fall/Winter): 507–534.

Malkmus, Doris J. 2008. "Primary Source Research and the Undergraduate: A Transforming Landscape." *Journal of Archival Organization* 6, no. 1–2: 47–70.

McCain, William D. 1940. "The Public Relations of Archival Depositories." *American Archivist* 3 (October): 235–244.

Pugh, Mary Jo. 2005. *Providing Reference Services for Archives and Manuscripts.* Chicago: Society of American Archivists.

Shirky, Clay. 2008. *Here Comes Everybody: The Power of Organizing Without Organizations.* New York: Penguin Press.

Theimer, Kate. 2010. *Web 2.0 Tools and Strategies for Archives and Local History Collections.* New York: Neal-Schuman.

Wosh, Peter J., Janet Bunde, Karen Murphy, and Chelsea Blacker. 2007. "University Archives and Educational Partnerships: Three Perspectives." *Archival Issues* 31, no. 1: 83–103.

Yakel, Elizabeth, and Deborah A. Torres. 2003. "AI: Archival Intelligence and User Expertise." *American Archivist* 66, no. 1: 51–78.

Zhou, Xiaomu. 2008. "Student Archival Research Activity: An Exploratory Study." *American Archivist* 71, no. 2: 476–498.

Approaches

Websites

Michele M. Lavoie

Introduction

As little as five years ago, most archival literature made only brief mention of the Internet as a public relations tool and often relegated institutional websites to the bottom of the list. Today, however, websites are as ubiquitous as any printed public relations literature and every bit as important. How often do you wonder about a brand or entity and immediately check out its website? What is your reaction to finding a poorly designed, ill-maintained site—or worse yet, no site at all? Will visitors to your institution's website have the same reaction?

The digital environment of today demands that archival institutions not only have a web presence but that they provide quality content to their would-be users. While the very thought of writing lines of code can be extremely daunting (see Figure 1.1 for a snippet of code from the National Archives and Records Administration website), archivists should not shy away from translating the traditional forms of public relations and outreach—brochures, pamphlets, even finding aids—to an online resource for its user base. Even the most technologically challenged archivist can create quality content that connects his or her institution with its intended audience . . . and leave the coding to someone else, if necessary.

This chapter will focus on the elements a successful website should include and why. It will not discuss such topics as HTML vs. XML, what software to use, or similar topics, as there are many other resources infinitely better suited for such discussions. Once you have determined what you want on your site, there are plenty of sources that will guide you in choosing a content management system or even how to encode a site by hand.

Getting Started

A well-done website is one of the most powerful tools an institution can use to promote its collections. The first step in creating a website is to

Figure 1.1. An Example of XHTML Codes from the National Archives Website

```
<!DOCTYPE html PUBLIC "-//W3C//DTD XHTML 1.0 Transitional//EN" "http://www.w3.org/TR/xhtml1/DTD/xhtml1-
    transitional.dtd">
<html xmlns="http://www.w3.org/1999/xhtml">

<head>
<title>Regulations for Using the National Archives</title>
<meta http-equiv="Content-Type" content="text/html; charset=iso-8859-1" />
<meta http-equiv="Content-Language" content="en-US" />
<link rel="icon" href="/favicon.ico" type="image/x-icon" />
<link rel="shortcut icon" href="/favicon.ico" />
<link rel="image_src" href="http://www.archives.gov/global-images/logos/nara-archives.gov-blue-100.gif" />
<meta http-equiv="imagetoolbar" content="no" />
<meta name="y_key" content="0e94d8e9e5732ec6" />
<meta name="description" content="Anyone can use the National Archives. You do not need to be an American citizen or
    to present credentials or a letter of recommendation. Information about holdings of and use of the Research Rooms
    of the United States National Archives and Records Administration" />
<meta name="date" content="2007-04-13" />
<meta http-equiv="PICS-Label" content='(PICS-1.1 "http://www.weburbia.com/safe/ratings.htm" l r (s 0))' />
<meta name="rating" content="general" />
<meta name="distribution" content="global" />
<script type="text/javascript" src="/includes/javascript/archives/oeTriggerParams.js"></script>
<script type="text/javascript" src="/includes/javascript/archives/oeLauncher.js"></script>


<script type="text/javascript">var sectionSearchOn = true;</script>

<script type="text/javascript">
var GB_ROOT_DIR = "http://www.archives.gov/includes/greybox/greybox/";
</script>
<script type="text/javascript" src="/includes/javascript/jquery.js"></script>
<script type="text/javascript" src="/includes/javascript/jquery.common.js"></script>
<script type="text/javascript" src="/includes/javascript/sortable/tablesort.js"></script>
<script type="text/javascript" src="/includes/javascript/sortable/customsort.js"></script>
<script type="text/javascript" src="/includes/greybox/greybox/AJS.js"></script>
<script type="text/javascript" src="/includes/greybox/greybox/AJS_fx.js"></script>
<script type="text/javascript" src="/includes/greybox/greybox/gb_scripts.js"></script>
<!--<script type="text/javascript" src="/includes/greybox/greybox/greybox.js"></script>-->
<link href="/includes/greybox/greybox/gb_styles.css" rel="stylesheet" type="text/css" media="all" />

    <script type="text/javascript">

    var GB_ANIMATION = true;
    $(document).ready(function(){
```

Source: http://www.archives.gov/research/start/nara-regulations.html.

assemble a team of stakeholders who will be responsible for developing and maintaining the site throughout its life cycle. These individuals can include other archives staff, library personnel, information technologists, the director or head of the institution, and even trustees. Each person should be chosen based on the particular perspective and expertise he or she brings to the table. Not everyone needs to have the same technological abilities, but if you have access to a website designer, you certainly want to ask that individual to join the group.

One caveat about website teams: too many cooks really can spoil the stew. Website by committee can spell disaster if there are too many people trying to voice too many opinions. The website team should be bound by one common goal—to promote the institution—and that goal should guide all actions taken in the development of the site's content and design. For this and other reasons, many experts on website design recommend drafting a one-sentence statement that summarizes the goal of the project. If (and when) the team finds itself at an impasse on a particular subject, refer to that summary statement to remind everyone what they are collectively trying to achieve; then ask how the task at hand can best accomplish that goal.

Planning, Planning, and More Planning

Like any undertaking, developing a website can falter right from the start if you do not plan accordingly. You cannot actually plan every aspect of a website; inevitably, some things will not develop as envisioned, and those initial objectives may change along the way—sometimes drastically. But this is true of every endeavor, and there must be a plan of attack to begin a project of this caliber. Whether you are on your own in a one-person shop or you are one of 20 team members, your team will need forethought, forecasting, and plenty of preparation to make the website successful.

The following sections will guide you through the murky waters of creating your own content, pulling it all together, and putting it out there for the wider world to partake.

Walk, Don't Run . . .

Creating a website to promote your repository and make it accessible to the outside world is an admirable goal, but it is not an endeavor into which one should rush headlong. Instead, you and your team should do some research before heading to the drawing table. Take a look at the public relations tools your institution is already using with success. Do you have brochures or pamphlets describing your collections? What signage do you have around the archives? What is your "brand"? The answers to any or all of these questions can provide the perfect starting point.

During the planning phase, the website team should also devote considerable time to reviewing what peer institutions have done with their sites to determine what websites can look and feel like. Searching for the phrase "archives and special collections" will yield thousands of hits on any search engine, so it would be useful to narrow your scope. Start with institutions such as the National Archives and the Library of Congress to see what is being done on a large scale, and then work your way down. Figure 1.2 illustrates the types of information that an institutional website can include. Consider reviewing the sites of peer institutions in your region or of members of a consortium in which your archives participates. National and regional professional conferences usually list participating institutions on their own websites for additional browsing.

Following are some additional resources for researching websites:

ArchivesNext blog, Best Archives on the Web Awards
http://www.archivesnext.com/?cat=30

Since 2008, archival issues blogger Kate Theimer has recognized archival institutions that have excelled in promoting their

---

Who Should Be on a Website Team?

1. Archivists who will be responsible for selecting content for the website
2. Information technology staff who will be responsible for creating and maintaining the website
3. Institutional officers responsible for public relations of the institution
4. A legal representative to make sure no copyright or trademark laws are violated
5. Anyone else who is interested in helping to publicize the archives through the website

Figure 1.2. The Homepage for the Library of Congress's Manuscripts Division Reading Room

Note: This homepage places front and center such information as hours of operation, featured collections, and links to various researchers' tools.
Source: http://www.loc.gov/rr/mss.

repositories in categories such as "Best use of Web 2.0 technologies" and "Best web experience."

Ready, 'Net, Go! Archival Internet Resources
http://specialcollections.tulane.edu/ArchivesResources.html

Although this site has not been updated since 2007, this service of Tulane University's Special Collections remains one of the most utilized clearinghouses for accessing archival websites.

Repositories of Primary Resources
http://www.uiweb.uidaho.edu/special-collections/Other
.Repositories.html

Created and maintained by Terry Abraham of the University of Idaho since 1995, this site provides links to archival institutions all over the world.

It helps to bear in mind the old adage, "Do not bite off more than you can chew." In terms of planning a website, especially one built from scratch, it is imperative to *plan big and design smaller*. This means that during the planning phase, you can dream as big as you want to and select all of the features that you want. But when it comes to the final version and its implementation, you should select only those features that accurately reflect your goals for the site but also are entirely practical and doable for your unique situation. Remember, you can always add more functionality to a working website as your experience broadens; attempting too much right out of the gate can spell doom for your project. Therefore, it is essential that your team determine the institution's objectives for the site.

Planning a website can be the longest part of the website creation process. Allocate enough time for planning in light of the proposed launch date of the site. The more people on the committee, the longer the planning process, but planners who do not take their time may miss important steps along the way.

Defining Your Goals

Your institution has already expressed its interest in creating a website to promote its collections. But what *exactly* is the goal? What results do you and your fellow committee members hope to achieve by creating this site? What are the standards by which you would deem it to be a success?

Most institutions' website projects have started with the same simple goal: to get more people to come through the door. While this is an admirable—and entirely achievable—goal, do not be afraid to think bigger and more broadly. Start at the beginning: What do you want the website *to do* or *to be*? What should visitors take away from it? Is the website just a digital billboard that provides only the barest of details, such as your institution's address and hours of operation? Or is the end result a virtual version of your archives, with digital collections, online reference services, and a slew of other interactive media? It is imperative that the website development committee members clearly define these goals *before* any coding starts. Otherwise, you will be amazed at how quickly that simple website you envisioned can spiral out of control!

Defining Your Audience

Think of a new grocery shop opening in a community that does not have access to a large number of stores. The introduction of a conveniently

Questions to Ask (and Answer Honestly) in the Website Planning Process
- What do you hope to accomplish?
- What information do you want to convey to your audience?
- Are there better ways of conveying this information?
- What have you already done that can be translated to the Internet?
- What would you like to try?

located shop where residents can purchase the items they need would naturally excite people who have been traveling further afield to shop.

Now imagine that after weeks of hype, that little shop opens its doors...and instead of the convenient little grocer they expected, the would-be shoppers discover that the store is entirely stocked with the barest essentials, with no selection and absolutely no variety. The disappointed visitors will leave, dejected, without finding what they came for, and, more important, without buying anything. Why shop at this store, which is more convenient but has no real substance, when they need to go elsewhere anyway to get the things they still require? Eventually no one will come and the enterprise will close, all because the shop owners did not consider their audience.

This scenario is no different from that of a website. Before you begin debating whether to write a blog or digitize everything in your collections to include on the site, take a moment (several, actually) to consider your target audience. Who are you trying to reach? Are you aiming for the usual group of researchers, or is the idea to branch out to new and potentially unexpected visitors? Will your users be schoolchildren, educators, curiosity hounds, professional historians, amateur genealogists—or all of the above?

In addition to traditional demographics, you will also want to consider how technologically advanced your target group is. If your audience will be a diverse group of users who vary greatly in terms of level of computer literacy, you will want to strike a balance between cutting edge and lowest common denominator. Your site will do no good for those still using dial-up connections if it launches with a large Flash introduction or automatically plays embedded YouTube videos in a constant loop. Conversely, if you are creating a site for users who are familiar with such ubiquitous facets of social media as Twitter, blog aggregators, RSS feeds, or content-sharing applications like Digg or Reddit, they may be easily disappointed by a sequence of static pages that do not allow them to customize the content for their intended uses.

Assessing Your Resources

One common misstep that archives often make is underestimating the resources required to create and maintain a website, especially one designed to promote public relations. A website that is not updated regularly due to lack of time or knowledgeable staff is a poor public relations tool. Therefore, an important part of maintaining a website is to determine what and who you will need to keep it functioning.

Staffing

Make friends with the Information Technology or Computer Support staff, if your institution has one. Put student workers or interns to good use. If you are in a college or university or have access to a nearby campus, are there any computer science majors who are looking for a project? Are there other community service programs that can provide free help (high school graduation requirements, Boy Scout/Girl Scout projects, etc.)?

Who Is Your Audience?

1. Who are you trying to reach by creating this site?
2. What type of content will this intended user group want to see?
3. How will they want to use the content?
4. How "tech savvy" is your intended audience? Will you have a web-surfing grandmother with a DSL connection, a schoolchild in China connecting via satellite, or a CEO in New York who still uses his AOL account from 1998? What features will appeal to—and can be utilized by—all of them?
5. Can you predict a change in audience in the near future?
6. What services do you want to offer through the website?

Take advantage of volunteers with this skill set. Any of these scenarios can be combined with a mentoring project—for example, you can bring together technology professionals with interested student workers.

If you have the resources, consider outsourcing the design to a local firm that can work with your website team to develop the site. This is an option if you do not have access to other technology support or if you are apprehensive about tackling the design yourself. An added benefit of outsourcing is the continued maintenance of the site. Of course, this option requires that you have a steady, reliable source of funding to pay for these services.

Funding

Money is required for a lot of things—hardware (e.g., server, computers, scanners, digital cameras, etc.), software (e.g., Dreamweaver, PageMaker, InDesign, PhotoShop), services (e.g., purchased server space, IT support for implementation), preservation (combination of hardware like external drives, DVDs, etc., and services like "cloud" space, someone to download and apply metadata, etc.). How are you going to pay for it all? Many archives are naïve about where the money is to come from when planning for a website, thinking that the site itself is automatically going to generate revenue from the day it launches.

Will people pay to access content on your site? Will they tolerate banner or pop-up ads if a commercial vendor such as Yahoo! hosts your site? What are the copyright issues of "selling" digital content from archival collections? What are other issues? If your site manages to generate a revenue stream from any of these activities, how long will it take for that revenue to offset the operational costs?

If your institution already has funding budgeted for marketing, consider redirecting some of those monies away from traditional efforts such as brochures, letterhead, and posters and instead apply them to creating and maintaining a website that will serve nearly all these functions in one location. Be realistic about the cost to create and maintain the site, starting with a specific period of time. Consider not only how much it will cost but also how long it will take to see a return on investment.

Maintenance

Other public relations materials, like brochures, pamphlets, or bookmarks, require a lot of up-front time and effort but, once published, can be used for a long period of time without further revisions (unless some bit of information needs to be changed). However, websites require constant maintenance long after the initial effort is expended. This applies to content, structure, location, and software and/or coding.

Time

One major component of site maintenance is the time required to keep the site current both in terms of content and design. Just as you must budget adequate funding for the hardware, software, and staffing to keep your site functioning properly, you must consider in advance the amount of time your institution can afford to devote to this upkeep.

In general, using your institutional website as a public relations tool requires at the very least a few hours every week. As mentioned several times throughout this chapter, a website becomes a hindrance if its information is inaccurate or outdated. Avoiding this situation calls for a certain amount of vigilance. Calendars must be updated on a weekly basis to include all of an institution's important events or to ensure that only the most current information is included. Special announcements come up frequently, and a website gives you the ability to get the word out quickly to as many people as possible. However, there is no way of knowing exactly how much babysitting your individual site will require.

Instead, consider the design of your site—which parts will demand the most time and attention? How is the calendar of events arranged? Even a simple linked list of announcements may need older items retired when new are added. Static pages in HTML often require more time simply to rewrite the code as needed, such as with a calendar composed of tables and cells.

If you plan to incorporate a staff blog, the frequency of posts should be determined by the availability of the staff person(s) responsible for writing those entries. A small staff of just a few people who wear multiple hats may not be able to blog on a daily basis if they are working at capacity already (as is usually the case in institutions of that size). Tweeting or updating Facebook statuses will require even more of someone's time, so you may wish to designate one or two individuals—such as a volunteer or part-time worker—who are not carrying a significant workload to take over those duties to avoid overloading your full-time employees. (See Chapter 2 of this book for a more in-depth discussion of the nuts and bolts of using social media to promote your archives, and see Chapter 3 for more detailed information about blogs.)

In addition to normal maintenance, an institutional website will require periodic review to continue to ensure overall quality. In a perfect world, content remains entirely relevant forever, no links are ever broken, and spelling errors or typographical errors never slip past a series of editors. However, this is the real world, and those problems happen to everyone at some point or other. Your institution should include periodic reviews into its overall website policy, even if only on a yearly basis. This period of review can also be used to add significant amounts of new content, such as a new digital collection or additional visitor resources.

Content Is King

Once you have established your goals for the website, you will find that the content has practically presented itself. Content derives from purpose and, in turn, design is determined by the content, regardless of whether the site is built from scratch by volunteers or generated by a content management system. Your website should contain a few key elements to help you in furthering the reputation and profile of your institution.

> Ultimately, users visit your Web site for its content. Everything else is just the backdrop.
>
> —Jakob Nielsen, *Designing Web Usability* (2000)

About Us

The basic element of any archives' website should be the section that describes the institution—everything from where it is to its mission and scope. The "About Us" section is the Internet equivalent of the brochure or tour guide: it should serve as the starting point for all who visit the site.

Some institutions choose to share minimal details, such as contact information, hours of operation, or a mission statement. Others provide a more detailed history of the founding of the archives, major milestones and events in the life of the institution, and a vision for the future. Some archives put short biographies of staff members online so that visitors can learn a bit more about the people who work there and their qualifications and interests. Some institutions have allowed their creativity and sense of humor to liven up these sections, as demonstrated by Figure 1.3.

"About Us" can also provide the perfect venue for a staff blog documenting the activities of the archives. Such a feature continuously generates (with proper upkeep, of course) somewhat dynamic content to punctuate the basic static information also found in this section. Including an archives' mission statement, coupled with an archivist's blog demonstrating how that mission is being carried out, can highlight an institution's efforts and generate good publicity.

The tenor of the "About Us" section should set the tone for the rest of the site. Your audience should have a better sense of the kinds of information and features they will find once they have visited this section.

How much do you want your virtual visitors to learn about your institution from visiting this section of the website? Do you want to show them photographs of the physical space or just give them a location? Do you want to share your archives' purpose, collection policies and scope, and other institutional information, or do you simply want people to know when you are open to the public?

The "About Us" section is a prime example of the importance of setting goals and defining your audience. Within the planning group, ask these fundamental questions: What do we want to tell our audience about this institution? How do we want to be seen? The answers should translate into each segment of the site, beginning here.

Contact Us

Similar to "About Us," the "Contact Us" section defines how you want to interact with your audience. Many sites simply list a mailing address, phone and fax numbers, and an e-mail address for a reference archivist. Others go a step further and provide individual staff information, particularly for institutions with more than one archivist or information professional, so that visitors can direct their inquiries to the appropriate individuals.

Many institutions utilize social media tools to feature a real-time "Ask-a-Librarian/Archivist" chat interface where visitors can type in a question and converse with an information professional on the other end. George Mason University's Special Collections and Archives

Common Elements of an Archives Website
1. About Us
2. Contact Us
3. News and Announcements
4. Events
5. Plan Your Visit
6. Make a Donation/Become a Member
7. Research/Using the Collections
8. FAQs
9. Digital Collections
10. Exhibitions

Figure 1.3. The Montgomery County (Maryland) Historical Society "About Us" Section

ABOUT US | MUSEUMS & EXHIBITS | LIBRARY & ARCHIVES | EDUCATION & PROGRAMS | GENEALOGY CLUB | MUSEUM SHOP | HISTORY & RESOURCES | GIVING

Home > About Us

Staff

Debbie Rankin, Executive Director

A lifelong resident of Montgomery County and a graduate of the College of Journalism at the University of Maryland, College Park, Debbie was named Executive Director in 2008. With a broad array of experience in non-profit management as well as development and marketing expertise, Debbie served as Executive Director at the Sandy Spring Museum and Development Director at BlackRock Center for the Arts. Debbie has also worked in advertising/public relations and served as PTA President/Vice President for over 5 years. As one of the first nominees for the Athena Award, presented by the Olney Chamber of Commerce, she is also a member of the Leadership Montgomery Class of 2009.

Image: *Gladys Neale Hilton (1895-2002) Married to Thomas Pickering Pratt, Jr.*
"She epitomizes grace, class and style"

Beth Hickey, Assistant Director

Beth, a native of Rockville, has worked in the museum and cultural heritage fields since the late 1990s when she found her calling as a MCHS high school intern. While working on an undergraduate degree in anthropology at Northern Arizona University, Beth worked as an archaeologist in Arizona and New Mexico. In 2003, she returned to MCHS as the Waters House Site Director for a year before moving back to Arizona to pursue a Master's in Anthropology. Although she enjoys working as an archaeologist, and occasionally misses being out in the field, Beth has discovered that her true passion is sharing the past. This is thanks to her experiences in public archaeology and at the Museum of Northern Arizona where she particularly enjoyed working with researchers and giving tours, in addition to caring for the archaeology collections. She looks forward to continuing the tradition of developing innovative programs at MCHS and fostering an appreciation of Montgomery County heritage in the community.

Image: *Kitty Poole, c. 1910, donated by the Poole family.*

Joanna Church, Director of Collections

Joanna works with the MCHS artifact collections and also researches, fabricates and installs most of the exhibits in the museums. A Montgomery County native, Joanna has a BA in anthropology from Grinnell College, and an MA in museum studies from the George Washington University. She has worked at MCHS since 1998 and is particularly fond of the textile and ceramic collections.

Image: *Mary Shaw Bennett, ca. 1895. Donated by Laurence Halstead.*

Note: The society's staff combined vintage photographs from its collections with staff biographies to create a whimsical addition to this page.
Source: http://www.montgomeryhistory.org/about_staff. Courtesy of the Montgomery County Historical Society, Maryland.

includes an "Ask an Archivist" chat feature, illustrated in Figure 1.4, that complements the additional contact information already available on the site. While this type of feature may not be the best solution for more complex queries, interactive features like chatting allow an audience to feel more engaged with the site and the staff.

Another feature to consider for a "Contact Us" section is an online form on the page that allows users to submit an e-mail directly from the site. These forms can range from the exceedingly simple (fields for name, contact information, and question) to the complex, using drop-down menus and other actions to select a specific area of inquiry. Figure 1.5, from the University of Delaware Archives and Special Collections' website,

Figure 1.4. The "Ask an Archivist" Chat Feature, George Mason University Special Collections and Archives

George Mason University Libraries
SPECIAL COLLECTIONS & ARCHIVES

This chat feature is designed to allow our patrons to ask general questions about navigating our website, materials in our collection, and our access policies.

We do not accept document reproduction requests via chat and more detailed research questions should be sent to our email address: speccoll@gmu.edu.

You can also reach us by phone at 703-993-2220 or fax at 703-993-8911.
Chat is available during SC&A's normal open hours - Monday, Tuesday, Thursday, and Friday 10:00 AM - 4:30 PM and Wednesday, Noon-8:00 PM.

GMUArchives

gmuarchives is online

Type **here** and hit enter to send a private message.

edit nickname: meeboguest530132

get meebo

about **SC&A** | using **SC&A** | our **collections** | digitized **collections** | our **blog**

University Dissertation and Thesis Services   University Records Management   Oral History Program

Source: http://sca.gmu.edu/chat.html.

exemplifies a simple online form for submitting reference requests. Again, such features are not technologically challenging but do require forethought and planning. Where are such inquiries to be sent—to an account created specifically for reference requests or directly to the archivist's inbox? Who will maintain such accounts? Do you want the server to generate an automated response to inform the user that his or her request has been sent, or do you want to rely on the staff to personally respond to each submission?

Of course, a website designed to function as a public relations tool should welcome input and interaction between staff and audience. Do not hide information, such as placing e-mail addresses within blocks of narrative or relegating telephone numbers to the very bottom of long pages. Consider adding a footer or special sidebar to each page with contact information, thus encouraging visitors to send an e-mail or call and reinforcing how freely the information is shared. If you are concerned about users spamming or abusing forms, select those features that have more specific functions, such as requiring users to choose a subject for an online form from a list determined by the planners. Applications like CAPTCHA will verify an e-mail address before submission and prevent spammers from hijacking addresses and forms.

"Contact Us" Information Elements

- Street address
- Mailing address
- Special mailing instructions
- Telephone and fax numbers (can include staff extensions, etc.)
- E-mail addresses (individual accounts, general reference, information requests, etc.)
- Chat function (e.g., "Ask a Librarian")
- Online forms—reference requests, general inquiries, generic information, etc.
- "Follow us on Twitter/Friend us on Facebook"

Figure 1.5. "AskSpec" Online Submission Form Used by the University of Delaware Archives and Special Collections

AskSpec

AskSpec is the electronic reference service for the Special Collections Department at the University of Delaware Library. General reference questions from the immediate University community should be directed to **Ask a Librarian**. Non-University researchers with general reference questions should contact local school or public libraries.

AskSpec provides answers to brief factual questions concerning holdings in the Special Collections Department. Please consult our **collection focus** page, **list of previous exhibitions**, **list of manuscript and archival collections**, or **DELCAT**, the Library's online catalog, to find specific information about department holdings.

Please complete the form below and submit to **AskSpec**. We will send an acknowledgment within 24 hours that your inquiry has been received, Monday through Friday, excluding holidays. Questions received Friday will receive a response the following Monday. Every effort will be made to answer your question as soon as possible.

Please complete all fields

Name

Email address

Mailing address

Phone number (optional)

Research status   Please select from the li ▼

My question concerns   Please select from the l ▼

Your question (*please be specific*):

Source: http://www.lib.udel.edu/forms/askspec.php.

Finally, be realistic about your institution's ability to respond to e-mails, phone calls, and any other means of inquiry. If you are a one-person shop, do you have the time to answer each e-mail personally while fielding an increase in phone calls and in-person foot traffic?

News and Announcements

Much literature is available that discusses how archivists can interact with the media through such tools as news releases and press kits. The traditional rules generally still apply, except now all of these tools can also be located in one location: your website.

As such, your website should include a section where press releases, announcements, and other newsworthy items can be shared with your wider audience. This section is usually titled "News and Announcements" or something similar. You can also use phrases like "Updates" or "In the News"—whatever you feel will convey to your audience that this is the place to find the latest happenings at your archives.

Such announcements usually occur in two places: on a page specifically for these items, and in an area of the main homepage designated for happenings in the "spotlight." Any highlighted event on the site's main page should be significant so that it will catch the attention of your audience. On the "News and Announcements" main page, the more immediate or current news items should be posted at the top of a list of other items shown in reverse chronological order, conveying the importance of the higher items in the list.

Like any other type of announcement for traditional media outlets, the announcements you make on your website should answer the traditional "Five W's and H": Who? What? When? Where? Why? and How? Be sure to include links to any additional information (internally on your website or from an external source). (For a more in-depth discussion of writing press releases for archives, see Megan Sniffin-Marinoff's "In Print, On Air: Working with the Media" [1994].)

One issue to avoid is that of the ever-expanding page: your visitors do not need to see every press release or announcement your archives has posted in the past two years. Instead, create an archives of previous items older than a specific period of time (three months is a good default period) and remove them from the main page. Simply add a link somewhere on the page (usually at the bottom or perhaps on a right-side navigation pane) to these older posts so that interested parties can still get to them if they wish. Some content management systems like blog generators can automatically create these archives every month, depending on the frequency of the updates.

Another way of presenting your news items is by way of a "teaser" in which only the headline and the first sentence or two are displayed, followed by a link encouraging the visitor to "Read more . . ." That link can lead to a separate page where the entire item is displayed or it can expand the text block on the current page, depending on the functionality of your website. Generally the "teaser" language will need to grab readers' attention enough to convince them to follow the link. However, the text should be informative enough that they still come away with a sense of the "Five W's and H" regardless of whether they read on or not.

Events

Some archives create separate pages for their upcoming events as another way of calling attention to them by devoting more space to their description. These pages can then be linked to calendars and announcements. Distinct page URLs can be included in related websites, press releases, posters, news articles, radio announcements, and other media outlets. If your website is part of a larger institutional site (such as that of a college or university), these pages can easily be accessed through other parts of the site as well.

This practice is particularly useful for recurring or annual events. The majority of the common information, such as what the event is and what activities it entails, will remain the same with only periodic alterations as needed. Details that are subject to change—date, location, or possibly

What Kinds of Announcements Can I Make?

- New accessions
- Completion of collection processing or editing project
- New director/significant change in personnel
- Exhibition opening
- Guest speaker or lecturer
- New digital collection made available
- Awarding of a grant
- New publication based on collection
- New feature to website (blog or other social media application, digital images, live chat, etc.)
- Change in hours of operation
- Membership/donation drive kick-off announcements
- Special programming
- Construction of a new building/ground-breaking ceremony

Events to Highlight

- Annual awards (include submission guidelines and deadlines, as well as past winners)
- Annual lectures
- Ceremonies
- Concerts/performances
- Conferences/symposia
- Fundraisers
- Meetings
- Open houses
- Outings
- Tours
- Workshops

Information Your Visitors Will Find Useful

- Hours of Operation
- Online form for requesting an appointment (if applicable)
- Directions (including public transportation, if applicable)
- Maps (e.g., Google Maps, MapQuest, rail and bus routes, campus maps, floor plans)
- Parking
- Accommodations (particularly if your institution has an established relationship with a local hotel)
- Dining options
- Local attractions, including related repositories
- Images of your buildings, campus, community, and so on

topic—can be edited for each event occurrence. To establish the history of the event, you could include other content such as titles of lectures within a series, photographs or video from previous events, or lists of awardees for an annual prize.

Plan Your Visit

One of the easiest ways to encourage people to cross the threshold of your archives is to provide them with the information they need to visit in person. Titling this section "Plan Your Visit" or "Visit Us" or "Directions, Maps, and Parking" will leave your audience in little doubt of where to find this type of instruction, although you may want to locate its link near the "About Us" and "Contact Us" sections. The practicality of this content makes it less exciting than other sections, but its provision sends a message to the would-be visitor that your institution welcomes the traffic. This section, along with "About Us," can truly demonstrate the goodwill of the institution.

Including little niceties such as lists of accommodations, restaurants, and local attractions encourages visitors to consider making a longer trip to spend more time in the archives and in the area. For example, Figure 1.6 shows the area hotels and restaurants listed among the visitor information on the Mississippi State University Libraries' website. Explore the possibility of establishing relationships with those local attractions: for example, in exchange for being listed on your website, hotels or restaurants in the area can offer discounts to your visitors.

This section is also a good opportunity to describe how the benefits of being a member or "friend" of the archives can enhance their visit, such as discounts on photocopies or on admissions to an affiliated museum. Even though you want people to view your website and then come and visit, realize that many patrons live far from your archives and cannot visit. Do not tailor your website for the patron who will later make a physical visit. Also plan for the website to be used by geographically distant researchers.

Make a Donation/Become a Member

In his *Developing and Maintaining Practical Archives*, Dr. Greg Hunter (2003) points out that public relations and marketing are often treated as synonymous in the archival profession. While the two are certainly not mutually exclusive, a website offers yet another opportunity for encouraging your audience to support your institution. Their presence on the website indicates their interest in the institution, and a description of the variety of ways in which they can contribute would not be amiss.

At a minimum, a section on donation or membership should list the benefits of such a contribution—tax breaks, discounts, certain privileges, complementary tickets to events, or other advantages. This section should also present an account of the programs or activities their contribution will help to fund. People like to know that their gifts are being utilized for causes in which they believe and support. Taken together, this

Figure 1.6. Hotel and Restaurant Information on the Mississippi State University, University Libraries' "Visitor Information" Page

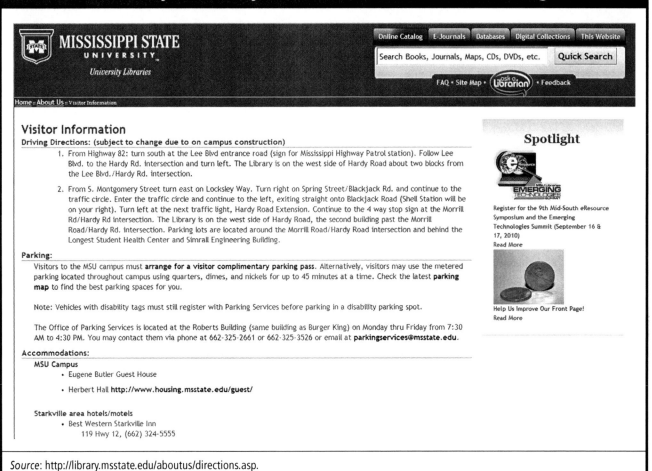

Source: http://library.msstate.edu/aboutus/directions.asp.

information can help to persuade your audience to make a contribution beneficial to both your institution and themselves. These details can also be reiterated in an electronic brochure or other similar collateral that your would-be donors can download for later perusal.

One of the easiest ways to increase the likelihood of contributions is to make available online all the materials an individual would need to become a member, make a donation, or create a bequest. If you would like people to join your institution as a member or become a "friend"— whichever terminology you use—be sure to include a secure form that they can submit electronically or print out and mail, whichever option suits their needs. Ideally people would have the option of paying online through the website with a credit or debit card or electronic check, for convenience and speed. However, you must take into account whether your website can support these types of transactions and guarantee the level of security required for online financial transactions. Check with your information technology staff and your financial institution to determine if you can offer this convenience. If your site cannot accommodate the requirements, explain to your audience that you cannot accept payments online at this time but then provide the appropriate forms and instructions on how to submit payment.

Some visitors may be considering adding your institution as a benefactor of their estate or granting a one-time lump sum or an annuity (often referred to as "planned giving"). Such an action requires the appropriate legal terminology to establish a bequest from the estate. The website team should work with the institution's legal counsel and financial advisors to supply sample wording that can be copied and pasted into a person's will. The Mount Vernon Ladies' Association—although technically charged with stewardship over more than just an archives—has a significant amount of information on its website dealing with major and planned gifts, including bequests and donations of real estate and life insurance (see Figure 1.7). Other institutions group together information on the donations of historical materials as well as monetary support (see Figure 1.8).

Figure 1.7. The Website for George Washington's Mount Vernon Estate and Gardens' "Suggested Bequest Language" Page

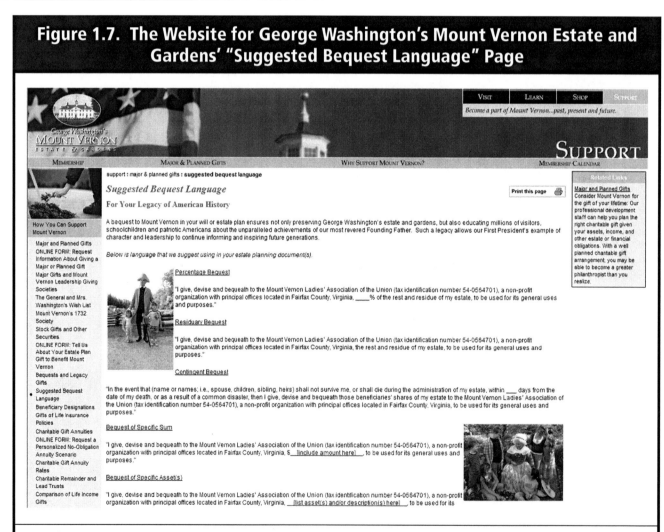

Source: http://www.mountvernon.org/support/donations/index.cfm/pid/992/. Courtesy of the Mount Vernon Ladies' Association.

Figure 1.8. The "Donations" Page for the University of Kentucky's University Archives

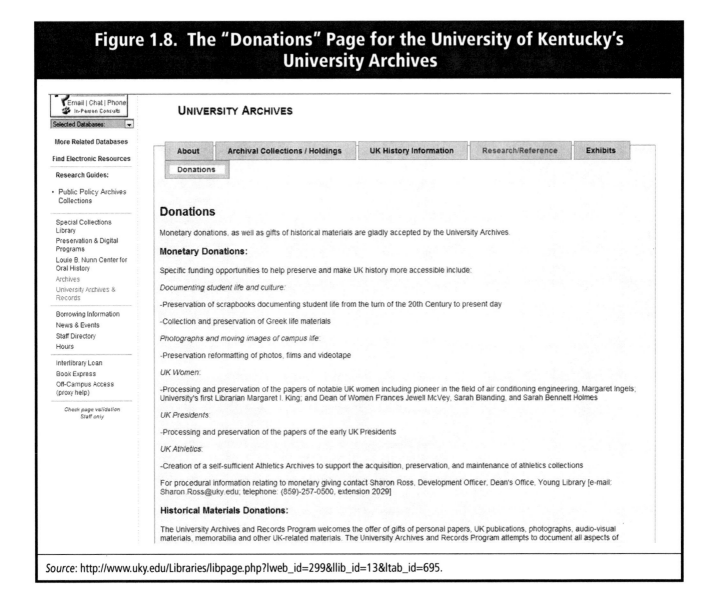

Source: http://www.uky.edu/Libraries/libpage.php?lweb_id=299&llib_id=13&ltab_id=695.

Research/Using the Collections

The most common goal of any repository using its website as a public relations tool is to get people to make use of the collections, be it in person or over the Internet. To achieve this objective, the website should include guidance and instruction on what one can find in the archives and how to access the collections. The information in this section should inform users of what to expect when preparing for a research project within a particular archives. Although each institution is different, there are many similar rules and regulations to be followed.

You want your users to be as informed as possible before they show up on your doorstep. You already have your policies and procedures in place, so you can easily share these on the website. By putting this information online, you are preparing your users to comply with your rules and regulations (or at least giving them the opportunity to do so).

Issues to Address for Visitors

Availability of materials

Upon arrival:
- Registration
- Belongings—use of lockers, restrictions on cell phones, and so on
- What is permitted in the archives
- What is not permitted in the archives
- Instructions on requesting materials, number of boxes allowed out at one time, and so on
- Photocopying, reproductions (photocopying, scanning, etc.)

Getting ready to leave the archives:
- Returning materials
- Checking out
- Following up

Licensing/permission to publish

One word of caution: you want to present your policies in as neutral a manner as possible to avoid sounding dismissive and unapproachable. Using less formal language to explain the rules can make you sound less overbearing and more welcoming, which is a key point in relating to your public. You can also add some explanatory language that your print materials may not have been able to accommodate due to space restrictions—for example, a trifold brochure can only contain so much text, whereas a webpage can go on indefinitely (although you certainly want to avoid that). Take the opportunity to explain to your users why you are asking them to leave their jackets and bags in lockers and use only pencils (see Figure 1.9). A user who understands the reasoning behind the rules and regulations is less likely to question them once onsite.

You should also provide instructions for and an explanation of any requirements you have regarding advanced notification of visit or a reference letter, if applicable. Provide forms that users can print and fill out in advance or, even better, submit online. For reference letters, consider including a template of boilerplate language so that the user can see what information is required. Your users are probably working with limited time and budget for research trips and will appreciate the time they will save by using the tools on your site. The result will be users who are well prepared for their visit to your archives.

This section should also include a discussion of the tools available to your researchers in searching the materials. This is also a great way to promote your collections by highlighting online catalogs, findings aids, subject lists, and search functions. You should also include access to any "Ask a Librarian/Archivist" live chat function you may offer so that users can ask a question in real time, and you should provide access to reference blogs so that users can review what other researchers have been doing with your collections. One suggestion regarding design: separate out links for these tools; do not place them only in blocks of texts. Separating links into sidebars or bulleted lists draws attention to them instead of asking the reader to discern a colored link in black text. You put too much effort into encoding finding aids and adding search terms to hide these tools away!

FAQs

Another useful section for many archives is the Frequently Asked Questions, or "FAQs." These predicted sets of questions and responses have become a ubiquitous part of almost any website and can encompass a range of topics. Particularly useful FAQs include multiple sections that inquire about the institution, what types of resources are in the archives, and even how to use the website. The benefit of including a section of these frequent questions is to ultimately save time for your staff as well as for your visitors by preempting the repetition of such mundane details as "Can I take materials out of the archives?" or "What is your policy on scanners or digital cameras in the reading room?"

Some archives also use the FAQs to answer questions regarding popular research subjects relating to their collections. For example, the

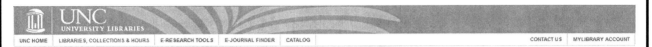

Figure 1.9. Online Guidance for the Users of the University of North Carolina University Archives' Southern Historical Collection

UNC UNIVERSITY LIBRARIES

UNC HOME | LIBRARIES, COLLECTIONS & HOURS | E-RESEARCH TOOLS | E-JOURNAL FINDER | CATALOG | CONTACT US | MYLIBRARY ACCOUNT

Southern Historical Collection, Southern Folklife Collection, University Archives and Records Management Services

Southern Historical Collection, Southern Folklife Collection, University Archives, General Manuscripts

USING MATERIALS IN THE SEARCH ROOM

Welcome. We hope that your research visit will be pleasant and productive. Thank you for taking the time to familiarize yourself with our search room policies and procedures. These policies and procedures are an effort to balance the needs of researchers with the security and long-term preservation of our unique holdings. We greatly appreciate your cooperation.

SEARCH ROOM
- Researchers will examine all collection materials in the search room.
- Unless otherwise directed, please sit at a small table and face the security cameras at the front of the room (double doors).
- Food, beverages, pens, purses, bags, folders, binders, notebooks, and books are prohibited.
- Return all materials to the window.
- NEVER exit the search room with collection materials.
- Upon leaving, present all items (e.g., laptop, notes) for inspection.
- All requests will be made on call slips.
- Complete and submit one call slip per collection, call number, or interview.
- The Library strongly recommends use of digital cameras for duplication of unrestricted materials. Photocopying is strictly limited and not available for same-day delivery. The Library reserves the right to prohibit duplication at the staff's discretion.

HANDLING OF MATERIALS
- At all times, please be gentle.
- Keep the documents flat on the table.
- Pens are prohibited.
- Do not place any items (e.g., a laptop) on top of materials.
- Do not remove metal fasteners (e.g., staples, paper clips, pins).
- Remove only one folder at a time from a box and use a place holder supplied by the archivists.
- Keep materials in original filing order. Do not re-organize materials.

USE

Source: http://www.lib.unc.edu/mss/pspol/using.html.

National Archives has FAQ sections on census records, genealogical research, and congressional records, with a link to the FAQs in the header of each page. While some of these questions may overlap with information in other sections such as "About Us" or "Researching / Using the Collections," they can reiterate certain policies or instructions that bear repeating.

Digital Collections and Online Exhibitions

This chapter is not a discussion of how to create virtual archives through finding aids, digital collections, and online exhibits—there are plenty of other resources on those topics. However, you should consider these features as public relations tools as well, because they are visual representations of your collections that allow the outside world a glimpse of your archival holdings. Why else would you put digital surrogates online, if not for your audience? Why go through all the hassle otherwise?

When planning for a digitization project, consider your audience and the manner in which you will deliver these materials to them. How will they approach a digital archives? Do not scan just to scan, or you will be at risk of wasting your efforts. Again—just as with the website as a whole—define your audience and goals before embarking on any type of digitization project.

Scanned images or digital photographs should represent the highlights of your collections, the jewels in your archival crown. The content (images and metadata) can be detailed descriptions or just "teasers." Offering a reduced version of an exhibition can also perform the same function. These "teasers," such as the University of Kentucky's "Explore UK" online exhibition (see Figure 1.10), can entice visitors to the website to become visitors to the "brick and mortar" archives because they want to see more. Note too that the "Explore UK" site offers visitors a chance to interact with the institution through various forms of social media. See Chapter 7 for more information about digitizing your photographs.

Figure 1.10. Digitized Materials Highlighting the History of the University of Kentucky and Encouraging Visitors to "Explore UK"

Source: http://exploreuk.uky.edu/exploreukhome.html.

A Word about "Web 2.0"

Other chapters in this manual address various "Web 2.0" technologies such as blogs, so there is no need to discuss those here (see Chapters 2 and 3). However, when developing content for your website, it would be best to determine how new social media can be utilized to enhance the user's interaction with the site. As mentioned elsewhere, reference blogs and tweets from the staff can help connect archivists and researchers.

Another consideration of how new technologies are changing the face of websites is the rise of smart phones and other mobile devices with Internet capabilities. Most of the intended audience will access your site from a traditional computer, but more and more individuals are using mobile devices to access content on the go. Therefore, if you have the technological capability to do so, explore the idea of creating a mobile version of your website that offers much of the same content in a simpler form. Of particular importance would be the "Plan Your Visit" information, as this would enable the user to look up last-minute directions or the phone number for the research room.

Ok, So Now What? (After It's Up)

All the planning in the world and top-notch content cannot guarantee that visitors will flock to a website. Still, it is the institution's responsibility to maintain the site and adapt it as needed, and this will require continuing effort.

Tracking Statistics

For years web counters have been able to display how many visitors have viewed a particular site or webpage. However, there are more sophisticated counters that can capture more useful information than simply a graphic depiction of the number of visitors who have clicked on the site since a particular date. These counters can be made visible if desired, but usually they run unseen in the background, gathering data on not only how many people access the site, but also what site they were viewing before moving to yours and what pages they saw on your site.

Additional information can be collected directly from the visitors themselves. When conducting a reference interview or responding to an e-mail inquiry, ask the individual if he or she came by the information about your archives through the website, and, if so, how did he or she locate the site? On what pages did they find the information they sought? Keep careful statistics for use in justifying budget requests, applying for grants, or performing other maintenance activities. You will also want to track whether your reference requests in general experience an increase, because this could indicate that the website has broadened your public profile.

Site Surveys

Once the site has been live for a period of two or three years, you may wish to conduct a survey of website visitors to ascertain how well the site is functioning. A survey can ask questions regarding all facets of a site: usability, navigation, content, design, and layout. There are numerous vendors available for creating and conducting surveys, so do not worry about designing one yourself. What you will be responsible for is determining what exactly it is that you want to learn about your site and then writing the questions to ascertain that information.

Be aware that, as with any survey, you will need to cast a wide net to gather sufficient data for analysis. Most would-be survey takers are selected at random by the survey application, but the design allows those selected to opt out of participating. As such, many people will most likely opt out at first, so you must allow the survey to run for a significant period of time, such as six months, depending on your needs. At the end of that time, review the results and find out how well your site is fulfilling its mission. If you find areas of improvement, it may be time to revisit your original plans and adapt them as necessary, even if you have not yet reached your established period of review.

Conclusion

Websites have, for the most part, become the public face of many archives, and we should embrace this development. If your archives already has brochures, pamphlets, press releases, and various forms for your users, then you have already created much of the preliminary content. Whether dynamic or static websites can encompass nearly all of these public relations tools and offer additional content, such as digital representations of collections and interactive tools for researchers. Every archives, big or small, should develop a Web presence to connect with their current and intended audiences. The types of content discussed in the preceding paragraphs will form the basis of a solid, informative site that will meet the needs of your users and increase your archives' public profile.

THE PLAN

1. Make sure your marketing plan includes the goals and objectives for your website.
2. Include in your plan a statement creating a website committee and delineating the members' duties and responsibilities.

References

Hunter, Gregory S. 2003. *Developing and Maintaining Practical Archives: A How-To-Do-It Manual.* 2nd ed. New York: Neal-Schuman.

Nielson, Jakob. 1999. *Designing Web Usability: The Practice of Simplicity*. Indianapolis, IN: New Riders Publishing.

Sniffin-Marinoff, Megan. 1994. "In Print, On Air: Working with the Media." In *Advocating Archives: An Introduction to Public Relations for Archivists*, edited by Elsie Freeman Finch, 40–53. Metuchen, NJ: Society of American Archivists and Scarecrow Press.

Additional Resources

Abraham, Terry, comp. 2010. "Repositories of Primary Sources." University of Idaho Archives and Special Collections. Updated in September. http://www.uiweb.uidaho.edu/special-collections/Other.Repositories.html.

Everson, Bart. 2000. "How the Web Works Part VII: Planning Your Website." Xavier University, Center for the Advancement of Teaching. http://cat.xula.edu/tutorials/planning/.

Finch, Elsie Freeman, ed. 1994. *Advocating Archives: An Introduction to Public Relations for Archivists*. Lanham, MD: Society of American Archivists and Scarecrow Press.

Public Relations Society of America (PRSA). 2011. "Public Relations Resources and Tools for Communication Professionals: PRSA." Accessed June 7. http://www.prsa.org/.

Pugh, Mary Jo. 2005. *Providing Reference Services for Archives & Manuscripts*. Chicago: Society of American Archivists.

Stielow, Frederick. 2003. *Building Digital Archives, Descriptions, and Displays: A How-To-Do-It Manual for Archivists and Librarians*. New York: Neal-Schuman.

Theimer, Kate. 2011. *ArchivesNext* (blog). http://www.archivesnext.org.

Tulane University Archives. 2007. *Ready, 'Net, Go! Archival Internet Resources*. Updated April 20. http://specialcollections.tulane.edu/ArchivesResources.html.

Social Media

Lauren Oostveen

Introduction

Social media presents an extraordinary opportunity for archives to market themselves to new and existing audiences. Social media can strengthen relationships with current researchers and act as a timely avenue to address queries. These tools can also expose archives' collections and services to an entirely new audience, thereby increasing visibility and relevance.

Andreas Kaplan and Michael Haenlein (2010: 59) define social media as "a group of Internet-based applications that build on the ideological and technological foundations of Web 2.0, and that allow the creation and exchange of user-generated content." Web 2.0 refers to user-generated content like blogs, microblogs, and social networking sites. In contrast, with static websites controlled by companies that are not interacting with their audience, websites that are built on user-generated content are populated by text, photos, videos, and other media that can come from anyone.

Blogging (see Chapter 3) is an excellent way of sharing information about your institution online. Blog usage began to spread in the late 1990s (Seminerio, 1998) but did not hit the mainstream until the mid-2000s (Massing, 2009). Like blogging, social media websites such as Facebook, YouTube, and Twitter have existed for years, but their popularity has increased drastically since 2007, becoming a part of everyday life for millions of people.

Just as radio and television called for new ways of marketing to be explored, social media can be used to reach a new audience and, better yet, interact and learn from them. One common misconception of archives often leans toward old, musty, and out of touch. Social media can help archives to change this view by offering an opportunity to communicate effectively through the channels people already use every day, providing a new way to research and teaching the online community about the relevance of archives.

Before You Start

Before jumping headfirst into the world of social media, it is important to consider who will be maintaining these channels. Will it be a team or a single person? Is social media outreach built into someone's job description, or will an already overworked archivist be updating these Web tools when he or she has the time?

At least one person in your organization should be designated to maintain social media channels, with at least an hour per day allotted to updating with new content, replying to queries, and so forth. Writing a social media strategy that fits in with your overall web strategy is also a good idea, as you can designate a "road map" for staff and determine measurable outcomes. You might want to designate the person as a member of your website development team (see Chapter 1).

Twitter

Learning the Ropes

Twitter is a social networking and microblogging service that enables its users to send and read other users' messages, called "tweets." It was founded in 2006 and in the past two years has become extremely popular, with individual users, businesses, organizations, and celebrities taking part (http://twitter.com/about).

Twitter provides a platform for archives to market themselves to users within their region and to the world at large. You can also use Twitter to connect with other archives, museums, and libraries, providing a valuable learning opportunity.

The basic premise of Twitter is to share (tweet) "what's happening" in 140 characters or less. A tweet can be text or text with a link to another website or image.

Those who subscribe to a user's tweets are called "followers." Users can send a tweet from Twitter.com, from a mobile Twitter application, or from one of the numerous desktop applications.

When signing up for Twitter, there are a few things to consider. First, your username should be simple, recognizable, and not too long. When a user re-tweets (RT), or repeats, one of your tweets, your username is included as part of your original tweet, so a longer username may make spreading your message more difficult. For example:

> @ABCArchives: A busy day on the research floor. Helping a lot of people with family history queries.

> @124Archives: Us too! RT @ABCArchives: A busy day on the research floor. Helping a lot of people with family history queries.

The profile section of your Twitter page will tell users who you are, where you are tweeting from, and what you are all about. Brevity is key, so this information must be concise. If you are tweeting for your institution,

Kate Theimer is a writer and commentator on the field of archives, specializing in the application of new technologies in archives. She is the author of *Web 2.0 and Strategies for Archives and Local History Collections*, published by Neal-Schuman in 2010. Theimer also writes the popular blog *ArchivesNext* (http://www.archivesnext.com/) and tweets as @archivesnext. These are her picks for the top five archives Twitter accounts:

1. Nova Scotia Archives & Records Management: @NS_Archives (http://www.twitter.com/NS_Archives)

2. The National Archives, UK: @UkNatArchives (http://www.twitter.com/UkNatArchives)

3. Special Collections Research Center, Swem Library at the College of William and Mary: @SwemSCRC (http://www.twitter.com/SwemSCRC)

4. Jewish Women's Archives: @jwaonline (http://www.twitter.com/jwaonline)

5. Deseronto Archives: @DeserontoArch (http://www.twitter.com/DeserontoArch)

under "Name" on the profile page, type your institution's name. Avoid acronyms, if possible. In the "Bio" section, if your institution allows it, type the name of the person who is updating the Twitter feed, as well as a few words about the institution. As Twitter is meant to be conversational, appearing as human as possible is recommended.

Biographies must be less than 160 characters, but a link to your website will provide more than enough information for curious users. You can include this in the "Web" section of the profile.

You can upload a photo or logo in the profile section as an icon to represent your institution. This image will appear next to your username in Twitter feeds. If you are going to use a photo from your collections, look for eye-catching images that will make sense, even when shrunk down into a small icon. Bright colors and lots of contrast help you stand out in your followers' feed.

You can also upload an image in the design section as your Twitter page's background. This image can be from your holdings, or one with text providing more information about your institution, or any other image that represents your institution.

Twitter allows you to update from its website, or you can download a desktop client or use a mobile application. From the website under "Home" you can tweet, see who is following you and who you are following, and find out who had "mentioned" you in one of their tweets (see Figure 2.1). You can follow a user by visiting their Twitter page and clicking "follow."

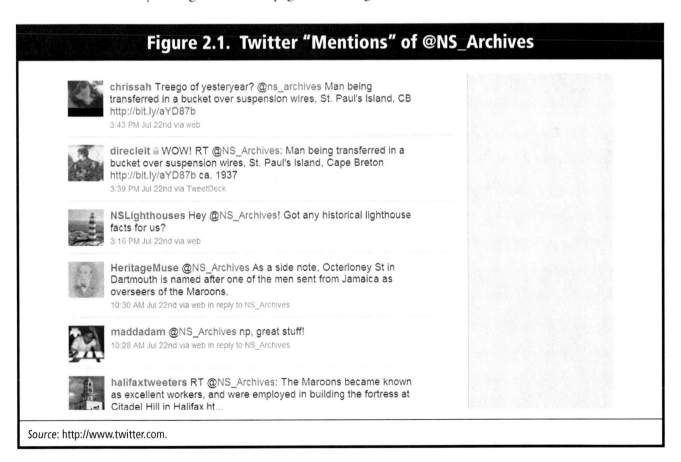

Figure 2.1. Twitter "Mentions" of @NS_Archives

chrissah Treego of yesteryear? @ns_archives Man being transferred in a bucket over suspension wires, St. Paul's Island, CB http://bit.ly/aYD87b
3:43 PM Jul 22nd via web

direcleit WOW! RT @NS_Archives: Man being transferred in a bucket over suspension wires, St. Paul's Island, Cape Breton http://bit.ly/aYD87b ca. 1937
3:39 PM Jul 22nd via TweetDeck

NSLighthouses Hey @NS_Archives! Got any historical lighthouse facts for us?
3:16 PM Jul 22nd via web

HeritageMuse @NS_Archives As a side note, Octerloney St in Dartmouth is named after one of the men sent from Jamaica as overseers of the Maroons.
10:30 AM Jul 22nd via web in reply to NS_Archives

maddadam @NS_Archives np, great stuff!
10:28 AM Jul 22nd via web in reply to NS_Archives

halifaxtweeters RT @NS_Archives: The Maroons became known as excellent workers, and were employed in building the fortress at Citadel Hill in Halifax ht...

Source: http://www.twitter.com.

While tweeting from the web is easy, the benefits of running a Twitter desktop application include the ability to manage several accounts at once, monitor keywords, update across different platforms (like Facebook), and follow tweets in "real time" (as opposed to refreshing the Twitter website to see the latest tweets). Twitter applications often include features such as link shortening, for example, bit.ly or tiny.url, and image hosting through partnering websites such as TwitPic. Link-shortening services allow you to condense long URLs into 20-character URLs, thus not taking up too much of your 140 character limit. Image-hosting services allow you to easily upload an image that can be viewed with a click on most Twitter clients. Link-shortening and image-hosting services also provide user statistics by tracking the number of users who have clicked your link and visited the website or image.

Twitter applications are very useful if you are managing multiple accounts, want to keep track of one or more hashtags (a keyword that appears with a number sign in front of it, e.g., #archives), or want to update across different websites, like Facebook. Clients can also be used to "schedule" tweets, which allow you to send a tweet at any hour of the day or night. Overuse of this is discouraged as you may not be available to answer questions regarding your update, and followers may be discouraged. Figure 2.2 shows an example of a Twitter client being used to monitor different accounts.

New desktop clients are created all of the time. There are also web services that serve as Twitter clients. Web services for Twitter include Hootsuite and Threadsy.

Desktop Clients for Twitter

- TweetDeck
- Twhirl
- Tweetie
- Ubertwitter
- Seesmic Twitter

Examples of Usage

Before you make your first tweet, consider what the purpose of your Twitter account will be and how it will fit in with your overall web strategy. Larger institutions, such as @LibraryCongress and @UKNatArchives, use their Twitter accounts to post links to events, press releases, and special announcements. Because of their size and reach, they gather followers without much effort, and this is a reasonable use of Twitter.

Smaller institutions have to use Twitter more strategically if they want to reach a larger audience. Building a relationship with followers through consistent, helpful, interesting updates is the best approach. These updates can be centered around different areas of work in the archives.

If you have digital exhibits, tweets can center around sharing these images and documents. Or you can share images of significance or general interest or that relate to a current-day event or issue in the news. An example of this type of Twitter account is @NS_Archives, a provincial archives from Halifax, Nova Scotia. Daily updates are made that link back to the institution's website, directing users to their online exhibits. Other archival institutions that use Twitter to promote their online exhibits and holdings include:

- CBC Digital Archives: Radio and TV clips, @CBC_Archives
- Deseronto Archives, @DeserontoArch

Figure 2.2. TweetDeck Used to Monitor Multiple Accounts

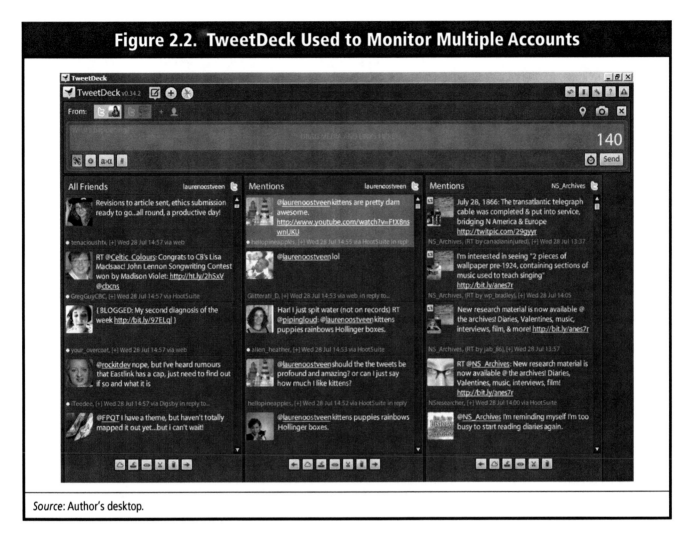

Source: Author's desktop.

Another interesting use of Twitter is to tweet entries from journals or letters in chronological order, so followers can relive an event or go through an experience in "real time." An example of this type of Twitter account is the Scott Polar Research Institute's tweets (@scottslastexp) following the diary kept by Captain Robert Falcon Scott during the British Antarctic Expedition (1910–1912). Beginning with the entry for November 26, 1910, the tweets follow Scott's ill-fated expedition until its last entry in 1912. Other examples of institutions using textual material from their holdings to create tweets include:

- John Quincy Adams (@JQAdams_MHS)
- The Orwell Prize (@TheOrwellPrize)
- The Redford Diaries (@Redford Diaries)
- Sponsored by The National Archives (UK), @UKWarCabinet

Twitter can be used to give updates on collections being processed, help people build their family trees, network with other archivists, and any other number of activities. Twitter's value to your institution is limited only by your time, resources, and imagination.

Audiences for Your Twitter Account

Audiences for Your Twitter Account

1. Other archives and archivists
2. Researchers and potential researchers in your archives
3. Government officials who fund or legislate for your archives or archives generally
4. Officials from your institution
5. Donors and potential donors to your archives

Twitter Terms

- **Follower**: Someone who has subscribed to your tweets
- **RT, or re-tweet**: To pass on someone's tweet to your own followers
- **FF, or follow Friday**: Recommending one or more users to your followers, typically on Fridays (hence the name)
- **Fail whale**: The image that appears on Twitter.com when the service is down
- **DM, or direct message**: To send a message to a user that only he or she can read; both users have to be following each other to DM
- **@**: Symbol that directs a message to a particular user and will show up in his or her "mentions" list
- **Hashtag or #**: A way to keep track of a "conversation" about a particular topic (e.g., #archives) or event (A popular use of a hashtag is for conference or special event attendees to add the conference's hashtag to their tweets. This is an example from the Association of Canadian Archivists' [ACA] 2010 Conference: @123Archives. The speaker just noted that @ABCArchives has the best Twitter feed ever. #ACA2010.)

Building Your Audience

After getting the hang of tweeting and establishing a good base of introductory tweets, you should start thinking about how you are going to build your audience. The best way to gain Twitter followers is to be helpful, informative, friendly, and human. Your tone should be light and, if at all possible, fun. Your tweets will be re-tweeted, and your account will be recommended to your followers' followers. This takes time and can sometimes feel frustrating to those who are trying to promote their archives. Avoid at all costs spam accounts or websites that promise hundreds of followers in minutes. You might gain a good number of followers, but they will not care about the content you are offering.

Your institutional website should include links to your social media accounts so that web visitors can easily find you. Reach out to those who are already making use of your services—they may not be aware of your participation in social media, and they will likely appreciate learning about your presence on Twitter. They may appreciate the opportunity to interact with your institution in a fresh way. This goes for other social media websites.

You can target potential followers by searching by location (great for city, state, or university archives) or by looking for lists (Twitter users can organize who they are following into subject-based lists, i.e., "authors"). To search for users by location, use the Advanced Search tool on Twitter's website (http://search.twitter.com/advanced). Once you have found users you think will be interested in your tweets, try following a few active accounts. This will introduce your account to them. Not all will follow you back, but it is likely that some will.

Lists are a great way to find potential followers. Of particular use are @archivesnext's Archives and Archivists on Twitter lists (http://twitter.com/archivesnext/archives-on-twitter). Following other archival institutions or archivists on Twitter is a great way to see different styles of communication and keep in the loop with idea sharing, trends, and announcements.

Overall, Twitter is about interaction. You should tweet more than once per day (four or five tweets per day, not including replies, is sufficient for most) and reply to questions and comments in a timely fashion.

Facebook

Facebook is arguably the most-used social media site, and archives have found that creating a Facebook page is useful for reaching researchers, potential researchers, and donors. This section discusses Facebook and how it can be used by archives.

Setting Up a Page

Facebook is a social networking tool that launched in February 2004. It has grown from a small website that was exclusively for university students to a site with 500 million registered as of summer 2010. On Facebook, users can add people as friends—people they know, friends, family, colleagues, and so on—and send them personal messages (like e-mail) and public messages (posting to their "wall," or personal homepage) and update their profiles with personal information, photos, and so forth to notify friends about themselves. The interaction with friends is surrounded by scores of applications that allow a user to plan events, share photos, write notes, play games, and countless other activities—all within the Facebook platform. A Facebook Page offers an institution the best opportunity for the greatest exposure (http://www.facebook.com/FacebookPages).

To start a Facebook Page, you must first sign up for Facebook, which involves providing an e-mail address and some measure of personal information—whatever you are comfortable with sharing. There are many privacy concerns that surround Facebook and how it uses personal information. Be sure to explore the privacy settings under the "Account" tab on the top of the page.

You can create a Page using the "Ads and Pages" tab. By creating a Page, you are making yourself an administrator. You can add other administrators by clicking "Edit Page" and "Add" above the Administrator column.

Much like filling out your personal Facebook profile, you will be asked to give information about your institution, such as your hours of operation, your website, and general information about your institution. Keep information about your archives short and informative, no more than a few paragraphs. For example:

> [Archives X] acquires, preserves, and makes available the state's documentary heritage—recorded information of significance created or accumulated by government and the private sector over the past 300 years.
>
> We maintain a strong tradition of client service. Each year we assist thousands of researchers and general-interest visitors, both onsite and online, in finding out more about themselves, their families, their communities, and their state.

On the left-hand column of the Page, the "About" section of your page will be displayed. That space can be used to describe what your organization is all about, as well as greet visitors to your Page. Along the top of your Page, the most recently tagged photos of your institution will appear in a row. These can be images of your holdings, your building, special events, and so forth. In the "Info" section you can enter important information such as hours of operation, your website's address, parking availability and access to public transit, and other information that is relevant to your researchers. For example:

> Welcome to the Archives' page! Every day we share significant dates from [location] history paired with items from our holdings.

When 25 or more people are connected to your Page, you can select a username for the Page by visiting http://www.facebook.com/username.

Kate Theimer's Picks for Top Five Archives' Facebook Pages

1. U.S. National Archives (http://www.facebook.com/usnationalarchives)
2. Alabama Department of Archives and History (http://www.facebook.com/AlabamaArchives)
3. Sophia Smith Collection, Smith College (http://www.facebook.com/SophiaSmithCollection)
4. The British Postal Museum & Archives (http://www.facebook.com/British-Postal-Museum-Archives/)
5. Archives of Appalachia (http://www.facebook.com/ArchivesofAppalachia)

What to Know Before Setting Up a Facebook Page

1. Who is your intended audience?
2. What type of content do you want to provide? Just announcements, discussion threads, or something else?
3. How "busy" do you want your page to be? Minimal content or dynamic content that changes often?
4. Who will have control over posting content to the page?

The Page username must be at least five alphanumeric characters in length. Keep your Page username as short and clear as possible, as usernames allow you to easily promote your presence on Facebook. You can employ this username in marketing material, like your website, brochures, and business cards. Take caution when selecting a name for your Page—once selected it cannot be changed.

Much like Twitter, Facebook allows you to upload an icon to represent your institution. A logo, item from your holdings, or other image will appear in users' News Feeds, a "homepage" where statuses, photos, videos, and so forth from friends and Pages appear, alongside any updates you make, so choosing a distinct image to represent your Page is important.

Building a Community

The premise of a Facebook Page is to build a community of people around your organization. You can use the Page to keep them informed about events, give research suggestions, share images, and offer anything else that you think will be helpful and interesting. Because the Page operates within Facebook, you can use different applications in sync with your Page.

For example, if you are having a special event, simply press the events tab on the left side of your Facebook Page. Facebook Page updates— which can be anything that sparks a conversation—can be 420 characters, somewhat longer than Twitter's 140 characters (http://bit.ly/fJmdg2). If you are using Twitter and Facebook to promote your organization, you can post the same updates, but use Facebook to post an expanded update. Update at least once a day to keep fans interested in your Page.

Post updates on the Wall of your Facebook Page. At the top of your Page, you are given the opportunity to make a text-only update; "attach" a photo, video, or link; or ask a question. To stand out in a Facebook users' Feed (where updates from all friends, pages, and events appear), it is a good idea to attach an accompanying photo or a link with a thumbnail image.

An excellent example of a popular Facebook Page is that of the New England Historic Genealogical Society (NEHGS; Figure 2.3). As of April 2011, the Page had almost 8,650 fans. Figure 2.3 illustrates the Info section of a Facebook Page as well as featured photos along the top.

Although Facebook Pages can be customized to allow or disallow "fans" to post comments on a Page's Wall, the NEHGS Page demonstrates the positive aspects of fans posting. The society's CEO posts stories of interest, and a staff member responds to research queries. Fans are active throughout the day, posting queries, photos, and stories relevant to the Page. This keeps the content fresh, giving fans a reason to check back often. The discussion area is also home to ongoing conversations between fans and the Page's administrators. This area is ideal for answering research questions or highlighting particular topics.

Ryan J. Woods, director of Internet Technology at the New England Historic Genealogical Society, thinks that NEHGS's Facebook page has been a useful tool for marketing member subscriptions:

Reminder

You can use many of the same desktop and web clients to manage both Twitter and Facebook.

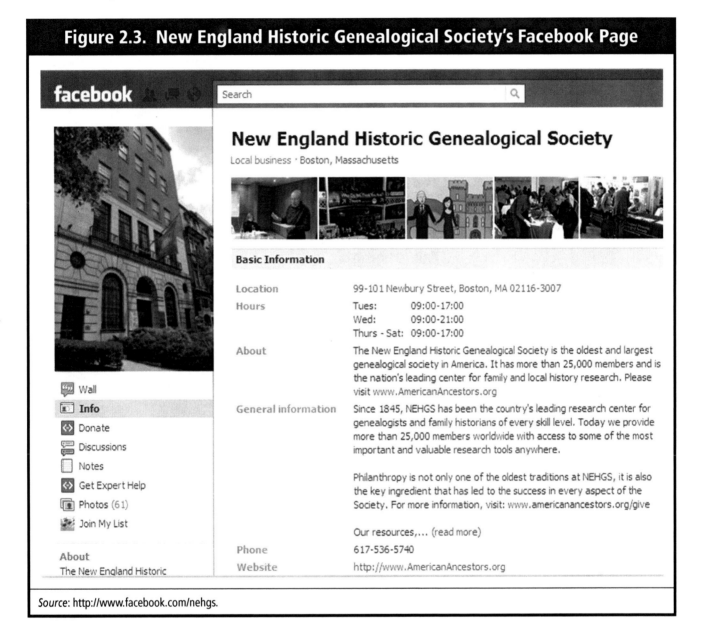

Figure 2.3. New England Historic Genealogical Society's Facebook Page

Source: http://www.facebook.com/nehgs.

Last July (2009), we posted an announcement on our Facebook Wall that we would give a discount on a new member subscription for anyone who mentioned the Facebook ad. At the conclusion of the month, we garnered 500 new members to NEHGS through the Facebook announcement, the single most successful membership promotion on record. (Ryan J. Woods, e-mail, July 29, 2010)

Page Insights and Statistics

Facebook Insights (http://www.facebook.com/insights/) provides Page administrators with statistics about the use of a Page. By understanding and analyzing these statistics, administrators can better understand what users want from a Page.

There are three different categories within Insights—general information on a Page (fan and activity increases or decreases), information about fans (demographics, daily active users, location, media use, etc.), and interactions (likes, comments, unsubscribes, and other activity). Figure 2.4 illustrates graphs on the Insights page. You can use information that you gather from Facebook Insights to determine what your fans do and do not like. You can then create posts that will garner more attention.

The Facebook Page also provides a weekly update on Page activity. This update arrives in the administrator's inbox once a week with valuable statistics on the increase or decrease in users, Wall posts, "likes," and Page views.

Advertising

In summer 2010, Facebook hit the 500-million-member mark, making it by far the largest social network on the planet. Administrators of Facebook Pages looking to reach some of those millions of users may

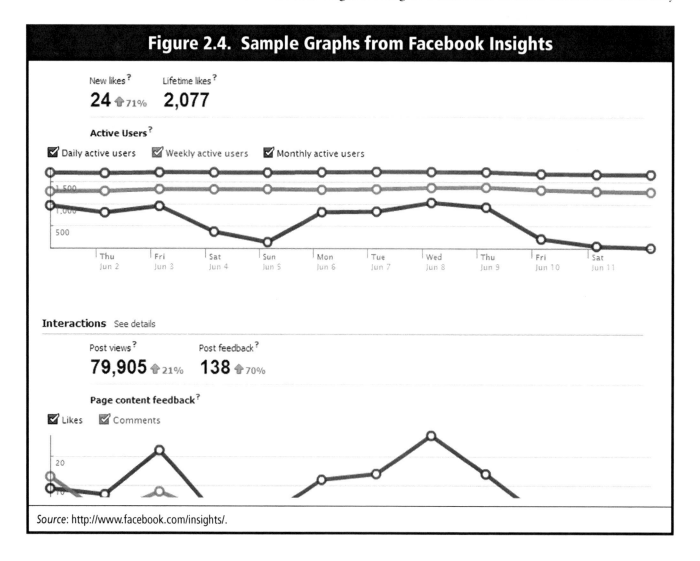

Figure 2.4. Sample Graphs from Facebook Insights

Source: http://www.facebook.com/insights/.

want to use Facebook Ads (http://www.facebook.com/ads/) to direct users to their Pages. To place an ad, go to the top right menu of your Facebook Page and click on the link for "Promote with an Ad." This will take you to a page where you can choose a photo (like your Page's display photo) and 100 characters of text to describe your Page.

The next step allows you to choose the audience for your advertisement. The first category is location. If your institution is a niche, local organization and you do not wish to market outside of your region, you can choose to promote to a particular area. Otherwise, you can promote your Page to all U.S. Facebook users aged 13 and up. See Figure 2.5 for an example of the reach of an advertisement directed at a particular demographic.

Other demographic targets include by gender, relationship status, and languages. The Likes and Interests section allows you to target specific users, such as those with history degrees, an interest in genealogy, or a connection to another archival institution. After you enter a term into the Likes section—for example, history—Facebook will populate a list of similar terms that you can select to broaden your scope (in the example, entering history may bring up archaeology). Facebook advertisements operate on a "pay per click" payment method. You must enter your maximum expenditure for one day, and Facebook will generate the fee per click based on that number.

Figure 2.5. Example of Facebook Ads Selection Process

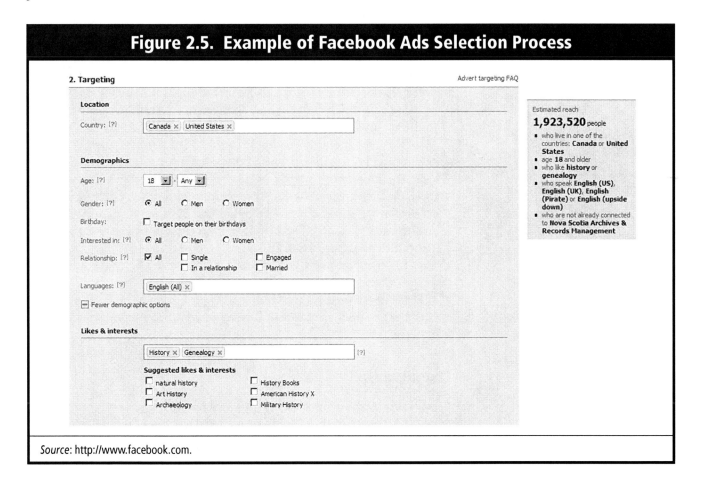

Source: http://www.facebook.com.

Facebook Groups

Facebook groups (http://www.facebook.com/groups) are useful for organizations, clubs, or special events that wish to keep their members informed and connected. Unlike a Facebook Page wall, any update you make on a group's Wall is directly connected to your personal profile. Group administrators can send e-mail updates to members' inboxes as long as the group has fewer than 5,000 members. This component makes groups useful for short-term marketing pushes, whereas Pages are best for maintaining a long-term relationship with fans.

Groups are not viewable unless you are already a member of Facebook (unlike Pages, which are indexed by Google). Groups also allow administrators and members to send bulk e-mail invitations to join the group.

A popular use of a Facebook group is for conference or event attendees. Organizers of the Association of Canadian Archivists' 2010 conference created a Facebook group for the conference and invited attendees via e-mail. The group successfully marketed conference workshops and allowed delegates to interact with one another before the conference began (http://on.fb.me/batMcK).

Flickr

Flickr is a photo-sharing site that allows archives to post photographs in downloadable or non-downloadable formats for sharing with the public.

Flickr is owned by Yahoo! To sign up for a Flickr account, you must already have a Yahoo! log-in or sign up for one. After signing up, you will be asked to provide information about your institution, a web address, your location, and an avatar (a photo that represents your institution). All of this information will appear in your Flickr profile page. Providing helpful and informative details about your institution is always a good idea. The Library of Congress's Flickr profile links to the Library's other social media, explains the origins of its photography collection, touches on the institution's views on tagging and commenting, and relays its institutional mandate. The profile page also features any photos of the institution that have been "tagged" (see pp. 45–46), Flickr contacts (uploads from contacts will appear on the Flickr homepage and under the "Contacts" tab), and group memberships.

Flickr allows users to quickly upload single images or multiple images in "batches" to online accounts. There are two different kinds of accounts: free and "Pro."

Signing Up

Free accounts allow users to upload 100 MB of images each month. If a free user has more than 200 photos on the site, they will only be able to see the most recent 200 in their "photostream." The other uploaded photos are still stored on the site, and links to these images in blog posts remain active. Free users can also contribute to a maximum of ten "group pools." If a free account is inactive for 90 days, it will be deleted.

Pro accounts allow users to upload an unlimited number of images and videos every month. Photos can be placed in up to 60 group pools, and, as shown in Figure 2.6, Pro account users have access to account statistics.

If your institution plans on using Flickr extensively or as its main online photo gallery, buying a Pro account is advisable. Not only does a Pro account provide extra space and unlimited photos in your photostream, it also offers statistics on your images and videos. The "Your Stats" page will break down your most-viewed photos (on a single day or overall), referrers to your photos, views on your account, and other useful measurables.

Photos on Flickr are searchable by their title, description, and "tags"—usually a short list of descriptive terms that apply to the photo. Each photo can have a maximum of 75 tags. Images are searchable by tags, so the higher the number of descriptive tags, the easier it will be to find your photo.

Once you have uploaded your photos and given each a title, a caption, and perhaps a few tags, it is time to organize your photostream using collections and sets. A "set" is a group of photos that have something in common, whether it is the topic of the photos, a photographer, a time period, or any other linking quality.

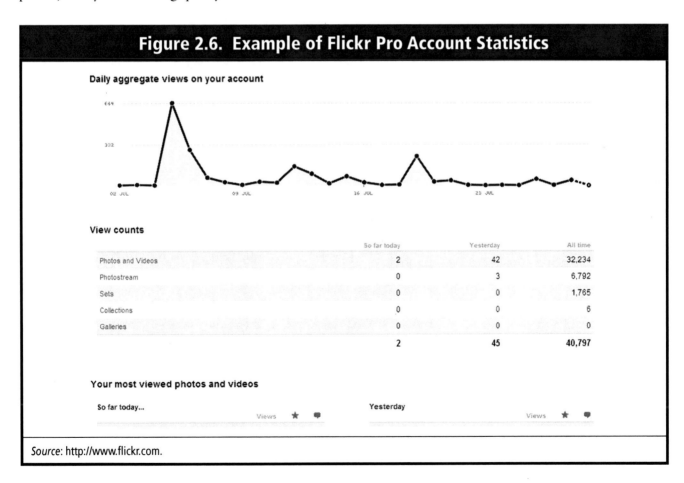

Figure 2.6. Example of Flickr Pro Account Statistics

Daily aggregate views on your account

View counts

	So far today	Yesterday	All time
Photos and Videos	2	42	32,234
Photostream	0	3	6,792
Sets	0	0	1,765
Collections	0	0	6
Galleries	0	0	0
	2	45	40,797

Your most viewed photos and videos

So far today...   Yesterday

Views ★ ◆   Views ★ ◆

Source: http://www.flickr.com.

Reasons for Having a Flickr Account

1. To share your photographs with the world
2. To advertise your photographs to researchers, media outlets, and others for sale
3. To solicit assistance in identifying photographic content, such as persons and places in the photograph

To create a set, click the "Organize & Create" tab. There you will have the option to arrange your photos by dragging images into the "organizer" area to organize your latest batch of uploads, or other content, such as tagged photos, non-tagged photos, photos from a particular date, and so forth.

Once you have determined which photos to place in your set and have dragged them into the organizer, you can batch edit the permissions (who can view, comment on, and tag your photos), add tags, add a location for the set (if your photos share a common location), edit titles and captions, and, finally, add the photos to a new or existing set. These sets will appear along the right sidebar of your Flickr page.

Simply put, a collection is a set of sets. If you have a variety of historical photos in sets, and they share a common theme, you can make them into a collection. For example, if you have some sets featuring photos exclusively from the 1890s, you can place those sets into a collection under that decade.

The Wisconsin Historical Society joined Flickr in 2010 and has already found success in using the tool. Visual Materials Curator Andy Kraushaar describes how the Society uses Flickr to promote its image bank on its website:

> When we post a new gallery of related images on our image database, we always select about 20 or 30 images to post on Flickr as a means of letting our Flickr followers know about the new gallery. Every image has a link back to its Wisconsin Historical Images entry if anyone would like to get more information about the image or possibly buy a print of the image. Flickr is not the primary route that most people take to get to our image database, but it has definitely been worth the investment we have put into it. (Andy Kraushaar, personal communication to author, July 2010)

Kraushaar also suggests that it is important to "interact with the people who are actively commenting on your images . . . as a means of getting your site out there" (Andy Kraushaar, e-mail to author, July 21, 2010).

The Commons

Any archives or historical society can easily join Flickr and participate using free or Pro accounts. Some institutions may wish to further their Flickr experience by applying to be a part of the Flickr Commons. The Commons on Flickr is "home to the world's public photo collections." It was created to show Flickr users "hidden treasures" from archival institutions around the world. Users are invited to participate in the Commons by adding their tags and comments to further describe the items.

A variety of archives, museums, libraries, and historical societies currently participate in the Commons, including the George Eastman House, the Library of Congress, the Brooklyn Museum, the Nationaal Archief, the National Archives and Records Administration, the State Library of New South Wales, and the Smithsonian Institution. As of summer 2010, 45 institutions from around the world were participating (http://www.flickr.com/commons/institutions/). The demand for institutions to join the Commons became so high that no new institutions were accepted for the remainder of 2010. No update has been made to the registration page as of April 2011.

To participate in the Commons, photos must have "no known copyright restrictions." Flickr's definition of "no known copyright restrictions" is as follows:

1. The copyright is in the public domain because it has expired;

2. The copyright was injected into the public domain for other reasons, such as failure to adhere to required formalities or conditions;

3. The institution owns the copyright but is not interested in exercising control; or

4. The institution has legal rights sufficient to authorize others to use the work without restrictions. (http://www.flickr.com/commons/usage/)

Each institution involved in the Commons also posts its own rights statement, which is usually a link back to its own website.

Members of the Commons receive an outstanding number of tags and comments on their images. Tags and comments describe the content down to minute details and sometimes identify people or locations within photos that were previously unknown. Figure 2.7 shows their most popular 150 tags.

Jennifer Gavin of the Library of Congress, the founding member of the Commons, wrote about the Library's success with Flickr in a January 2010 blog entry on its website:

Figure 2.7. Top 150 Tags on the Library of Congress's Photos

1910s 1911 1912 1913 1940 1940s 1941 1942 1943 4x5 aircraft airplane al alfredpalmer alfredtpalmer america americanleague architecture army athlete aviation bainnewsservice baseball baseballplayer battleship beard blackandwhite boat boxer boxing building bw california cap car chicago children city clouds color colorized crowd cymru delano detroitpublishing dress factory farm fashion field flag flags football fsa georgegranthambaincollection glassnegative greatmustachesoftheloc hat hats historicalphotographs history horse horses house howardhollem howardrhollem illinois ireland iwd jack jackdelano landscape largeformat lf libraryofcongress man manhattan men military mountains moustache mustache nationalleague navy new newmexico newyork newyorkbaseballgiants newyorkcity newyorkgiants nl norway ny nyc october october1942 old parade people philadelphia photochrom plane pologrounds portrait railroad river royalty russelllee seated ship sky slidefilm snow soldiers sport sports stadium standing street suffrage suit texas train transparencies transparency trees uniform uniforms unitedstatesnavy us usa usmc usn usnavy vintage wales war wartime washingtondc water white woman women worker workers worldwar2 worldwarii ww2 wwii york

- This is a list of The Library of Congress' 150 most popular tags. You can see all The Library of Congress' tags here.

Source: "The Library of Congress' Photostream," Flickr, http://www.flickr.com/photos/library_of_congress/tags/.

Flickr Terms

- **Photostream:** The way in which Flickr displays the photos and videos uploaded to the site
- **Tag:** A keyword or category label applied to a photo or video
- **Group pool:** A collection of photos on a common subject added to by multiple Flickr members
- **Set:** A group of photos that falls under the same heading
- **Collection:** A set of sets
- **Gallery:** A collection of up to eighteen public photos or videos of Flickr members' videos or photos
- **Note:** Text that will appear on the photo itself; often points out something about the image

Kate Theimer's Picks for Top Five Archives YouTube Channels

1. George Eastman House (http://www.youtube.com/user/GeorgeEastmanHouse)
2. Iowa State University Library Special Collections Department (http://www.youtube.com/user/ISUSpecialCollection)
3. British Film Institute (http://www.youtube.com/user/BFIfilms)
4. U.S. National Archives (http://www.youtube.com/user/usnationalarchives)
5. New-York Historical Society (http://www.youtube.com/user/nyhistory)

Acceptable File Formats for YouTube

- WebM files
- .mpeg4, 3GPP, and MOV files
- .avi
- .mpegps
- .wmv
- .flv

As of today, there have been more than 23 million views of the images and more than 27,700 Flickr community members call us a contact. In two years, we have loaded more than 8,000 images in two collections (historic photographs and historic newspapers) in 12 sets on diverse topics. . . . Over a thousand records in the Prints and Photographs online catalog have been enhanced with information from the Flickr Commons community. More accurate and detailed information in our catalog, with links to interesting histories, makes the pictures not only easier to find but easier to understand. (Gavin, 2010)

YouTube

YouTube is a video-sharing website on which users can upload, share, and view videos. Since its launch in 2005, YouTube has become exceedingly popular, with two billion videos being viewed every day as of mid-2010.

Since 2006, YouTube has been owned by Google (http://www.google.com/press/pressrel/google_youtube.html). To create an account with YouTube, you can use a preexisting Google account. With an account, you can comment on and rate videos and upload your own videos. You can upload up to ten videos in a single uploading session on YouTube. Each video must be under 2 GB and less than 15 minutes in length. As the file is uploading, users can enter information about the video (title, description, tags, and category). As with Flickr, the more information provided for a video, the easier it will be to find.

In June 2010, YouTube launched an online video editor at http://www.youtube.com/editor, which is extremely useful for those without the often expensive software associated with editing. The video editor allows users to easily trim and combine multiple clips, add audio tracks, and preview the finished product.

If your institution is looking to share videos on YouTube, it is a good idea to set up a YouTube channel. To customize your channel, log in to YouTube and the "My Account" link at the top of the page. Then scroll to the "Channel Settings" section.

There, you can enter a new title and description for your channel, as well as select a new video to use for your profile picture. You can brand your YouTube channel to coincide with your institutional website by selecting a color scheme and a background image for your page. You can add personal information, such as your name, gender, age, and location, or stay with adding only information about your institution. It is strongly advised that you include a link to your main website so that YouTube users can learn more about the institution.

Comments on videos in YouTube channels can be easily moderated. You can designate who can comment on videos by going to your Account page and clicking the "Channel Info" link. There, choose an option under the "Who Can Comment" section, and then click the "Update Channel" button.

A good example of an archives' YouTube channel is the National Archives and Records Administration's (NARA) page. As shown in Figure 2.8, the channel is branded with the NARA's logo and colors and features in-depth information about the organization. Just as Flickr users organize photos into sets and collections, YouTube users can group related clips into playlists. NARA's channel features playlists on World War II, the 1940 census, the March on Washington, and more.

To create a YouTube playlist, click "New" (next to the "Playlist" button) in the "My Account" section. Write a name, description, and any tags you would like to include. Then, choose whether you want the playlist to be public or private. To add videos to the playlist, go to the "My Uploaded Videos" section, and check off the videos you would like to include in the playlist, then click "Add To" and select your playlist.

While YouTube is a perfect fit for archives looking to share their film collections, one of the most popular examples of an archives using YouTube is the University of Manitoba Archives. The archives took photos from one of its most popular collections, the Dr. T.G. Hamilton séance photographs and set the photos to some eerie music. The result is a creepy four-minute long video that has garnered over 170,000 views and more than 550 comments. Figure 2.9 shows one of the scary images that has made the video so popular.

What Can You Post on YouTube?

1. Videos in your collections
2. Videos of events your archives has held or sponsored
3. Interviews with archivists, donors, or researchers about specific collections

Figure 2.8. NARA's YouTube Channel

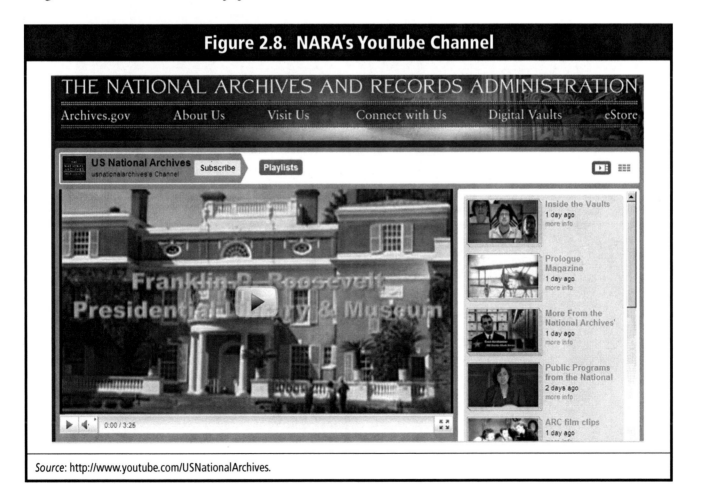

Source: http://www.youtube.com/USNationalArchives.

Figure 2.9. T.G. Hamilton's Photos of Ectoplasm

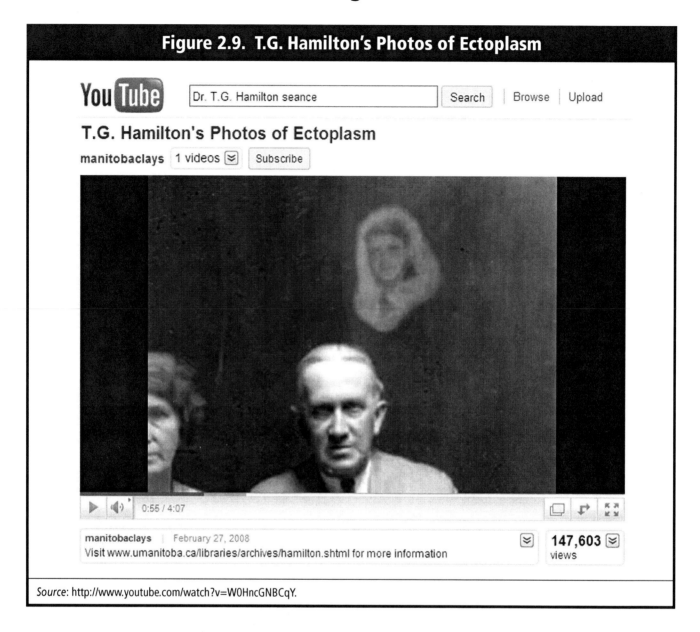

Others

New social media applications are being introduced every day, making it a necessity to keep up with technology news via websites like TechCrunch and Wired. If your area has a social media meet-up, make an effort to attend and learn from the people present. Meet-ups, such as podcamps or informal gatherings (e.g., Halifax, Nova Scotia, has a Third Wednesday social media meet-up), usually involve getting together to discuss an aspect of social media and technology while providing an opportunity to network.

One dominant trend in social media is the "mashup." A mashup is a webpage or web application that uses and combines elements of two or more sources to create new services. An example of a mashup that seems custom-made for archives is Historypin, created by We Are What We Do (WAWWD). Historypin combines Google Street View with its users' "old" photos. Photos are superimposed over present-day locations to show what the location looked like, or what was happening there, "way back when."

By using a combination of Google Maps and Street View, an archives can pinpoint the location of a photo in its holdings. To add a photo to the Historypin map, first sign up for the service using your Google account. Once you have signed in and provided some minimal personal information, you can start adding photos.

Lucia Komljen, of WAWWD (the organization that founded History pin), says that Historypin offers archives an exciting new opportunity to share their collections with a wide audience:

> Historypin gives all these amazing local archives around the world the chance to take their often underexposed content to a much bigger audience. Historypin has hundreds of thousands of visits from all over the world every month and they are finding the Maps and Street View features really engaging and simple to use, so we will know that they are making their way round a lot of content.
>
> Beyond just looking at these archives images, users can now interact with them, which is where things start getting exciting on a local level. As users add stories and memories to archives images and then start to add local pictures of their own, families and communities can come together around local history, bringing it back to life. (Lucia Komljen, personal communication to author, July 2010)

To begin, click "Add Your Photos" on the top of the screen. Select your photo from your computer or from a website. You can add up to five photos at one time. You will then be prompted to provide information about the photo. You can then apply a title, description, tags, and a "story" to the photograph. If you want the description to link back to your own website, you can associate a link with the photo.

To place your photo on the map, enter an address that is relatively close to where your "pin" will go. Then click "Pin to Street View"—this will take your photo into Street View, where you can line up your photo with the present-day setting. To line up your photo correctly, use the "Show/Hide" button to hide the photograph and navigate Street View until the location looks right. Consider the angle and placement of the photographer. To finish lining up the photograph, click the "Show/Hide" button again to bring up the image, which can be scaled up or down to fit the scene. When you are confident that you have a good match, click "Save" and then "Finish" to complete "pinning" your photo. Your photo will then be viewable on the Historypin world map and can be found when someone looks up your area of the world. Figure 2.10 shows a properly lined-up "pin" at scenic Peggy's Cove, Nova Scotia.

Komljen says that because archives have been the most creative users of Historypin, WAWWD is looking to develop features on the website to help archives:

Lucia Komljens's Favorite "Pins" on Historypin

Pins like the one on Elizabeth Street in New York (pictured at http://bit.ly/aB6ahp) really show the power of the Street View comparison and we are hoping that images like this will inspire hundreds more of the same community to be shared.

The one of a grandfather and grandson shelling peas on the front porch in Livonia, MI (pictured at http://bit.ly/al1bqG), is not the best Street View match but it's such a lovely shot and gets to the heart of the intergenerational power of the project.

A bit closer to home for us, there are some amazing London shots...showing how different and yet how similar life was in some parts of the City 100 years ago, like the smart banker on his way to work (http://bit.ly/cmqu7D) in 1905. (Personal communication with author, July 2010.)

Figure 2.10. Peggy's Cove "Pin"

Source: http://www.historypin.com.

[Archives are] relishing the chance to share their collections in a new way and reach new people. Recently, we have been collaborating with local archives to help develop some new features that will particularly help archives. These include being able to add special archival information to images (photographer, archives number, etc.) as well as create special collections on the site. (Lucia Komljen, personal communication to author, July 2010)

Another shift in social media is the move toward mobile applications. Twitter, Facebook, Flickr—they all have mobile applications that make on-the-go updating easy. Building a custom application for your organization is a somewhat expensive and very technical undertaking that likely cannot be done in-house but will make your collections more accessible than ever. North Carolina State University Libraries' WolfWalk is an example of a great mobile application that blends the past and present (http://www.lib.ncsu.edu/dli/projects/wolfwalk/).

After the application is installed on a smart phone (usually an iPhone, iPod, Blackberry, or Android phone), students can take a guided historical tour around campus. Their mobile devices will detect their current locations using GPS and then give detailed information about nearby buildings and other places.

Other mobile applications include Foursquare and Facebook Places, which allow you to "check in" to different locations. On Foursquare, the person who checks in to a location the most often will become the "Mayor." Check Foursquare and see if people are already checking into your archives. Fun promotions can be built around this concept, such as, for example, a gift certificate for the researcher who checks in the most during a month.

Conclusion

Social media offers an extraordinary opportunity for an archival institution to market itself online. With minimal staff and often no budget, a single update on Twitter, Facebook, Flickr, or YouTube has the potential to reach thousands of people. Communicating effectively through social media channels helps to build a relationship with an online community who otherwise might not be aware of your institution's value.

The best way to learn how to use social media is to sign up on your own for the services and go for it. Having personal accounts on these websites allows you to learn the ropes at your own pace.

You can measure your success with social media by counting the number of followers, fans, image views, tags, and comments, but the real value in these tools is the relationships you can build between your institution and the online community.

Those who would not necessarily come into an archives to research but are interested in learning about history are given an opportunity to explore archival holdings in a new way. Social media can assist in breaking down the "old and musty" archives stereotype and share your institutions' holdings far beyond the reach of a typical press release or brochure. For more examples of "archives 2.0" social media tools, visit Kate Theimer's excellent Archives 2.0 wiki at http://archives2point0 .wetpaint.com.

Why Keep Up with New Social Media Technologies?

1. Your researchers and donors might use a technology you are not using, and you need to reach them where they are.
2. The more places you are on the social web, the more people you will reach.
3. It is good to know what sites are out there and which ones will work for your marketing purposes and which ones will not.

THE PLAN

1. Create a social media policy that specifies who has control of posting content to each site and who has oversight, and make this a part of your marketing plan.
2. Make sure boilerplate content for social media sites is approved before you join.
3. If you use photographs or audio/video from your archives on social media sites, make sure you have copyright or fair use permission, and document this as an addendum to your marketing plan.
4. If you use Flickr and are going to allow downloads of the images, create a photo reproduction policy (or use the one in Chapter 7 of this book) and put it in your marketing plan.

References

Gavin, Jennifer. 2010. "Library's Flickr Site Celebrates the Taggable Twos." *Library of Congress Blog*, January 15. http://blogs.loc.gov/loc/2010/01/library%E2%80%99s-flickr-site-celebrates-the-taggable-twos/.

Kaplan, Andreas M., and Michael Haenlein. 2010. "Users of the World, Unite! The Challenges and Opportunities of Social Media." *Business Horizons* 53, no. 1: 59–68.

Massing, Michael. 2009. "The News about the Internet." *New York Review of Books* 56 (August 13): 29–32. http://www.nybooks.com/articles/22960.

Seminerio, Maria. 1998. "The Open Diary Takes Off." *ZDNet News*, December 1. http://news.zdnet.com/2100-9595_22-101090.html.

Theimer, Kate M. 2010. *Web 2.0 Tools and Strategies for Archives and Local History Collections*. New York: Neal-Schuman.

Additional Resources

"5,000,000,000." 2010. *Flickr Blog*. September 19. http://blog.flickr.net/en/2010/09/19/5000000000/.

"The Commons." 2011. Flickr. http://www.flickr.com/commons/usage/.

Facebook. http://www.facebook.com.

Facebook Places. http://www.facebook.com/places.

Flickr. http://www.flickr.com.

Foursquare. http://www.foursquare.com.

Historypin. http://www.historypin.com.

Smarty, Ann. 2008. "Facebook Group vs. Facebook Fan Page: What's Better?" *Search Engine Journal*. October 1. http://www.searchenginejournal.com/facebook-group-vs-facebook-fan-page-whats-better/7761/.

Theimer, Kate. *Archives on Twitter*. Twitter. http://twitter.com/archivesnext/archives-on-twitter.

Twitter. http://twitter.com.

Wisconsin Historical Society. "Wisconsin Historical Images' Photostream." Flickr. http://www.flickr.com/photos/whsimages/.

YouTube. http://www.youtube.com.

Zuckerberg, Mark. 2010. "Facebook Hits 500 Million Members." *Facebook Blog*, July 21. http://blog.facebook.com/blog.php?post=409753352130.

Blogging

Lisa Grimm

Introduction

Blogging has come a long way since its 1999 definition as "a Web site that contains an online personal journal with reflections, comments, and often hyperlinks provided by the writer" (Theimer, 2009). Most current blogs are far removed from the confessional stereotype of the format's early days; for many sites around the Web, the term *blog* often suggests little beyond the publishing platform. For our purposes, *blog* will be defined for archives and archivists as a more informal website with multiple entries that may be organized by date and/or keyword, typically with user comments available—but this definition is flexible enough to encompass almost any aim.

Given the informal origins of blogging, it is not surprising that many archives blogs offer a more personable, and seemingly less structured, avenue of communication between the archives and its potential users—but the blog format is flexible enough to serve needs as diverse as basic outreach to replacing the online public access catalog (OPAC). Archives' blogs go beyond offering the basic information that should be found on every archives' website (collection information, location, opening hours, contact information, and the like) and can help elucidate what "really happens" in the archives—increasing transparency and offering users a chance to see what goes on behind the curtain.

Some blogs offer something of a hybrid format combining more than one style, but most fit quite well into one of the following broad categories, as defined.

Repository blogs often have multiple authors, depending on the size of the institution—but, as in the analog archives world, small staffs and lone arrangers are just as prevalent online. They may highlight items from the collection or publicize upcoming events or the archival staff's daily tasks. However, they serve to promote the institution, not individual staff members (which is not to say that archivists who write for repository blogs are not recognized for their work; in general, though, these blogs have a more collective goal).

Categories of Blogs
- Repository blogs
- Processing blogs
- "Catablogs"
- Archival content blogs
- Personal archives blogs

Processing blogs have become more popular in the past three years as the profession moves toward a wider notion of transparency; decisions about processing styles and collections management decisions are often documented in these blogs. Processing blogs are something of a subtype of the repository blog, but they tend to be a stand-alone feature that focuses on the specific task at hand rather than on the other activities of the archives. They can be a useful tool to demonstrate to donors action being taken on collections (either a single collection or a number of different collections), but they must be used with caution. This will be discussed in further detail later.

"Catablogs" use the blog format to replace the traditional online catalog (whether it be an OPAC or simply a list of finding aids). Given that archival materials are not always well served by typical library technology tools, the ability to customize the display and content blogging software provided offers the archivist a more granular way to provide access—often down to the item level, where required—as will be discussed later in this chapter.

Archival content blogs may be hosted by an institution but are quite frequently the province of the nonarchivist. These are "real-time" diary or journal entries of historic materials reproduced in an online format, ranging from the well-known, such as the online *The Diary of Samuel Pepys* (Figure 3.1), to those from local history collections such as the *Joshua Hempstead Blog* (Figure 3.2), maintained by the New London County Historical Society.

Personal archives blogs are maintained by individual archivists, who typically comment on the state of the profession (or encourage discussion of the profession) or disseminate information to other archivists, without the constraints necessary in an institutional blog. Given the many demands on the time of most archivists, why should they consider blogging? In short, it's a simple tool that widens access while helping the archivists involved maintain their professional profiles—without ever leaving the office.

A number of blogs and their sponsoring institutions are discussed in this chapter. See the sidebar for links to all the websites and blogs discussed herein.

A History of Blogging by Archives

Blogging as a recognized offshoot of generic web publishing developed in the late 1990s, with the launch of some early blogging platforms, including LiveJournal and Blogger, in 1999. Movable Type and WordPress joined their ranks in 2001 and 2003, respectively, with the early 2000s seeing a huge spike in the number of blogs produced (and, not infrequently, later abandoned—this applies to blogs of every stripe, not simply archives blogs). The archives world joined the blogosphere when the University of Georgia's Special Collections posted a few entries online in 2001; Phil Gyford joined the fray in 2003 with his blog, *The Diary of Samuel Pepys*; and African American Studies at Yale University's Beinecke Library started the *African American Studies at Beinecke Library* blog in the same year.

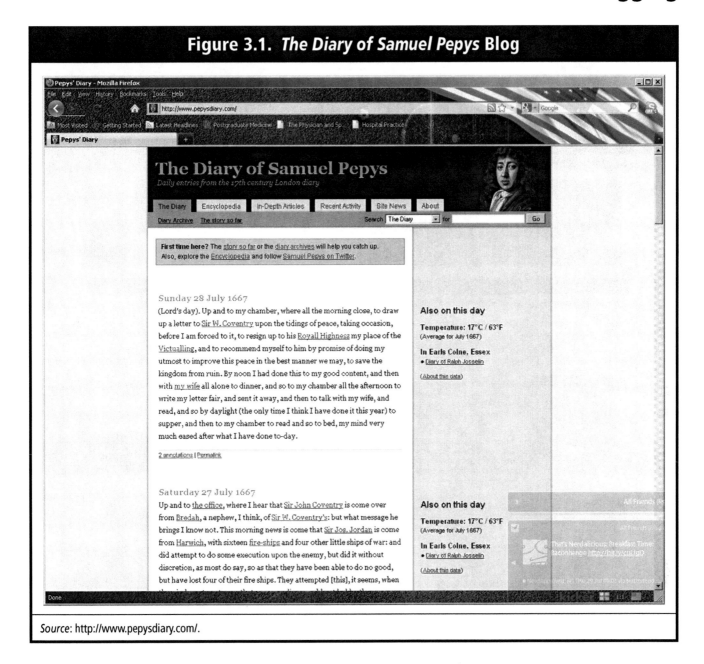

Figure 3.1. *The Diary of Samuel Pepys Blog*

Since 2005, the number of archives-related blogs has grown exponentially (especially insofar as institutional blogs are concerned), and they have gradually expanded not only their user bases, but their various aims and links between other organizations have grown and changed as well. The role of the archives blog is becoming ever more important as archives use other social media to promote and provide access to their institutions.

Why Archives and Archivists Should Blog

It is a given that most archivists have very full plates, but the benefits of blogging far outweigh the time spent working on a blog. This section

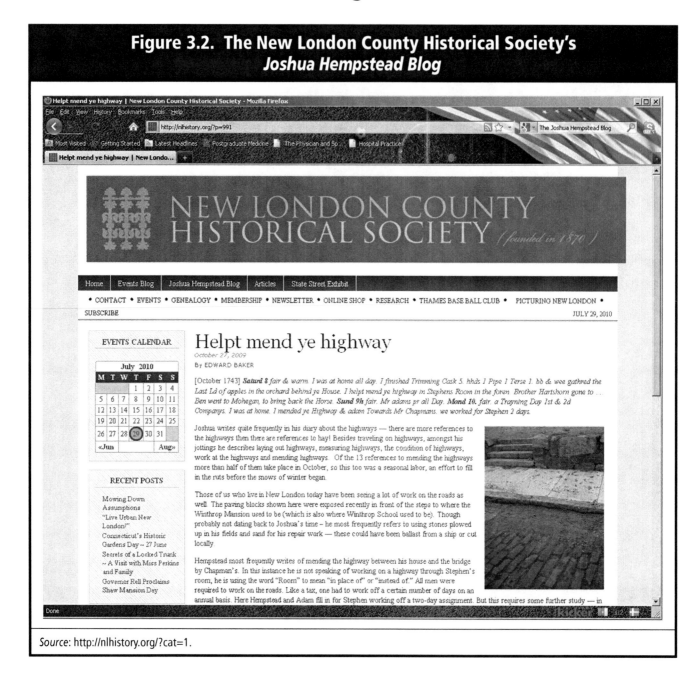

Figure 3.2. The New London County Historical Society's *Joshua Hempstead Blog*

Source: http://nlhistory.org/?cat=1.

examines the benefits more fully, beginning with basic promotion of the archives.

The institutional blog serves to raise the public profile of the archives and typically highlights (or hosts) exhibitions, events and programming, or recent research. Rather than waiting for users to find them, archival institutions can proactively promote specific collections or raise awareness of funding needs through blog posts. One of the strengths of this approach is that the archivists at the institution have control over how they present themselves and their content (Leonard, 2009). It can be much simpler (and more targeted—promoting your blog to the right audience will be addressed later) than a finding aid that may or may not be found by an interested researcher. Northwestern University Archives went through a number of iterations with its blog before hitting on the right mix of tone and promotion to bring new audiences to their collections, resulting in a successful blog and a rise in research requests, as well as a higher institutional awareness. Repositories are increasingly using their blogs for references purposes; Dickinson College documents and shares each reference request, including what was discovered and links to any relevant scanned images, on their blog, proving quick access for researchers as well as those responding to reference requests (Figure 3.3).

At first glance it might seem that the chief audience for a processing blog is other archivists, but processing blogs also help to increase transparency

Figure 3.3. Dickinson College Archives and Special Collections' Reference Blog

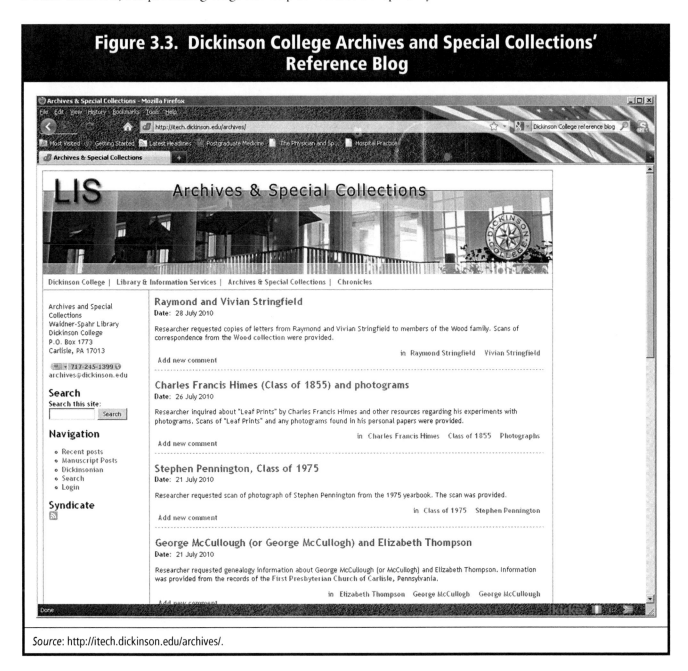

Source: http://itech.dickinson.edu/archives/.

and demystify what archivists do for a more general public. They can also help to support fundraising efforts—one of the Historical Society of Pennsylvania's processing blogs, *Processing the Chew Family Papers*, highlighted the processing of the Chew Family Papers, showing donors specifically where their dollars went in their "Adopt a Collection" initiative. The blog also served to highlight decisions made during processing and announced when the finding aid was completed, thus linking back to more traditional resources. Other processing blogs focus on technique or education, while some serve to document grant-funded projects, thus becoming part of the larger historical record in the process. The *PACSCL Hidden Collections Project* blog is one such example; it documents the project from a variety of viewpoints, from managerial to student worker, offering both a high-level view of the project as well as input from those involved in the day-to-day processing. New discoveries, as well as logistical challenges, are both documented on the blog—and the interactive nature of the format has even helped connect descendants to the collections in this example (Smerz, 2009).

A number of successful catablogs have been inspired by the University of Massachusetts's *UMarmot* blog, which uses the blog format to provide a number of access points into each record:

> Each UMarmot record contains a brief description of each collection, including the collection name, size, and date range, a brief description of its contents, selected subject terms, and links (when available) to detailed finding aids and other online resources. Each record is also indexed under one or more general subject categories, which may be selected using the drop-down menu on the right side of the page. (Special Collections & University Archives, University of Massachusetts at Amherst, http://www.library.umass.edu/spcoll/umarmot/?page_id=561)

With readily customizable blog tools such as category tags (see Figure 3.4), collections can be easily browsed and sorted using a number of criteria (Kramer-Smyth, 2009). Each collection is an individual blog entry, and a user can narrow a search to a specific collection or can find a group of collections related to the same subject—allowing for discovery of related collections without accessing each individual finding aid. The flexibility of the blog format is of particular utility for archival material that is not necessarily well served by traditional OPACs—and it also aids an archives that lacks the IT support necessary to support the OPAC.

For you, the individual archives blogger, setting up and maintaining the blog demonstrates your technical and writing skills—it is an easy way for potential employers or collaborators to discover your work—and it can help to raise and maintain your professional profile. Creating your own forum to discuss professional issues shows your professional commitment, and while you may have opinions with which others disagree, if you present yourself professionally, it should still prove a benefit. As a professional development tool, a personal archives blog can be very useful. There is a large and growing community of archives bloggers, and your blog can help you connect with them. The audience gained through blogging can help burnish a resume—or even give added credence on grant applications

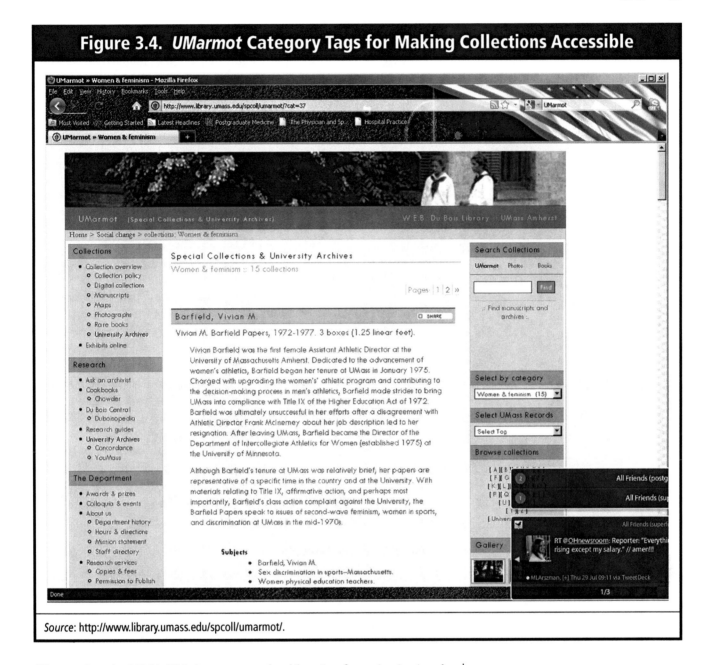

Figure 3.4. *UMarmot* **Category Tags for Making Collections Accessible**

Source: http://www.library.umass.edu/spcoll/umarmot/.

(Kramer-Smyth, 2009). This is not to say that blogging for an institutional blog will not provide similar benefits; as with any online activity, it adds to your digital footprint, but it will be generally understood that the voice and opinions you express on one may be quite different from the other (see "Setting Policies," pp. 65–67).

Creating a Blog

Making the decision to blog might be easy, given the benefits—but the subsequent design and setup tasks may seem daunting. By breaking down the process into a number of phases, blog creation can be made simple.

Options and Choices for Blog Setup

There are a number of options to consider before starting a blog:

- What platform will you use?
- Will the local IT department host it, or will you use the hosting options offered by the blog platform?
- What sort of layout and template will best serve the blog?

If these sound overwhelming, it's worth taking a step back to look at the organization's current skill set. While advanced technical skills are not required to start or update a blog, some basic HTML and Photoshop skills can improve the look and feel—and those more advanced skills (including cascading style sheets, or CSS, interface design, and basic system administration) do open other avenues for hosting and development described later in this chapter.

First, some definitions are in order. A *hosted blog* is one that resides on the servers provided by the platform—most commonly, Blogger or TypePad. But a *self-hosted blog* must still be stored somewhere; the difference is that you are providing the hosting. A few pros and cons for each option are shown in the sidebar. This is one of the most important choices you will make in the life of your blog—while you can always move to a self-hosted option later, it will require a bit of migration work. Weighing your (or your organization's) skill set at this point is crucial; while setting up a self-hosted blog is a great way to learn some basic system administration and coding skills, it's not your full-time job. If, on the other hand, you have those skills in-house, the greater level of customization and freedom offered by a self-hosted solution may be ideal. This is not to denigrate the hosted option—it's a fast and efficient way to get out information, but it's worth noting that it is an option you may outgrow.

Setting Up a Self-Hosted Blog

In addition to the skills mentioned earlier, templates can be more fully customized (or even built from scratch) if you or another staff member

HOSTED VERSUS SELF-HOSTED BLOGS		
	Hosted Blog	**Self-Hosted Blog**
Pros	• Fast, simple setup—no complex coding skills required • Software updates are automatic • Free	• More control over the blog's look and feel via back-end code • Some hands-on maintenance can be required for software or plug-in updates • More "professional" look and feel, if desired, with custom URLs
Cons	• Less control—over both code and content (which may be a factor when linking to historical material) • Outages may occur and the host may not back up your site • Generic URLs	• More technological expertise required • Cost may be a factor—while the platforms themselves are free, the hosting and any domain registration fees will need to be covered

have more advanced XML and CSS skills. If your institution is paying an outside company to host the blog, you will need either a staff member with some basic system administration skills, such as database creation and software installation, or access to an IT department that is committed to taking on those tasks.

With most current web hosts, setting up a blog is a fairly straightforward process. Once you have set up an account with the host, you or another staff member who is the administrator accesses a web panel, which typically features a graphical user interface, to complete the steps required to get the blog ready to go. Typically all that is required is the registration of a URL and the creation of a database and installation of the blog software (usually WordPress or Movable Type); both are straightforward processes for most technologically inclined people, and in most cases there is extensive documentation offered by the hosting company for these steps. As staff turnover and loss of institutional knowledge is always a concern, it is wise to keep documentation of required usernames, database names, and passwords—but in most cases the web panel will need very infrequent tending. Choosing the right option for your organization's current technology setup can save headaches down the line.

Setting Up a Hosted Blog

In contrast to the self-hosted process, setting up a hosted blog is quite simple—all it requires is filling out a few online forms, although some customization is certainly possible.

Updating: Author versus Administrator

Once you have chosen a platform and hosting option, it is time to make some policy decisions. How often can the blog realistically be updated? Regular updates are the biggest factor in maintaining reader interest, so it is wise to spread out this responsibility, if at all possible. An ideal baseline is no more than a week between updates; more than a month makes the blog look like it is no longer used. To that end, creating multiple user accounts and rotating responsibility for updates can be a useful element. Although the terminology may vary somewhat among platforms, there are always two levels of user accounts—one for authors and one for administrators.

If you are a less technologically inclined user, an author account still gives you plenty of control over the look and feel of your post. (All of the above options, which are available whether choosing a hosted or self-hosted option, come with a WYSIWYG—or "what you see is what you get" editor—with an interface akin to what is found in Microsoft Word or other word-processing software; there is little to no code involved). While an author account keeps you locked out of the administrative side of the blog—you will not have access to the template code or the ability to create new users—you will not "break" anything by creating and editing your own updates. It is advisable to have more than one administrator, however, to deal with any unforeseen issues in case the main administrator is unavailable.

What You Need Before You Set Up a Self-Hosted Blog

- Web space provided by your institution through its web hosting account or an account with a provider
- Some system administration skills (or a willingness to learn)
- A URL for your site—either registered with the host or through a domain name registrar

---

Step-by-Step Guide to Setting Up a Hosted Blog

1. Choose a provider. Blogger or TypePad are most common for hosted blogs, but there is a version of WordPress available as well.
2. Create your account. This is where you'll name your blog and choose its URL (e.g., http://yourarchives.blogger.com).
3. Choose one of the provided templates, or upload one of your own; examples are available in a simple web search.
4. Add further authors to your blog, if applicable.
5. Start adding content!

User accounts may be generic so that each post seems to have an institutional author—for example, the username could simply reflect the name of your archives—or accounts can be user-specific. The generic name will seem more formal, while the individual user option gives each staff member who posts an opportunity to highlight some of his or her work in a way that can be seen by the wider archives community. The administrator who sets up individual accounts should have every user's password in case a user forgets his or her password.

Configuring the Blog

Whether using a hosted blog or setting up your own, the next step is to configure the blog itself. The major duties here include choosing a template and setting up user accounts. Even with hosted blogs, there is still ample room to customize the look and feel of the blog. It is not necessary to use one of the templates already supplied (each platform has quite a few out-of-the-box options), although the setup process is considerably faster if you use an existing template. The downside is that it will have a less professional look. As mentioned earlier, a staff member with a little bit of skill in XML and CSS can quickly modify a template to create a more unique look; a wide variety of templates for each platform can be easily found via a web search.

Depending on your institutional policies, you may be locked into a template chosen by your parent organization, or you may have the opportunity (and challenge) of choosing and customizing your own template. The major blogging platforms all offer a number of pre-installed templates, but your site will look more professional, and more unique, if you go beyond those options.

While a web search will turn up a dizzying array of options, first consider your in-house technical skills—a basic understanding of HTML, CSS, and web graphics can go a long way toward creating your own look and feel. Consider how text- or image-heavy your blog is likely to be; a two-column layout may be perfect, or you may prefer a three-column layout to include sidebar widgets (e.g., blog archives, related links, logos, or featured items). Variations on both themes (as well as others) are widely available. Be sure to choose a template that will not overwhelm the reader—simplicity and clean lines will highlight your content more effectively than bells and whistles. It may well be worth testing a few templates to see which is the best fit, and it's always possible to change templates later, whether as a means of refreshing the site or to take the look and feel in a different direction.

As mentioned, there are two options for user accounts, administrator or author. All that is required to create these accounts is an e-mail address for each user. It is also possible to create different levels of publishing authority. Some users can be given authority to approve blog posts before they go live. This function may be particularly useful when employing temporary or student workers who contribute to the blog but who may require a bit more editorial guidance.

Setting Policies

It is important to decide early who will have editorial authority over what is published on the blog (obviously, this does not pertain to individual bloggers to the same degree it does to institutional blogs—but it is still worth remembering that what you write on a blog is publicly available). Will someone act as the blog's sole editor, or will there be an editorial board who decides what is published? In either case, your institution may require adherence to its existing policies; even if you are not using your employer's servers or IT support, it may still be wise to stay within their guidelines. The blog can be a useful tool to highlight the value of the archives to the institution, so be sure to carefully frame issues such as lack of funding or institutional support (if, indeed, it is decided that the archives' blog is an appropriate forum to point out such problems).

While the voice and tone will no doubt vary among authors, ensure that all writers understand any constraints (whether official or diplomatic) under which they are operating. Share with authors this advice about writing for the Web: the blog may be read on a phone or other hand-held device, so the copy should appear in easily digestible "chunks." This holds true for readers accessing the site from a computer as well. You are not writing for an academic audience, so stay away from long, dense blocks of text. Provide context, but try to keep things broken up with images or other media (see Figure 3.5).

The blog's editor should formulate a policy on comments. All blogging software includes several options for comments—allowed, moderated, or closed (none allowed). In many cases, archives blogs can generate interesting discussion, but comments sections can also be plagued by spam. If you start out with "free" comments, it is simple enough to switch to moderating (or even closing) comments later—although it may be necessary to delete unwanted commentary or outright spam.

The decision to allow open comments or moderated comments or not to allow comments at all will depend on your institution's goals for the blog, as well as other policies, workflow, and (later) traffic. As mentioned earlier regarding the PACSCL example, comments can provide an avenue for interested external parties to become involved with the organization and its materials. While one might assume that a small archives blog will generate considerably less traffic than a pop culture blog, less traffic does not necessarily mean the blog will be unnoticed by comment spammers. Implementing the moderated comments option ensures that your blog will not be inadvertently advertising pharmaceuticals, but someone must monitor the site to allow appropriate comments. Of course, even with freely open comments, this can become an issue, and if your site is, indeed, targeted by spammers, cleaning up the mess they leave behind may end up taking longer than moderating comments as they come in. By contrast, the delay between posting and approving comments for a blog that has heavy traffic may somewhat stymie that blog—but in any event, you can revisit the decision on handling comments at any time.

Figure 3.5. Using Images to Break Up Dense Text to Keep from Overwhelming the Reader

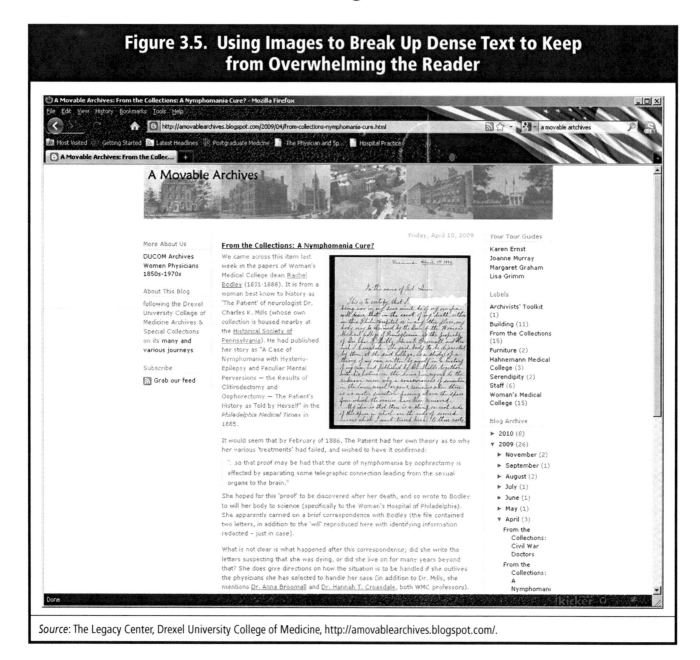

Source: The Legacy Center, Drexel University College of Medicine, http://amovablearchives.blogspot.com/.

Some suggested best practices for keeping your blog fresh and professional are really little more than common sense:

1. Choose and write for your audience, whether that is the general public, other archivists, funding bodies, or your institution, but remember that those beyond your ideal audience will be able to find what you have written.

2. Use proper spelling and grammar and check your work before posting it. The blog may be informal, but it's still no place to be sloppy.

3. Include images and use keywords in each blog post; they maintain reader interest. If you can link those images to larger

versions with rich metadata, you are giving potential users another avenue of discovery for your collections.

4. If you choose one staff member to be the "gatekeeper" who is required to approve any blog posts, ensure he or she can do this in a timely fashion. A stale blog post will read as such, even when you're talking about history.

5. Stick to a reasonably regular publishing schedule wherever possible.

While these points chiefly apply to institutional archives blogs, individual bloggers can still take note; as previously discussed, you should have no hesitation in taking on controversial archives-related topics as long as you adhere to the usual guidelines of professional discourse. The additional common sense rules for individual archives bloggers are self-evident:

1. Do not say anything about your employer you would not mention in any other public setting.

2. If you find your archives blog frequently strays onto other topics, it may be time to start a second blog—stick to your subject.

3. Even for an individual, a regular publication schedule is vital—readership will drop away just as quickly when updates become scarce.

Syndication

Once the blog has found a basic rhythm as far as tone and update frequency, promotion becomes a key concern. Typical methods involve connecting with other archives bloggers, using other social networking tools, including Facebook and Twitter, or sending e-mail blasts for each update. This may seem like engaging in public relations for the sake of public relations, but these additional tasks as part of each blog update should not become too onerous—and some require only one-time setup.

Syndication of the blog is the fastest way to get updates out to a wider audience, and it is a very straightforward process—once a few terms are defined. RSS (Really Simple Syndication) is one of the most popular syndication formats. Essentially, it creates a "feed" that other sites can automatically pick up or to which individual readers may subscribe. It may sound intimidatingly technical, but even the novice blogger can use RSS feeds to increase readership (Hrastnik, 2006). Your blog has a built-in RSS feed to which individual readers may subscribe by clicking the supplied orange logo (Figure 3.6), but sending this feed to an aggregator (typically, a subject-specific site that "collects" and distributes feeds) ensures it will be found by many new readers.

In the archival world, ArchivesBlogs is the best-known aggregator—using RSS feeds, it automatically displays new archives blog posts as they

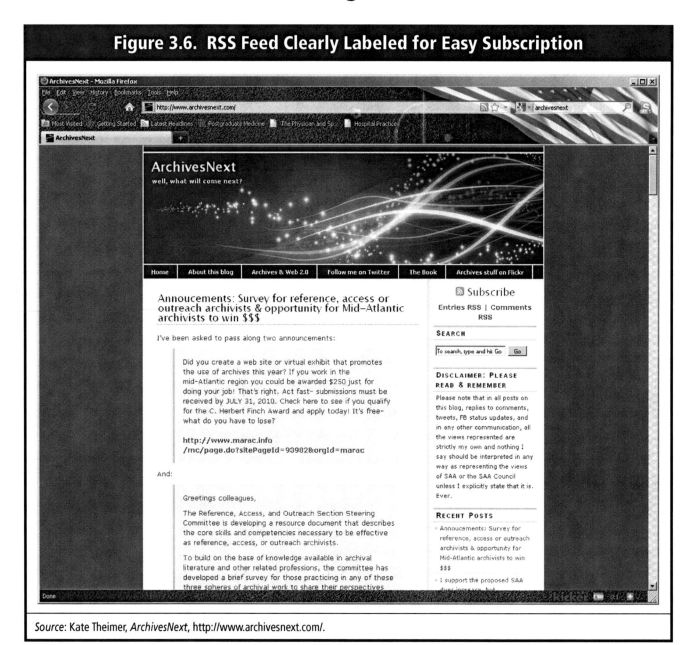

Figure 3.6. RSS Feed Clearly Labeled for Easy Subscription

Source: Kate Theimer, *ArchivesNext*, http://www.archivesnext.com/.

go up. Blogs are sorted by language, and the most recent blog posts are displayed both on their websites and on their Twitter feeds. Most readers and subscribers are other archivists, so if that is your target audience, getting the URL listed on ArchivesBlogs will certainly drive traffic to the blog.

RSS feeds are also a useful way for you to ensure that your blog will be found in the Web 2.0 world—feeds can be added to Facebook accounts, mobile apps, and e-mail accounts. Readers have content delivered directly into the device or platform they use most often. For this reason, it is wise to set your RSS feeds to allow full content to be accessed by these various methods; the option to limit to just the first few words can be off-putting to end users.

If the goal is to publicize the site beyond archivists, seek out an aggregator by subject and consider how researchers find your facility at present. Archives with a particular strength in women's history may find more success publicizing their sites via those websites, while an institution placing an emphasis on a specific author or historical figure may wish to ally with other related blogs and sites.

Generic syndication services are also useful, especially if the goal is to gain a more general audience; it is well worth ensuring that the site is listed in Technorati and Google Blog Search. Making your blog "findable" by adding it to these sites should be part of your initial setup; as a courtesy, you may want to wait to add your blog to ArchivesBlogs until it is clear you have a viable blog with a record of regular updates. Facebook offers a number of blog syndication options as well; using the RSS feed as a tool, the blog can be "fed" to any or all of these outlets. (See the sidebar on p. 56 for links to these and other services.)

Depending on your organizational policies, it may be wise to apply for a Creative Commons license for the blog; this will offer some protection from commercial entities scraping text and images and using them without permission—although for this reason, it is also advisable to watermark any images you use on your blog. Keeping track of where users are coming from can also help ensure that material is not being reused elsewhere without permission. Also, having a Creative Commons license will protect the institution from most copyright infringement problems that might occur. All comments are considered part of the Creative Commons.

Tracking Your Progress

A number of free tools and resources are available to help you analyze how popular the blog is and what users are searching for. These data points can help you tailor future posts to users' interests and can also aid you in making decisions about which collections to highlight. Institutional archives may also find an additional benefit, perhaps discovering that a relatively unknown collection has a wider group of potential users and using those statistics to plan future budgets or grant opportunities. Google Analytics is one option to consider; StatCounter is another. Both tools are free and provide reports such as visitor paths, popular pages, search terms, and maps of where visitors are coming from. (See the sidebar on p. 56 for links to these tools.)

Conclusion

As with any technology, blogs will become dated if software is not regularly upgraded—the same is true for the look and feel of the blog. While it is not necessary to have a designer on staff, it can help to have someone with a good eye for detail to provide these infrequent refreshers. Keeping the blog's documentation up to date is also very

RSS feeds allow your readers to easily find your latest posts by subscribing to your feed. It is also a simple way to allow your content to be picked up by blog aggregators (websites that pull in content from a number of websites), helping you to reach a wider audience—wherever it might be.

Resources for Evaluation of Your Blog's Business
- User statistics: Google Analytics, StatCounter, or a package provided by your host
- Google Webmaster Tools: Helps improve your site's ranking as well as alerting you to broken links and code improvements

important—but, as mentioned earlier, updating does not need to go much beyond usernames, passwords, and some brief technical information. It should be enough to deal with staff turnover; as a general rule, a departing staff member should no longer have access to the institutional blog, regardless of how pleasant the terms of parting are. And it cannot be emphasized enough that frequent blog posts will help drive traffic, while infrequent posts will do little to bring new users to an archives. Blogging can be a real time commitment for the busy archivist, but it can reap real-world rewards through increased archives use, wider awareness, and a more connected place in the archival profession.

THE PLAN

1. Formulate a set of goals you want to accomplish with your blog, and place these in your marketing plan.
2. If you have a person or persons who will be posting to the blog, give them written authority to do so in your plan and give them duties and responsibilities.
3. If you establish guidelines for your blog and for posting to your blog, put these in your plan.

References

Hrastnik, Rok. 2006. "Use RSS to Increase Your Traffic Now, Part 1." *Marketingstudies.net.* Accessed October 12, 2009 (no longer available). http://rssdiary.marketingstudies.net/content/use_rss_to_increase_your_traffic_now_part_1.php.

Kramer-Smyth, Jeanne. 2009. "Spellbound Blog: Using Blogs as a Professional Development Opportunity." *The Interactive Archivist: Case Studies in Utilizing Web 2.0 to Improve the Archival Experience.* Chicago: Society of American Archivists. http://lib.byu.edu/sites/interactivearchivist/case-studies/spellbound-blog/.

Leonard, Kevin B. 2009. "Blogs and Blog Marketing: Bringing New Users to the Northwestern University Archives." *The Interactive Archivist: Case Studies in Utilizing Web 2.0 to Improve the Archival Experience.* Chicago: Society of American Archivists. http://www.lib.byu.edu/sites/interactivearchivist/case-studies/blogs-at-nu/.

Smerz, Courtney. 2009. "The Hering-Knerr Family Papers and a Peek into the Hilles Family Papers." *PACSCL Hidden Collections Processing Project: Revealing the Unknown Stories of the Philadelphia Region* (blog). December 4. http://clir.pacscl.org/2009/12/04/the-hering-knerr-family-papers-and-a-peek-into-the-hilles-family-papers/.

Special Collections & University Archives, University of Massachusetts Amherst. 2011. "What Is in UMarmot?" *UMarmot.* http://www.library.umass.edu/spcoll/umarmot/?page_id=561.

Theimer, Kate. 2009. "Web 2.0 Tools and Strategies for Archives and Local History Collections." *ArchivesNext* (blog), June 9. http://www.archivesnext.com/?p=294.

Additional Resources

"Blog." 2011. *Merriam-Webster Online Dictionary.* http://www.merriam-webster.com/dictionary/blog.

Daines, J. Gordon III, and Corey L. Nimer, eds. 2009. "Web 2.0 and Archives." *The Interactive Archivist: Case Studies in Utilizing Web 2.0 to Improve the Archival Experience.* Chicago: Society of American Archivists, May 18. http://lib.byu.edu/sites/interactivearchivist.

Dickinson College. 2011. "Archives & Special Collections." http://itech.dickinson.edu/archives/.

Drexel University College of Medicine Archives & Special Collections. 2010. *A Movable Archives* (blog). Last post October 1. http://amovablearchives.blogspot.com/.

Drexel University Libraries Archives & Special Collections. 2011. http://www.library.drexel.edu/blogs/collections/.

Earl Gregg Swem Library, College of William and Mary. 2010. *Mary Comes to the College with William* (blog). Last post March 11, 2010. http://womenatwilliamandmary.blogspot.com/.

Electronic Frontier Foundation. 2011. "Legal Guide for Bloggers" *Bloggers' Legal Guide.* http://www.eff.org/issues/bloggers/legal.

Gillin, Paul. 2009. "Why You Should Take Another Look at RSS." *Paulgillin.com*, April 21. http://paulgillin.com/2009/04/why-you-should-take-another-look-at-rss/.

Gyford, Phil. 2003. "About This Site." *The Diary of Samuel Pepys.* http://www.pepysdiary.com/about/.

Historical Society of Pennsylvania. 2008. *Processing the Chew Family Papers* (blog). http://chewpapers.blogspot.com/.

Kelly, Brian. 2007. "A Meta-Policy for Institutional Blogs." *UK Web Focus* (blog). February 1. http://ukwebfocus.wordpress.com/2007/02/01/a-meta-policy-for-institutional-blogs/.

Lally, Ann M., and Carolyn E. Dunford, 2007. "Using Wikipedia to Extend Digital Collections." *D-Lib Magazine* 13, no. 5/6. http://www.dlib.org/dlib/may07/lally/05lally.html.

Mancini, Anna. 2008. "From the HP Archives...." *The HP Blog Hub.* http://replay.waybackmachine.org/20090522135248/http://www.communities.hp.com/online/blogs/hparchives/default.aspx.

Matienzo, Mark A. 2006. "On What 'Archives Blogs' Are and What Archives-Blogs Is Not." *thesecretmirror.com* (blog), September 22. http://thesecretmirror.com/archivesblogs/responsetolannon.

———. 2011. *ArchivesBlogs.* http://archivesblogs.com.

New London County Historical Society. 2001. *Joshua Hempstead Blog.* http://nlhistory.org/?cat=1.

Rosenzweig, R. 2006. "Can History Be Open Source? Wikipedia and the Future of the Past." *Journal of American History* 93, no. 1: 117–146. http://chnm.gmu.edu/essays-on-history-new-media/essays/?essayid=42.

Simon, Nina. 2007. "Institutional Blogs: Different Voices, Different Value." *Museum 2.0* (blog), March 7. http://museumtwo.blogspot.com/2007/03/institutional-blogs-different-voices.html.

Theimer, Kate. 2011. "Blogs." *Archives 2.0* (blog). Last update March 9. http://archives2point0.wetpaint.com/page/Blogs.

University of Georgia Libraries, Special Collections. 2011. *Richard B. Russell Library for Political Research and Studies* (blog). http://rbrl.blogspot.com/.

Media Outlets

Stephanie Gaub

Introduction

As any disgraced celebrity can attest to, the media can make or break a career. The same holds true for archives and other cultural institutions. One false step with the local, regional, and national press can spell disaster for an organization. Therefore, it is important to have a positive relationship with the media so that they support you in both good and bad times. Respecting media deadlines, knowing who to contact, and understanding the tactics involved in fostering these relationships will prove beneficial for you and your institution.

Media outlets often have little understanding of what an archives does, while many archivists have minimal or episodic training in the areas of marketing and public relations. Despite this disconnect, both entities need each other. The media needs the archives to help with historical pieces, back stories, and filler on slow news days. Archivists need the media to help promote their activities and to respond to any controversies that may arise. "Archivists recognize their responsibility to promote the use of records as a fundamental purpose of the keeping of archives" (Society of American Archivists, 2005). To achieve this, it is important for archivists to have an understanding of the pressures placed on media representatives and the tactics involved in creating and sustaining mutually beneficial relationships.

Definition of Media

The media is generally understood to be the organizations and people who cover, report, edit, direct, and produce the news for television, radio, and newspapers. Each type of media has its own set of peculiarities that should be understood before embarking on a professional relationship. Media outlets can be print or online venues, as well as over-the-air broadcasts.

Print media, such as newspapers and magazines, often have deadlines that allow for changes, while television and radio spots are often live and

- Print
  - Newspaper
  - Magazine
  - Journal
- Online
  - Archives website
  - Other organization's website
  - Blog
  - Online newspaper
  - Online magazine
- Broadcast
  - Radio
  - Television

Goals of the Archivist Acting as Public Relations Professional

- Create, maintain, and protect the archives' reputation.
  - Make the archives easily accessible through finding aids and indexes.
  - Ensure that staff are friendly, helpful, and knowledgeable in the archives' holdings.
  - Speak to various groups about the archives and its holdings.
  - Maintain a file of all outreach to show how the archives is contributing to the community.
- Enhance the prestige of the archives.
- Present the archives in a positive light.
  - Join other cultural institutions to promote common goals.
  - Promote the archives in tourism through the local chamber of commerce.
- Create goodwill on behalf of the archives by offering classes to local educational institutions and other organizations and ask the media to attend and report.

spontaneous. Many outlets are guilty of encouraging instant sensationalism, which can be detrimental to an institution if a story is not worded or edited correctly. You should understand the nuances of each type of media as well as recognize an interesting news story. Cultivating friendly media contacts will help you tell a positive and informative story that will benefit the media outlet as well as the archives.

Cultivation of the Media

All media outlets report the news, but their methodologies vary. This will have an impact on the ways in which you interact with various news venues. In forging relationships, it is important to think like a public relations professional as well as an archivist and to adopt the primary goals of a public relations professional.

Developing Mutually Beneficial Relationships with the Media

When developing positive relationships, you must combine professional integrity with basic courtesies. "Please" and "thank you" go a long way in fostering mutual respect. Use the following basic principles for effective public relations:

- Use honest communication to maintain credibility.
- Network with media personnel.
  - Meet the publishers, editors, and journalists whenever possible.
  - Hand out brochures and pamphlets related to the archives.
  - If a person is new to the area, give him or her additional information about the community—a little kindness can go a long way!
  - Attend events at which the media will be present, such as ribbon cuttings, government meetings, and cultural events.
- Always ask the media for a deadline; if you cannot meet the deadline, explain your reasons and see if an extension is possible.
- Send public service announcements to all local television, radio, and newspaper outlets.
  - Think of events as party invitations—they are appreciated even if possible attendees need to decline.
  - Overlooking individual outlets can create ill-will.
- Always maintain an open, consistent, and impartial relationship with the media; be sure that all media outlets receive the same press releases and notices of a newsworthy story.
- Fairness of actions will result in reciprocity and goodwill.
  - When multiple media representatives are present, be sure to speak to each of them.
  - To create personal relationships, contact individuals rather than departments.

- Maintain two-way communication to build relationships.
  - Do not wait until you need the media to contact them.
  - Formally thank the media for their coverage of an event or publication of a story or photograph.
- Conduct environmental research and evaluation to determine actions or adjustments needed to maintain good working relationships.
  - Understand community issues that will benefit and potentially damage the promotion of the archives.
  - Maintain professional relationships with the media without showing favoritism.
- When calling a journalist, find out at the beginning of the conversation if he or she needs you to call back or can speak at that moment.
  - This is a professional courtesy that makes an impression and lets the reporter know that you understand the constraints placed on him or her.
  - After talking with the reporter, have materials ready to send to demonstrate that your public relations department is serious and well organized.

Television

Utilizing local television stations to promote your archives can be just as influential, if not more so, than using local radio stations. As with radio, there is a variety of types of television stations ranging from local stations to public broadcast stations. As museum public relations expert Susan Nichols has observed, "The truth is that television news departments need you just as much as you need them" (Nichols, 2001: 17). They do need to be able to locate you quickly and be satisfied that your story meets their needs. The following guidelines will aid you in responding rapidly and effectively:

- Know who makes the decisions at your local news stations.
  - Directors usually have the final editorial word.
    - In larger cities, directors are not directly involved in story selection.
    - In smaller cities, directors may also serve as anchor or assignment editor.
  - Assistant news directors, executive producers, or managing editors normally have time to plan stories for weeks or months before going on air; these individuals can be powerful allies and great assets.
  - News producers are primarily concerned with programs on air that night; however, they also have a say in which stories are covered.
  - Assignment editors are the busiest people in a newsroom, so get to know their assistants.
  - Some stations also have special projects or features editors who can be great contacts.

- Develop your idea into a news story by asking the following questions:
  - Why is it news?
  - Who will it affect?
  - Why should the viewing audience care?
  - Is there a link between your story and a larger news story?
  - Are there images to enhance the story (Nichols, 2001)?

- If being on camera makes you nervous, do not go on; a message delivered by someone who obviously lacks confidence will suffer as a result.

Radio

Radio is an enormous resource for public relations. Most people are exposed to radio on an almost daily basis. Some radio stations exist solely for informational purposes, such as National Public Radio (NPR) stations, while others focus on playing music geared toward their listeners. No matter what the station's objective, disc jockeys are always looking for interesting stories to attract listeners, and the Federal Communications Commission (FCC) mandates that each radio station devote a certain number of minutes to public service announcements. Your archives can benefit from such announcements, because you are one of the groups that the FCC had in mind when making the mandate. Following these guidelines will help to maintain a positive relationship with any radio station:

- Submit public service announcements.
- If possible, do not go on the air live; if you must do a live broadcast, know the subject and try to anticipate any questions that may be asked.
- Be aware that a taped interview will be edited.
  - Cultivate a trustworthy relationship with the radio station.
  - Formulate answers to questions that cannot be misinterpreted if taken out of context.

Print Media

When dealing with print media, it is not uncommon for an archivist to play the dual role of public relations professional and columnist. An archivist may submit press releases and public service announcements (see Chapter 5), as well as submit information and work hand in hand with writers. Members of the print media will also often call on an archivist when fact checking or looking for interesting information to include in a story. The following tips will help you to maintain a successful relationship with members of the print media:

- When serving as a source of information:
  - Become adept at writing interesting and well-written press releases.

- This will help get your story noticed as well as allow you to have better control over the "spin" of the story.
- Write the press release so that it appears to be a news story to help avoid editing on the part of the media.
  ○ Take time to know which columnists would be most interested in stories you can tell. Find out individual specialties and contact information.
    - Once you have determined a story in which columnists might be interested, contact them directly to pitch your idea.
    - Do not play favorites with a particular news outlet.

- When serving as the columnist:
  ○ Keep the paper's deadline in mind and always meet it.
  ○ Make sure your column grabs the reader's attention.
    - Begin with the most important information, as many readers will not finish the entire piece.
    - Choose fun topics rather than ones that may be controversial in nature; the point is to promote the archives and create a positive image.
  ○ Ask patrons and colleagues what they find interesting about the archives and use this information to create a story.

Determining Who within the Organization Talks to the Media

When working with the media, in addition to cultivating relationships, it is important to protect yourself and your organization: "[J]ournalists feel that they are being obstructed and are perhaps missing out on a much juicier story direct from the horse's mouth" (Runyard and French, 1999: 169). As such, archives must determine who has authority to speak with members of the media. Be sure to delineate such authority in your marketing plan.

Tips for Dealing with the Media

Dealing with the media in an appropriate manner can keep a good situation from going bad and a bad situation from getting worse. It is important to understand things from the media's point of view and have an understanding of where the media's interests lie. Many members of the media are also sensitive to the issues and pressures placed on cultural organizations. As a result, members of the media are usually receptive to receiving information that keeps them current with these organizations, people, and programs. To better deal with the media, it is important to remember the following basic guidelines:

- Plan in advance and prioritize events and issues that best meet the goals of the archives.
- Know the media; familiarize yourself with style, orientation, strengths, and weaknesses.

Determining Who Has Permission to Speak with the Media

- If your archives has a public relations or marketing department:
  ○ General inquiries regarding hours, policies, and activities will be handled by the staffs of these departments.
  ○ If the media's query is more specific, or sensitive in nature, it is important to determine who can best answer the questions and have the public relations or marketing staff member present along with the appropriate staff person.
  ○ The public relations and marketing staff should talk with other key staff members and give basic pointers for dealing with the media.
    - Nothing is ever "off the record."
    - If you are unsure of how the information will be used or think that the story may not directly reflect the conversation, ask for more information and/or stop the interview.
- If your archives does not have a public relations or marketing department:
  ○ First determine who can best handle the inquiry; often this is the director or department head.
  ○ Ask some probing questions of the media representative to determine the type of information he or she is seeking as well as the deadline.

- Be selective in the stories you promote; overemphasizing a minor story may be detrimental to publicizing a major story later.
- Know the deadlines and preferred method of submission for each media outlet.
  - Deadlines are usually listed in the newspaper or on websites.
  - You may need to call the media outlet directly to obtain format information.
- When contacting a journalist, have several stories ready to pitch and be able to get the point across in 90 seconds or less.
- Be aware that all information considered in the public domain should not be withheld.
- Have one person designated as the media contact so that the media outlet is not inundated with press releases and other marketing materials from your institution.
- Schedule your events so that you can take advantage of slow news days such as holidays and be sure to send invitations three to four weeks in advance.
- Send a yearly press kit or letter to reporters introducing yourself and your archives and its upcoming events and programs; be sure to include your contact information. (Kotler and Kotler, 1998)

What to Avoid

After working with the media for an extended period of time, it is natural for professional acquaintances to develop into working friendships. These relationships can prove harmful to the archives if you place too much personal trust in members of the media. Thus, it is important to remember that nothing is ever "off the record" when speaking with members of the media. Recognizing that the archives and the media do not have the same missions is important. Keep the following in mind to help steer a story away from potentially damaging publicity:

- Evaluate the goal of the media entity you plan to work with; most members of the media want stories that are newsworthy and grab people's attention.
- Do not argue with a reporter who has turned down your story.
- It is okay to send a suggestion to a reporter, but never tell a member of the media what to write.
- Understand how you as an archivist can control the direction of a story in which you are involved.
- Always promote the archives rather than your own opinion on a topic.
- Make sure that when promoting a specific collection, the collection donor is amiable to the media attention.

Handling Negative Press

Unfortunately, negative press is often the most common type of press coverage. Sensationalism attracts viewers, listeners, and readers and therefore increases ratings. Cultural institutions often are in the news as a result of some negative situation. Whether it is the theft of collections by a staff member, unethical actions by a board member, or an unflattering review of an exhibit, no archives is immune to the effects that bad press may have on support. For this reason, it is important to have a plan for dealing with the media in the event that your institution is at the center of negative news. The following list gives suggestions on how to deal with various types of negative press that an archives may face:

- Crisis management
  - A crisis is anything that can affect the archives and have an impact on its reputation:
    - Funding and staffing issues
    - Injury and damage to people, buildings, or objects
    - Injury and damage caused by others
    - Media attacks
  - Designate a communications center.
    - This should be the press office or director's office; if you cannot access your building, designate space that will serve as the communications center.
    - Have one or more telephones and Internet access available.
    - The director or designated media spokesperson will be the media contact; whoever it is should have formal training for dealing with the media.
  - Get a statement out to the media quickly, but remember that the first statement sets the tone and could be the only one on which the archives is continually judged.
    - A mass e-mail is acceptable.
    - Update information on your website, and make sure that all related press releases are on the website for easy access by all media representatives.
  - During disasters, human issues transcend collection issues.
    - Denials, "no comment," and blaming others are not acceptable.
    - The archives must begin by showing concern for the victim(s) and demonstrate that something is being done about the incident.
    - The archives must also take appropriate steps to control the situation.
  - If appropriate, set up a question-and-answer forum and invite the media.
  - Stay in control of the situation.
    - Continue to manage the story consistently and sensitively.
    - Issue regular bulletins to keep the media and the public abreast of the situation.
  - Once a crisis has ended, take steps to build confidence.

- Negative exhibit review
  - Promote the exhibit through as many other channels as possible to alleviate the impact of a single negative story.
  - Continue to enhance the positive relationship with the reporter.
    - Do not hold a grudge.
    - Put the incident behind you and move on.
  - Do not respond in print, as this will only prolong negative publicity; keep in mind that those who did not read the initial review may read the continued dialog, which will provide the story a longer life.
  - If there are factual errors, contact the editor to clarify these and ask for a correction, but do not raise the issue of unfavorable coverage.
  - Keep track of the reporters' future work; if negativity toward the archives persists, ask to meet with the editor and the reporter to determine the source of the problem.
  - Bad press often generates interest that good press doesn't, which may result in increased attention for your organization. (Runyard and French, 1999)

Conclusion

Forming good relationships with members of the local and national media can have a positive impact on your archives. It is important to understand the different types of media, their deadlines, and the types of stories in which they are interested and to treat them with the respect that you would expect to receive if you were in their situation.

In addition to forging amicable relationships with members of the media, it is also important to understand the dos and don'ts of dealing with the press, to know who has the authority and responsibility to speak to the media, and to have a plan of action for facing negative or unwanted publicity. Having all of these actions in place will make it easier to work with members of the media and enable you to present your organization in a positive light. The main goal is good representation of the archives to elicit trust and interest in what you do. Maintaining positive relationships and getting information to the media in an expedient and timely manner will go a long way to ensuring that your archives is positively presented to the public.

THE PLAN

1. Make a list of all the media outlets you want to reach in your marketing efforts, and attach this list to your marketing plan.
2. Figure out who will be the authority on matters related to the media, and include this in your plan.
3. Formulate some crisis management guidelines for dealing with negative press, and include these in the plan.

References

Kotler, Neil, and Philip Kotler. 1998. *Museum Strategy and Marketing: Designing Missions, Building Audiences, Generative Revenue and Resources*. San Francisco: Jossey-Bass.

Nichols, Susan K., ed. 2001. *Taking Charge of Your Museum's PR Destiny*. Washington, DC: American Association of Museums.

Runyard, Sue, and Ylva French. 1999. *Marketing & Public Relations Handbook for Museums, Galleries & Heritage Attractions*. Lanham, MD: AltaMira Press.

Society of American Archivists. 2005. "Code of Ethics for Archivists," February 5. http://www2.archivists.org/code-of-ethics.

Press Kits and News Releases

Russell D. James

Introduction

Archivists regularly curate physical and online exhibits, coordinate special events, and lead workshops and conferences, but they often devote less time publicizing these events than they might. Proper press coverage informs audiences and creates a positive image for the archives. Relatively few archivists have enrolled in marketing courses or public relations workshops.

This chapter covers the basic elements of preparing press kits and writing news releases. Archivists who implement such strategies will increase visitors and participation in their carefully planned events. Although an integral part of the working lives of many professions, press kits and press releases are usually not something an archivist deals with. Instead, such things have traditionally been left to the public relations and marketing departments of the parent institution (university, corporation, etc.). Now, however, many archivists are realizing the need to market themselves and their archives using public relations tools that are perhaps new to them. This chapter will guide you through the creation of these two marketing tools.

Press Kits

Press kits are collections of public relations materials about the archives and staff that are preassembled and distributed to media contacts to inform them about the repository. It includes material about the archives and the people who work there. Press kits may include demographic information about the archives, use statistics, financial data, photographs, and curriculum vitae. They need to be carefully planned and constructed to achieve the institution's goals.

Although usually a part of the marketing program of larger organizations, press kits can give archivists an added edge when dealing with media outlets. Not every reporter or blogger will know about the archives and the staff who work there. Having a press kit guarantees that anyone who is involved in the marketing of an archives (from the archives staff to reporters) will have ready access to the who, what, when, where, why, and how of the archives.

Archives Information

Press kits offer opportunities to tell the archives' story. Spend one paragraph outlining the history and significant figures who built the collections. Another paragraph might offer background information on the nature of the archives, as well as basic collecting policy and outreach information. Include the archives' mission statement. Graphs, charts and visually engaging statistics attract attention and offer appropriate background material for events. Use Figure 5.1 as a starting point for writing this important press kit page.

Figure 5.1. Archives' Holdings Crib Sheet

1. How many volumes of rare books do you have? _____
   List important rare book volumes:

2. How many manuscript collections are in your care? _____
   List important manuscript collections:

3. How many organization/government archival collections are in your care? _____
   List important archival collections:

4. How large is your map collection? _____
   List important maps in your collections:

5. How large is your newspaper collection? _____
   List important newspapers in your holdings:

6. How large are your microform holdings? _____

7. What is the physical size of your collections (cubic or linear feet)? _____

8. What are the dimensions of your reading room/research area? _____

9. How many researchers can you accommodate at one time in your reading room/research area? _____

Journalists appreciate financial information. Provide succinct donor data, highlighting significant contributors and grants. Discuss specialized functions, such as preservation laboratories and reformatting labs. Discuss the size and nature of your staff, collection use statistics, and recurring annual events. To help you construct this portion of your press kit, use Figure 5.2.

Staff Information

People matter, so be sure to include information about yourself and other staff members in the press kit. Each kit should include brief biographical information about key staff members, similar to the information one encounters in book jacket blurbs. Biographies should be personable and professional.

Include photographs of the archivists in press kits. It is a good idea to include multiple formats, including prints, TIFFs, and JPEGs. Provide

Tips for Creating Graphs and Charts for a Press Kit
1. Strive for easy readability.
2. Prepare both black-and-white and color versions.
3. Create both print and electronic formats.
4. Include contact information and dates on every graph and chart.

Figure 5.2. Checklist for Creating the "Archives" Part of the Press Kit

1. How many archivists, staff, and volunteers work in your archives?

2. How many researchers do you serve each year?

3. Is there a special subject many of your researchers come to visit you for?

4. What are the demographics of your researchers (ages, fields of study, places of origin)?

5. Do you have any collections that are special to the community?

6. What is your most-used collection and why?

7. Have you had any famous researchers visit?

8. Have there been any award-winning books or documentaries written or produced using some of your collections?

9. Are there any special services you provide to your holdings (preservation, microfilming)?

10. Are there any special services you provide to the public?

11. Do you hold tours and, if so, when and for how many?

12. Are there any special events you hold regularly (conferences, speakers series)?

---

master copies to publications so that they can adapt the visual to their own publication standards.

Include a short curriculum vitae for each archivist. This allows the media outlet to select more detailed information and to highlight data that will appeal to their target audiences.

News Releases

A news release is a short summary of an event that is distributed to media outlets for mass market consumption. News releases can appear in print or electronic form. They can announce leadership changes, successful fundraising programs, special events, and important acquisitions. When writing a release, you need to strike a balance between providing succinct information and adequate detail. Planning, writing, editing, and distributing are the simple sequential steps in the process.

Planning

News releases require some up-front planning. Before sitting down to write, you should first gather lists of potential media outlets, then obtain information about the subject of the press release, and finally assemble materials needed for actual writings.

Media outlets range from newspapers and news magazines to radio and television stations to blogs and web-based resources. They may be local, statewide, regional, national, or international in focus and coverage. Your first step in choosing outlets is to answer the following questions:

1. What type of coverage do you need or want? What is the geographical reach of your story?

2. Is the event/story a time-sensitive news item or a public interest story?

3. Do you desire a fully developed news story or a brief blurb?

Newspapers and news magazines often provide short stories and coverage of archives events, such as exhibit openings or lectures. Archivists often succeed best at the local level, because their events typically attract local audiences. Note that radio and television stations regularly run public service announcements. On-air media outlets typically read only short paragraphs, so you must capture the essence of your event in a few short sentences.

Your most important planning activity will involve compiling a list of media outlets and contact information, which should be maintained in a simple database. Each database entry should include the name of the media outlet, names of editors and reporters, contact information (telephone numbers and e-mail addresses), and notes regarding format preferences.

Note that keeping track of interesting information about media personnel, such as names of family members and pets, can also help you create a good relationship with them. The more that you can personalize contact, the more likely you are to develop a positive relationship.

Contents

Good press releases rarely exceed four paragraphs, though the length of each paragraph depends on the material covered in the release (U.S. Department of Agriculture, 2011) and should never exceed two double-spaced pages. They can include photographs, if you have those. If members of the media need additional information, you can provide them with press kits and offer to make additional information available.

Headlines

Good headlines should be brief—no longer than 75 characters—and should capture attention. Headlines should be interesting, informative, truthful, and tantalizing. A good headline tells the story in about seven words and is a crafty, clever tool used to get the attention of readers and cause them to ask for more.

Headlines are often the thing most put off or ignored by many press release writers. Some feel that the headline is not that important, but it could very well become the headline of a story written about the subject of your press release. A good press release writer treats the headline like it is so important that it becomes the foundation the rest of the release is written around.

After writing a press release, read the title again and ask yourself, "Does the press release explain this and expand on this"? If the answer is "yes," then you have done your job. If the answer is "no," perhaps you should come up with another headline; or, if you really like the headline, rewrite the press release, making sure this integral question about the relationship between the headline and the release is answered in the affirmative.

First Paragraph

The first paragraph of any news release is most important in captivating readers. A good first paragraph will address the classic *who, what, when, where,* and *why* questions. It should also contain lively writing filled with action verbs. Media outlets often will use only the first and fourth (contact information) paragraphs of your release, so it is critical to provide the most important information here. Follow these guidelines when writing your first paragraph:

Who: Who is involved, who is speaking, and who is conducting the activity?

What: Explain the event with a brief description.

When: Provide the complete name and date of the event.

Where: Provide the full name of the place where the event will be held with directions or a URL link.

Why: Explain why this event will interest readers.

General Comments Concerning News Releases

1. Despite your best efforts, you cannot mandate that a news outlet use your release.
2. Media outlets will rarely use your complete press release.
3. A news release calls attention to your event, but it is not a script that the outlet will follow.
4. Media outlets may not always use your releases in the manner that you intended.

News Releases: Writing Tips

1. Double-space the entire press release.
2. Use one-inch margins on all sides.
3. Use a common font and font size throughout the news release.
4. Avoid qualifier words, such as *could, would,* or *should.*
5. Do not use contractions.
6. Standardize your presentations of dates and times throughout.
7. Indent all paragraphs.
8. Use third person when writing.
9. Find a good editor to read your release before distributing it.

Hints for Writing Headlines

1. Do not use helping verbs that take up valuable space.
2. Do not use punctuation unless absolutely necessary.
3. Do not use archival jargon.
4. Ambiguities in meaning may attract attention.
5. Headlines need not summarize the event, but they should entice the reader.
6. Sensationalism can create additional interest.
7. Get to the heart of the matter immediately.
8. Novelty sells.
9. Use consistent and easily recognizable font sizes, such as Times New Roman or Arial.

If you successfully answer these five questions in your first paragraph, you will have accomplished your most important objectives.

Second and Third Paragraphs

These paragraphs allow you to elaborate on the details provided in the initial paragraph and promote the event more carefully. Elaborate on the facts contained in the first paragraph by providing details that cannot be included in abbreviated form.

Be careful, however! Most factual mistakes are made in the second and third paragraphs. Make sure that all of your facts are correct. Also, the second and third paragraphs are the "meat" of the press release, so ensure that you are not vague or ambiguous. If you are, then rewrite until everything is clearly explained.

Though the second and third paragraphs both typically amplify the first paragraph, most supporting quotations are included in the third paragraph. Be sure that you obtain permission from any individuals you cite in your release.

Fourth Paragraph

The final paragraph simply provides contact information for your archives. Include full names and titles of all persons, as well as phone numbers and e-mail addresses. Mention the availability of more detailed press kits, as well as the existence of additional physical or online materials. Brief factual information is included here.

Media outlets also recognize two different conventions for concluding your release. At the bottom center of the release, include one of the following "slug lines": ### or -30-. This indicates that the release has ended and that any ancillary material (such as letterheads or mottos) below this line should not be included. Figure 5.3 shows a sample news release.

If you want more coverage from your press release, include your archives' social media sites. For instance, giving your Twitter account to a reporter could mean one more follower. But if that reporter gives your Twitter account in the story, then you may get hundreds more followers. Although it is not recommended that you mention all of your social media sites, including one or two may give you some additional exposure from the press releases.

Photographs

Follow these guidelines for including photographs with your release:

1. If a press release has photographs, they should accompany all copies of news releases, not just some of them. If you are distributing the press release electronically, then this is not a problem, but do not pick and choose which media outlets get photograph copies and which do not. Such choices can result in negative public relations. If there are no photographs included with the press release, then that is okay; just send the release.

Figure 5.3. Sample Press Release

PRESS RELEASE
Sunflower Archives, Franklin State University
May 31, 2104

ECCENTRIC SUNFLOWER ARTIST TO DAZZLE VISITORS

The Sunflower Archives [WHO] presents the paintings and sculptures [WHAT] of renowned regional floral artist Joshua T. Solismajor [WHO] in a multisite exhibit at the Beermaster Planetarium on the Franklin State University campus [WHERE] from Tuesday, May 16th to Tuesday, June 20th, 2010, open every day from 8:00 a.m. to 5:00 p.m. and on Sundays for an additional showing from 7:00 p.m. to 9:00 p.m. [WHEN]. The public is invited to a free gallery opening at the planetarium on May 20th from 2:00 p.m. to 5:00 p.m., with light refreshments and a cash bar provided. No reservations necessary for attendance at the opening. The works of Mr. Solismajor cover the gamut of representations of the sunflower in art, literature, poetry, and history, and different media are used throughout the exhibit pieces. Anyone interested in sunflowers, flowers generally, or niche artwork will find this exhibit to their liking. [WHY] Directions to the planetarium and additional information about the artist and the exhibit are available on the archives' website at http://www.sunflowerarchives.com/ or by calling (101) 555-3456 weekdays during business hours.

The exhibit, titled "The Sunflower Escape," contains the collected works of Mr. Solismajor from the drawings he made in his early days of sunflower worship through his collegiate days of learning to paint in different media (watercolor, acrylic, oils) to his midlife crisis of sculpting sunflowers from any and all materials available, including trash refuse and household items such as jewelry, flatware, computer printers, and used toothbrushes. The exhibit is even laid out in a sunflower pattern, which visitors see toward the end of the exhibit, which winds its way up the stairs and onto the observation platform of the gallery. Mr. Solismajor and his favorite cat (appropriately named "Sunflower") will be present at the exhibit opening.

Joshua Solismajor is one of the major plant artists of our age. He draws, paints, and sculpts sunflowers exclusively. No one really knows what his real name is because he changed it during his adolescence. Mary Frugan of Art World says of Solismajor, "He is truly a great artist and the beauty of his creations is only overshadowed by the eccentricity of his nature." Solismajor's work has been mass-produced and sold as prints by ShellMart, earning the artist millions of dollars. Local art critic Eric "Dopey" Lighthouse says of Solismajor's works, "They are beautiful, but the beauty grows as you travel through his life from adolescence to middle age." Though all the artwork is sunflowers, each piece is so much different from and yet so much the same as the others.

Inquiries into the exhibit's particulars may be made to Mrs. Jenny Manuel, archivist at the Franklin State University at (101) 555-1666 weekdays during business hours or by e-mail at jennymanuel@frankstateuniv.edu. A press kit for the archives and supplemental materials for the archives, exhibit, and Joshua Solismajor are available upon request or by going online to http://www.frankstateuniv.edu/archives/sunflowers.

###

2. Include only visual materials that have been professionally shot and produced.

3. Labels on the back of the release should indicate photograph subject, date and place taken, copyright information, availability, and—if possible—a caption.

4. Provide digital photographs to media outlets with a resolution of 300 dots per inch (dpi). Media outlets can manipulate images to fit into publication conventions. Provide photographs in standard TIFF and JPEG formats, preferably on flash drives for quick transfer to reporters. (See Chapter 7 for further discussion of photographs.)

Electronic Press Releases

Electronic communication allows archivists to publicize events and send announcements to listservs, as well as customized electronic mailing lists geared toward your particular constituencies. There are different places to send press releases. The first is to individual persons and organizations, such as media outlets. This is the normal venue for sending press releases. However, there are press releases services on the web where you can send your press release and it can be picked up by media outlets. Because thousands of press releases are sent to these sites every day, you should target the recipients of the press release by following guidelines and suggestions in Chapter 4 on dealing with media outlets.

Working with Institutional Public Relations Departments

Most large institutions have their own public relations or media relations departments. These departments specialize in dealing with the media, so your public relations department's staff probably already has lists of media outlets in your region, templates for press releases, and formal approval procedures. In some instances, for example, when you receive a major grant, protocol may dictate that either a department in your institution or the foundation itself will initiate the press release. Public relations experts will benefit you by saving you time and effort, and it is important to work with them and respect their contributions.

You can assist your institution's public relations department in three ways. First, you can take the initiative and prepare your own press kit. This will ensure that the kit contains accurate information, and, once you have created it, the public relations department can offer helpful feedback.

Second, you can analyze the media outlets used by your public relations office and tailor those contacts to meet your own needs. You might be aware, for example, of archives-friendly blogs in your area that could have escaped the department's notice. Conversely, some media contacts may have no interest in your program. By working together, you can help professionals at your institution prepare more strategic and targeted approaches.

Third, always strive to provide clean, edited, error-free copy to your public relations department. Carefully edit your work; even "rough drafts" that you send to the department for approval should be polished and error-free.

Conclusion

Your press kit will prove invaluable as media outlets request information for your sponsored events and activities. It serves as your principal communications tool and should be kept current as situations change. News releases are your best tool to publicize individual events and activities. If you plan and carefully create press kits and news releases, you will have the ability to reach global outlets and carefully target interested local parties. Once you write your first press release, you will find that subsequent work will roll off of your keyboard faster than expected. By carefully following some standard procedures, you can create beautiful and thoughtful press releases that will help media outlets effectively promote your events and activities.

THE PLAN

1. Make a boilerplate copy of your masthead for press releases, and compile the standard information that will be included in your fourth paragraph. Include these in your marketing plan.

2. Make sure that the list of media outlets that you create is included next to your press release's boilerplate language in your marketing plan.

3. Designate one person to write or approve press releases, and specify that person's name, source of authority, and responsibilities in your plan.

4. Create a list of questions that staff will need to answer when filling out the staff biographies section of your press kit and place that list of questions in your plan.

5. Delegate authority to one person for maintaining and updating your press kit, and specify that person's name, source of authority, and responsibilities in your plan.

References

U.S. Department of Agriculture. Food and Nutrition Service, 2011. "Getting to the Core of Media Relations and Outreach." *Community Partner Outreach Toolkit*. http://www.commodityfood.usda.gov/snap/outreach/pdfs/toolkit/2010/Community/SNAP_community_Chapter06.pdf.

Additional Resources

Baverstock, Alison. 2002. *Publicity, Newsletters, and Press Releases*. Oxford: Oxford University Press.

Cohen, Ralph. 1985. *Effective Press Releases*. Pinegowrie, South Africa: Thomson Publications.

Loeffler, Robert H. 1993. *A Guide to Preparing Cost-Effective Press Releases*. New York: Haworth Press.

Solis, Brian, and Deirdre Breakenridge. 2010. *How to Generate Effective Press Releases for Social Networks*. Upper Saddle River, NJ: FTPress Delivers.

VandeVrede, Linda B. 2007. *Press Releases Are Not a PR Strategy! An Executive's Guide to Public Relations*. Scottsdale: VandeVrede Public Relations.

Newsletters

William Jordan Patty

Introduction

Newsletters are an effective public relations tool because they consist of multiple stories, images, and writers. Similar to press releases, newsletters promote the work of archives through stories. Unlike press releases, newsletters contain stories gathered together to create a single publication. An archives may publish a newsletter annually, quarterly, or monthly. Often enhanced with images, graphics, and other illustrations, the newsletter can serve as a lively way to convey valuable information to targeted constituent groups, both within and outside the institution. Archivists who create and disseminate newsletters may increase an archives' number of users and donors, as well as educate the public about their mission.

Combining newsworthy information with a targeted mailing list, newsletters are the most common serial publications produced by organizations both large and small. Approximately 50,000 corporate newsletters exist, and public, nonprofit, and other organizations also produce them. Most newsletters reach an internal readership, but approximately one-third also target external audiences (Smith, 2004). Many newsletters produced by archives are created for outside groups, although the newsletters can contain content that is also relevant to groups within the same parent organization, such as within a public library or university. If an archives is large enough, with many divisions, it can produce a strictly internal newsletter for news about different divisions and a second newsletter for the public at large.

Archivists can fill much of a newsletter with articles about collections, meetings, events, reports, personnel changes, and major operational announcements involving facilities and equipment. A major story or two from the parent organization might also be appropriate, such as announcements concerning the appointment of a new university librarian or the construction of a new library building (Arth and Ashmore, 1984). The newsletter is an opportunity for the archives to promote its resources with a visually appealing format, whether in print or online.

Steps to Creating a Newsletter

Purpose and Audience: Before investing time and resources, you need to consider two points: What is the purpose of writing a newsletter for the archives? What audience is the archives trying to reach? Answering these questions will help guide the entire process.

Content: Decide on the subjects, sources, and contributors. Images should illustrate all content. Articles should interest a wide audience and eschew technical language unfamiliar to those outside the archives profession.

Design: This process will be the most time-consuming for the first issue. Once you make decisions about the layout, fonts, and nameplate, you can base subsequent issues on that template.

Editing: You need to allow enough time for all of the stories to be completed, as well as for revisions. Most editing will be internal in the archives, but there may be a process for external editing depending on the larger organizational procedures established by the public relations office.

Delivery: Printing a hard copy requires more time and cost, but this method is helpful for sending directly to the audience as well as having extra copies for other distribution opportunities. An electronic copy might be posted on the archives website and accessible from most computers. A print/electronic combination usually works best to reach multiple audiences.

Regardless of the audience targeted by the newsletter, the information generates an interest in archives that is part of the larger public relations effort. Archivists use newsletters to educate the public on the importance of primary sources. Through this greater understanding of primary sources and other programs, an archives ultimately hopes to attract new researchers and patrons (Finch, 1994). With proper planning and design, the archives can create a newsletter that will serve as an important part of its broader public relations program.

Purpose

The primary purpose of the newsletter is to serve a particular audience and bring favorable attention to the work in the archives. Ideally, this might generate funding, but the primary purpose involves focusing on important daily work (Arth and Ashmore, 1984). Funding should not constitute the primary motivation for writing a newsletter. You can further identify the purpose of the newsletter by thinking about broader objectives and goals (Beach, 1995). For example, a goal of the archives might be to increase the number of volunteers, so one objective might be to use the newsletter to promote the interesting collections and the need for processing staff. A newsletter published by a university archives might include information about the new records management program to heighten awareness on campus (Figure 6.1). Notice the use of photographs to show "before and after" images of the records and a photograph of the records manager. The newsletter might also include information on new collections that would interest the outside researcher community and donors. A section that introduces new processing staff hired with a new endowment established by a donor would also be important to include.

Although archives are unlikely to create a newsletter to generate subscription revenues, the newsletter might attract monetary donations or collections that fit in with the archives' collection development policy (Beach, 1995). Most often, archivists create newsletters to attract more interest and use of the collections, programs, and services. In some cases, you may not have to focus so much on fundraising because that is the responsibility of another office within the larger institution. It is always critical to make sure that any solicitation of funds that you undertake in your newsletter is approved by your development office.

Even if there is a development office for your entire institution, the archives will probably want its own mailing list. Distribution outlets are important not only for newsletters but also for many other kinds of public relations activities. Of course, the mailing list may also be divided into appropriate groups if it is determined that not everyone should receive the newsletters or if researchers opt out of receiving promotional material (Pederson, 1987).

The newsletter serves another purpose by providing an outreach tool for the promotion and use of the collections. On the other hand, creating demands when the reference staff, for example, cannot provide a high

Figure 6.1. Example of Using the Newsletter to Promote a New Records Management Program at the Catholic University of America

ACUA Newsletter

The American Catholic History Research Center and University Archives

Volume 1; Issue 1 Fall 2006

CUA Records Management Program Begins

The archives office accomplished several records management goals over the past year. First, in May 2005, the archives hired Leslie Knoblauch as the records archivist. She secured approval from the Office of the President for the initiation of a formal records management program on campus. Meanwhile, the unofficial records management team of Timothy Meagher, Ph.D.; John Shepherd; Patrick Cullom; and Leslie Knoblauch held face-to-face meetings with key university administrators, such as the provost, the vice president for finance and administration, the vice president for student life and the general counsel about managing their records.

The Office of the President served as the pilot program, which included surveying records with the staff; reorganizing the office's primary filing system, including the indexing and organization of the main subject filing system; and creating and approving a retention schedule.

The archives also tapped the skillls of former CUA library director Adele Chwalek as a records management consultant. Her expertise led to significant weeding and reorganizing of the existing collection of CUA presidential records as well as integrating new deposits. Those include the records of presidents Byron, Ellis, O'Connell (David), Pellegrino and Walton. When it's completed, the arrangement of the President's

Records stored in the basement of a CUA building (left) and in the Archives after processing (right).

Assistant Records Manager Leslie Knoblach arranging a records consultation.

Office records will be a major accomplishment.

The archives staff made connections with other departments after the approval of the records management program, resulting in preliminary records surveys conducted with the schools of architecture and planning, engineering, and nursing; the departments of art, education and English, and public safety; the offices of facilities planning and construction, disability support services, public affairs, study abroad, treasurer, and vice provost and dean of graduate studies. Knoblach also processed the records of the athletics department and the archives, and produced finding aids and appraisal reports for both collections. The archives staff received a retention schedule. With these successes, Knoblach moves on in the future to the records of the Board of Trustees, the provost, alumni relations and development.

Inside:

ACUA Newsletter

Fall 2006

1

level of service is problematic. It is important to achieve a proper balance (Pederson, 1987). Too much time spent working on description, access, and preservation without properly promoting collections can be detrimental to the work of the archives staff. Without adequate promotion, collections will not receive the level of use that can justify the work spent on processing. By creating a newsletter, archivists can highlight all of their hard work. If the archives lacks adequate staff to handle additional research requests, the newsletter can also convey this information so that service level expectations are realistic.

Audience

Depending on the size of the archives, you can structure the newsletter to reach both an internal and an external audience. The internal audience might include other departments in a large archives or library while the external audience could consist of researchers, donors, and other archival professionals. In some cases, the archives might reach these multiple audiences with general interest articles. Articles should convey a sense of intimacy, as if the publication is a personal letter to its readers. Short, timely stories convey this better than lengthy, in-depth pieces that may be found in larger publications, such as news magazines and journals (Beach, 1995). Although newsletters have become more sophisticated with desktop publishing, including some with magazine-like qualities, they all attempt to deliver similar content that is timely and informative for the audience (Maxymuk, 1997). Whether that audience is internal or external, all readers will be most interested in short, informative articles that discuss archives work without professional jargon.

Archivists typically send out public relations-style newsletters to external audiences, institutional newsletters to internal audiences, and professional newsletters to other archivists, although it certainly is possible to combine these elements in a single publication (Maxymuk, 1997). You may decide to publish more than one newsletter with similar content but different targets, such as one newsletter for an internal audience and one for an external audience.

By delineating the purpose, goals, objectives, and audiences, you will improve the quality of the publication (Beach, 1995). If you are trying to attract volunteers, for example, it might not be effective to show only items from the collections. Rather, newsletters should include some photographs of people working so that potential volunteers could imagine themselves in similar situations (Figure 6.2). Include employee photographs along with stories concerning new programs, such as the establishment of a new records management program in the university archives. A photograph of the actual records manager will personalize the operation.

You can collaborate on newsletters with other local repositories because those repositories probably hold collections and organize programs of interest to similar audiences. By collaborating, the archivist can include richer content in the newsletter, but the logistics involved with

Figure 6.2. Example of a Donor List and a New Employee Profile in the Newsletter of the Butler Center for Arkansas Studies

BUTLER CENTER DONORS

DONATIONS

Rev. D. K. Campbell, Little Rock
Jan Emberton, Little Rock,
    in memory of Janet Clinton
Annabelle Clinton Imber, Little Rock,
    in memory of Gertrude Remmel Butler
Carl H. Miller Jr., Little Rock
Lynn Morrow, Jefferson City, MO
Bobby and Kathy Roberts, Little Rock,
    in memory of Gertrude Remmel Butler
Mr. and Mrs. J. Walt Stallings, Little Rock,
    in memory of Marie Ward Jones
David Stricklin and Sally Browder,
    Little Rock, in memory of Willie Oates

Rice Art Fund

Peyton and Betty B. Rice, Little Rock,
    in memory of Sam Sowell
Sarah and Michael Renner,
    Minneapolis, MN,
    in memory of Louis Austin Graham

Encyclopedia of Arkansas History & Culture

George E. Lankford, Batesville,
    in memory of Burnelle Regnier

GIFTS OF MATERIALS

Betty Sorenson Adams, Little Rock
Carol D. Anderson, Prescott City, AZ
Eliza Ashley, Little Rock
Bob Bailey, Little Rock
James W. Bell, Little Rock
Velma Block, Little Rock
Marcia Camp, Little Rock
Art Campbell, Little Rock
Catholic Business Women's Club,
    Little Rock
Central Arkansas Library System,
    Youth Services (BASE program)
Joel A. Cooper, Conway
Charles S. Curb, Clarksville
Robert England, Memphis, TN
John P. Gill, Little Rock
John Griffin, Searcy
Marie J. Griffin, Chicago, IL
Lawrence Harper, Little Rock
Susan Hogan, Lower Makefield, PA
Jean Jernigan, Little Rock
Michael Keckhaver, Little Rock
Guy and Anna Lancaster, Little Rock
Jeanne McDaniel, Little Rock
Jim McDaniel, Dallas, TX

Jo Melton, Little Rock
Beverly Mikita, Sherwood
Judge Morris S. Arnold, Little Rock
Brooks and Donna Nash, Cabot
Bobbie Newtown, Little Rock
Howard Norton, Vilonia
Ted Parkhurst, Little Rock
John C. Payne, Chattanooga, TN
Joyce Peck, Little Rock
Patsy Pipkin, Searcy
Mike Polston, Cabot
John G. Ragsdale, Little Rock
Herbert M. Russ, Colorado
Shirley Schuette, Little Rock
Mary Ann Stafford, Maumelle
Dana Steward, Little Rock
Virginia Cunningham Steward, Menifee
Rhonda Stewart, Little Rock
David Stricklin, Little Rock
John Sweeney, Fox
Ginann Swindle, Sherwood
John Truemper, Little Rock
Arzella Valentine, Pasadena, CA
Gordon Wittenberg, Little Rock
George Worthen, Little Rock

Butler Center Welcomes Shari Hays

Shari Hays joins the Butler Center team to help catalog new material and assist patrons with their research. Hays is not new to the Central Arkansas Library System (CALS). She has been employed by CALS for six years as Fletcher Library branch manager and then as a cataloger in the Main Library's technical services department. Hays has been cataloging Butler Center material for some time, but now will become a full-time Butler Center staff member. Hays will also perform book and pamphlet preservation work. Hays says, "I studied preservation in graduate school at University of North Texas when I was working on my master's in library science. I really enjoyed learning how to preserve, protect, and extend the life of fragile and precious materials." ∎

The Butler Banner   Page 7

Source: Used by permission of the Butler Center.

coordinating deadlines may serve as a considerable obstacle (Finch, 1994; Pederson, 1987). Make sure that the newsletter collaboration targets the specific audience that you want to reach. Sometimes goals and objectives for newsletter production and dissemination differ among archives, and it is important to understand these differences in the event that collaboration may not satisfy your purposes.

Creating the Newsletter

Newsletters vary from simple formats with few images to glossy publications that resemble magazines with in-depth articles and interviews. You can create much of the content with articles about collections, events, reports, personnel changes, and major operational announcements, such as construction or new equipment. A major story or two from the parent organization might also be appropriate, such as the appointment of a new university librarian or the dedication of a library building. You should also consider that newsletter stories might be repurposed into press releases (Arth and Ashmore, 1984). Purpose and audience should inform the entire process.

Content

When crafting the content of the newsletter, consider some basic questions. What are the subjects of the stories? Are the stories interesting? Do the stories cover a diverse range of topics? The intention is to make a connection with an audience already familiar with the archives and its work, as well as to keep the language direct and concise (Sandifer, 1996; Ten Cate, 1992).

You can use information directly from an annual report if that document is not widely distributed. Annual reports can be a good source for information for a "From the Boss" column or for some other statement from the director. In some cases, the archives newsletter can supplement a larger newsletter published by the public relations department of the parent organization. Typically, larger organizational newsletters select stories about the archives. They often cannot be used as a tool to reach a specific audience.

For the first issue of a new newsletter, you can use information from past publishing efforts, such as publications that have been prepared to explain repository, reference, or educational services. For example, the newsletter can include tips on beginning research or properly handling documents (Pederson, 1987). Often articles that include basic research methodology or tips for organizing research are well received. Consider making such items a recurring column. Such articles could have unanticipated benefits. An audience member who sees the care that you take in preserving materials, for example, might consider your repository an ideal place to deposit a family collection.

Surveys and Frequently Asked Questions (FAQs) also offer excellent sources of information. When the same questions arise on a regular basis, it indicates that there is considerable public interest in a topic, and you can make good use of this in developing stories. Frequently published newsletters also offer ideal opportunities for publicizing upcoming events (Pederson, 1987). Less timely publications, however, really cannot take on this function. Content must remain current. Timely publishing means professional publishing.

Donor and volunteer lists also provide interesting content. By highlighting donors and volunteers, the archives recognizes their contributions and also illustrates widespread interest in the archives. Further, this constitutes another opportunity to enlighten newsletter audiences. Readers may be unaware, for example, that the archives accepts audiovisual

Options for Repurposing Material

Press releases: These essentially consist of individual stories that can be rewritten into fully developed articles. Press releases already contain basic facts, but archivists can include additional context and colorful language to transform them into newsletter articles.

Annual reports: Annual reports similarly contain numerous facts that can serve as the basis for several stories and columns.

Collection information: Frequently asked questions concerning collections can generate ongoing columns filled with interesting facts. These might focus on such topics as the oldest item in the collection, the scope of the material, and the story behind the founding of the archives.

Internal documents: The archives staff regularly create documents concerning reference, educational outreach, and acquisitions. This offers useful data for explaining the preservation and service activities in the repository.

Upcoming events: Most archives sponsor events and lectures that offer good newsletter fodder. You can include information about the nature of the event, time, place, speaker biographies, and similar materials. Visual materials also can enhance the presentation.

Donor and volunteer lists: Archives maintain documentation about donors and volunteers. Details concerning innovative volunteer projects and fascinating donations make outstanding articles.

materials. Donation lists can highlight the diversity of records and materials in the repository and stimulate new contributions. When listing donors and volunteers, however, it is always important to notify them and obtain permission first.

By writing an ongoing column or series (see Figure 6.3), you or a volunteer can update readers about particular works and about new research materials that have been uncovered (Arth and Ashmore, 1984). Discussions of rarely used but important collections provide another possibility for a story. You can use the archives' primary source material, neighborhood stories that emerge from the records, and similar ongoing treatments to bring projects to the attention of readers.

Other popular newsletter features include the ways in which nontraditional researchers, such as television producers, use the repository (Finch, 1994). Again, such stories expand readers' understanding of the significance of the collections and the ways in which they can serve broader purposes.

Contributors

Archivists often enlist staff members and volunteers to help write stories, edit copy, select photographs, and meet publication deadlines (Arth and Ashmore, 1984). This allows for greater departmental participation and creates a sense of ownership concerning the product. In some cases, the public relations office can help. Professional press photographers, for example, can take quality photos at archives events. Generally, though newsletter production will remain in archival hands.

Researchers and donors are excellent sources for articles (Figure 6.4). Researchers sometimes make discoveries about collections that archivists have overlooked. Donors have an excellent knowledge of collections before processing. They sometimes connect with general audiences in ways that archivists cannot always accomplish. They may have readily available abstracts that require minimal editing. An added sidebar can highlight donations to the archives as well as the donors. A sidebar can also illustrate how collections arrive at an archives, in turn attracting researchers. To ensure that donors and researchers turn in stories you can use, make writing guidelines available to them.

Archival administrators often delegate newsletter assignments to staff, and editors have relatively free reign over stories and contents (Arth and Ashmore, 1984). However, because the newsletter reflects the quality of work conducted at the archives, editors need to allow supervisors time for a final review. In addition, administrators and editors need to reach consensus on the contents of the various articles.

Once stories have been written, you can file them for later reference and for repurposing in news releases and web-based resources (Ten Cate, 1992). You can file articles concerning projects that have not been completed in time for newsletter deadlines and then use them in future issues. In Figure 6.5 (p. 104), notice the article on the lower section of the page that updates readers on an ongoing project. Good

A Newsletter Committee

It is a good idea to form an official newsletter committee so that more than two or three people will work on production and editing. When forming a committee:

1. Delineate duties for each committee member, such as writing articles, developing topics, updating mailing lists, and editing.
2. Note the existence of the committee and its responsibilities in your marketing plan.

Figure 6.3. Example of an Ongoing Series about Publications Created with Documents from the American Catholic History Research Center and University Archives

The American Catholic History Research Center and University Archives

Book Corner

By Associate Archivist John Shepherd

Over the decades a variety of scholars and writers have used our records as source material to write history. Works on the life and legacy of Monsignor George G. Higgins, a renowned 'labor priest,' have been in the forefront lately, with the most recent being *César Chávez, the Catholic Bishops, and the Farmworkers' Struggle for Social Justice* (University of Arizona Press, 2006) by Marco Prouty, Ph.D. Based upon research in the papers of Monsignor Higgins, this is a condensed version of Prouty's doctoral dissertation from The Catholic University of America. His sympathy for César Chávez, a hero of almost saintly proportions to many Hispanic Americans, does not blind him to Chávez's shortcomings in building a strong farm workers union that could sustain itself beyond the heady days of boycotts and hunger strikes of the 1960s and 1970s. He also discusses the roles of the three churchmen who, as members of the Bishops' Ad hoc Committee on Farm Labor in the 1970s, were crucial to the accomplishments of the nascent United Farm Workers union in receiving labor contracts from growers, many of them Catholic, as well as the passage of significant legislation by the State of California. These men, Cardinal Roger Mahoney, Bishop Joseph Donnelly of Connecticut and the aforementioned Monsignor Higgins, strongly supported the farm workers when many of their clerical colleagues were indecisive or even hostile.

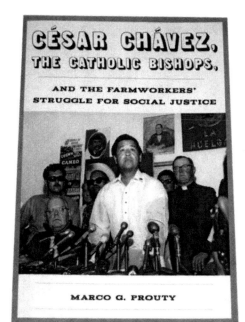

Additional works based largely or in part on research from our collections include studies such as *American Catholics and the Mexican Revolution, 1924–1936* (Notre Dame University, 2006) by Matthew A. Redinger and *Uncharted Territory, The American Catholic Church at the United Nations, 1946–1972* (CUA Press, 2006) by Joseph S. Rossi, S.J., as well as biographies such as *Steadfast in the Faith, The Life of Patrick Cardinal O'Boyle* (CUA Press, 2006) by Morris T. MacGregor, *An Archbishop For The People, The Life of Edward J. Hanna* (Paulist Press, 2006) by Rev. Richard Gribble, *The Holocaust and Catholic Conscience, Cardinal Aloisius Muench and the Guilt Question in Germany* (Notre Dame University, 2006) by Suzanne Brown-Fleming and *Ambition and Arrogance, Cardinal William O'Connell of Boston and the American Catholic Church* (Cobalt Production, 2007) by Douglas J. Slawson.

Such works are encouraged by Dorothy Mohler Research Grants, which help defray research and travel costs for those using the collections, which are especially rich in American Catholic social welfare organizations and social theory as well as American labor history. The winners for 2007 were Jeanne Petit, associate professor of history, Hope College, awarded $250, to use the papers of the National Catholic War Council for an article, " 'A Real Piece of Americanization Work': Gender, Race, and the National Catholic Community Houses, 1918–1922" and research for a Web project on "Women and Social Change" based at SUNY Binghamton. Carrie Schultz, a Ph.D. candidate in history, Boston College, received an award of $250 to use the papers of the National Catholic Welfare Conference, NCWC, and Catholic Boy's Brigade (among others) for her dissertation " 'Let the little children come to Me': Catholic Children's Moral Development in the United States, 1920–1965." Amy Koelinger, assistant professor of religion at Florida State University, was awarded $500, also to use the papers of the NCWC for a book project, *Rosaries and Rope Burns: Boxing and Manhood in American Catholicism, 1880–1970.*

Figure 6.4. Example of an Interview with a Researcher

Researcher Profile
Interview with Rebecca Brueckmann

Rebecca Brueckmann doing research in Special Collections. Photograph by Valerie Robertson, 2009

Berlin, Germany resident **Rebecca Brueckmann** spent four weeks in the Special Collections Department last summer, doing research for her master's thesis.

Please tell our readers a bit about yourself.

I am 25 years old and a master's student of contemporary history at Humboldt University in Berlin, Germany.

Can you describe your research?

I am researching historical sources for my thesis on the 1957 desegregation crisis of Little Rock Central High School. I concentrate on "massive resistance," i.e., segregationists' resistance to the civil rights movement, with a particular interest in gender-specific aspects and historical discourse analysis.

My main focus is the segregationist group, the Mothers' League of Central High School. After reading the research of Phoebe Godfrey and Graeme Cope, I wanted to learn more about the Mothers' League and their significance in the escalation of the 1957 desegregation crisis. I am trying to analyze the role of women in the segregationist movement and the ties of the Mothers' League to the Capital Citizens' Council of Little Rock. Of particular interest is the women's rhetoric, politics, and forms of protest, in light of the traditional roles of most women in the 1950s. The role of the Mothers' League is sometimes overlooked in the history of the 1957 desegregation crisis.

I have been looking at a number of collections. The most important were the Sara A. Murphy Papers, the Little Rock Central High Integration Crisis Records of the FBI, the Arkansas Council on Human Relations Papers, the

Virgil T. Blossom Papers, the Orval Eugene Faubus Papers, the Citizens Councils of America Collection, the Elizabeth Huckaby Papers, as well as the *Southern School News*. Upon completion of my work in Fayetteville, I went to the Arkansas History Commission/State Archives in Little Rock to look at the Justice Jim Johnson Collection and more newspaper articles from the *Arkansas Gazette* and the *Arkansas Democrat*.

What were your impressions of Fayetteville and the University?

My visit to the Special Collections was a wonderful experience. The staff was kind, helpful, professional and skilled. Employees helped me a lot with my research and made me feel at home. This made everything so much easier. I finished earlier than expected, which gave me an opportunity to explore Fayetteville.

My research visit to the University and Fayetteville was not only a very educational and enriching experience for my studies, it was also a great vacation in lovely, natural surroundings. I love Berlin. It is an amazing city, but it can be a bit "too much" at times. I enjoyed the summer weather in Fayetteville; it was the best I have experienced in many years.

Gift Enables Purchase of Civil War Era Letters

Dr. William H. Cobb, retired history professor at East Carolina University in Greenville, N. C., recently made a generous gift to Special Collections in honor of Dr. Walter L. Brown, University of Arkansas emeritus professor of history. Cobb studied with Brown while he was a graduate student in the 1960s.

Cobb wanted his gift to be used for the purchase of materials documenting the history of Arkansas. The gift was used to purchase Civil War era letters written from Helena by an officer in the occupying Federal army.

Brown, who started teaching in 1954, retired from the University in 1990. He was editor of the *Arkansas Historical Quarterly* from 1958 until his retirement. In May of this year, the University dedicated the foyer in Old Main in honor of Brown.

Tom W. Dillard noted, "Individual gifts such as this are absolutely critical to the functioning of Special Collections."

Anyone wishing to honor a living person or memorialize the deceased may do so by contributing to the department's Arkansas materials acquisition account. Interested persons should contact Tom W. Dillard, Head of Special Collections at tdillar@uark.edu or at 479-575-5576.

Source: Used by permission of the University of Arkansas Libraries Special Collections.

articles can also serve as examples for potential contributors, as well as informational resources for processors. Ultimately, content is the most important aspect of your newsletter, so spend the most time developing it and follow the suggestions in this section to make sure that you are producing high-quality material.

Design

Graphic design decisions remain instrumental in creating really attractive packages. Indeed, some graphic design decisions will influence content. The placement and arrangement of text columns and images can determine article length. Such predetermined lengths offer advantages in working with contributors and should be stipulated in your newsletter writing guidelines.

Once you or the committee have determined the layout, you will need to choose a typeface for various sections of the newsletter, including the body, headlines, and subheads (Maxymuk, 1997). Graphic design may seem tedious at first, but consistency and design pay long-term dividends. Templates can be created for initial issues and used in subsequent numbers. Some software programs, such as those offered by Corel or Microsoft, have newsletter templates built into their software suites. Use those to your advantage. Preset templates can be modified, and only minimal revision may be necessary to meet your needs.

When you work on your first issue, it may be necessary to seek professional assistance and consultation to help you make difficult decisions. Public relations departments may prove especially useful in negotiating such troublesome problems as proper color schemes. Great variations exist in the ways in which colors appear on different computers and monitors (Pederson, 1987). Some institutions have specific requirements for colors, graphics, texts, and fonts that are used by offices and departments. Always clear your template with the proper institutional authority before proceeding.

Images found in the archives collections will prove useful in helping to create a unique nameplate. A newsletter title may simply consist of the name of the repository followed by the word *newsletter*. As with other graphic design elements, the nameplate is used more than once (Maxymuk, 1997). Asking for title and image suggestions is a great way to include archives staff in the creative process and can encourage "buy-in" from important constituents.

Some optional graphic design elements can improve the professional appearance of the newsletter. The page numbers, or folios, can be placed in the header or footer on each page. In addition to the page number, headers and footers should contain the publication name and issue information (see Figures 6.3 and 6.5, pp. 101 and 104). The back page is referred to as the *mailer*. It typically consists of the logo, address information, and perhaps a table of contents or interesting photo (see Figure 6.6). In the example shown in Figure 6.6 (p. 106), the back page consists of a mailer and an Arkansas history quiz. The masthead, which is placed on the front page of the newsletter, can contain names of contributors,

Figure 6.5. Example of a Column by the Department Head at the Butler Center for Arkansas Studies

A Word from the Center

David Stricklin, Head of the Butler Center

The question I am asked most often is, "When is the move into your new building?" Creating the new Arkansas Studies Institute (ASI) complex (see the cover story, pp. 1–2) has been a long process, to say the least. I've been at the Butler Center for almost four years, and the basic design for the ASI was already in place when I got here. Weekly meetings began at about that point. We have spent so much time with the architects and contractors—Polk Stanley and East-Harding, respectively—that when this is all over we're going to have to go into some kind of therapy program to deal with separation issues!

Any big project takes time, and this one has been particularly complicated, especially because of the structural and conceptual problems of trying to make one whole out of three buildings from three different centuries. New construction on one must blend with adaptive reuse of the other two. The 1882 Porbeck–Bowman Building turned out to be an especially tough one to save, but I am so pleased we were able to do so. It will be a wonderful place in which to work, and its rescue is an inspiring Arkansas success story.

I feel quite confident in giving you an answer to the aforementioned, oft-asked question: The next *Butler Banner* you receive will have either an announcement of the date of the ASI grand opening or pictures from that event. Make plans to come and see the new ASI. I feel quite confident in saying something else: You will be very proud of the Institute.

One sad note: Bill Norman, a devoted friend of the Butler Center and of the *Encyclopedia of Arkansas History & Culture*, passed away recently. Bill was a banker with a passion for Arkansas history and a particular fascination with the ways technology could be used to share the state's history with people around the world and in every corner of Arkansas. We will miss him a great deal and always remember his many acts of kindness and expressions of encouragement.

Thank you all for your own acts of kindness and expressions of encouragement as we move forward in this venture. ∎

Forgotten: The Korean War Project

This summer, the Butler Center launched an initiative to document and preserve Arkansas's role in the Korean War. "Forgotten: The Arkansas Korean War Project" is an attempt to fill the documentary void related to the war. Often overlooked or overshadowed by events to follow, the Korean War has fallen into a vast no-man's-land in the American psyche, somehow lost between the headiness of World War II and the anguish of Vietnam. According to Max Hastings, one of the leading historians on the Korean War, "United States losses in three years were only narrowly outstripped by those suffered in Vietnam over more than ten." In addition to the personal cost, the worldwide political ramifications of the war were huge and still linger today. Yet the war is one that most Americans would rather forget. Unfortunately, this has meant that the sacrifice of our men and women in uniform has often been overlooked. We believe it is time to change that.

The Butler Center is soliciting information from Arkansans who were on the battlefield as well as those left home. Of particular emphasis is the acquisition of letters, photographs, diaries, and other written records of Arkansas's Korean War veterans. Our oral history campaign will allow veterans to share their personal memories.

Jim Mullings, 1950

In addition, we are sending out a questionnaire to all interested Korean War veterans.

Since launching the project, we have made contact with a number of Korean War veterans. Our first response came from Jim Mullings of Claremore, Oklahoma. Mullings, a Paris (Logan County) native, was a member of the Arkansas National Guard when it was mobilized for federal service. After arriving in Korea in January 1951, he served as a gunner on a 155 mm self-propelled artillery piece affectionately known as "Bulldog's Bark." Mullings shared doz-ens of his snapshots from the war with us as well as newspaper clippings and other documents. Serving as the guinea pig for our first Korean War oral history, he performed admirably, and we were lucky to get some fascinating insights into the war. One particularly interesting story revolved around him unwittingly giving two North Korean spies a ride in his Jeep. He also recounted the difficulty of seeing the suffering of the civilian population. Through his words, Mullings was able to offer a candid portrait of what it was like for a young Arkansas boy to be thrust into a war in a faraway place. Such interviews are a veritable gold mine of information. And most importantly, they are a vital and irreplaceable piece of our collective history as Arkansans.

If you are a Korean War veteran, or if you know of one, please contact us about the project. It is our intention to see that Arkansas's Korean War veterans finally get the respect and recognition they deserve. Though nearly sixty years separates us from the event, it is important for us not to lose sight of the sacrifice that these men and women offered for their country. Through this project, we hope to make sure that they will never be forgotten. ∎

Contributed by Brian Robertson, Butler Center Manuscripts Coordinator

Source: Used by permission of the Butler Center.

the full name of the repository, and contact information. Short sidebars expand on points found in longer articles (Maxymuk, 1997).

Newsletter designers should consult Section 508 of the Americans with Disabilities Act to make sure that newsletters meet federal disability access requirements (U.S. Government, 2010). Although compliance may not be mandatory, Section 508 makes reading easier for your potential audience. You might make compliance mandatory in your own marketing plan.

Editing

The use of a specific style guide, such as the *Chicago Manual of Style*, may not be necessary, but it will help you maintain consistency and uniformity. Public relations departments often have style guides that can easily be adapted and implemented. Without a coherent brand or style, newsletters will appear poorly written and sloppy and will be an unfortunate reflection on their parent institutions.

Professional printers will require additional editing time, and there often are limited opportunities to make substantial edits. Errors often creep into the process as printers are less conversant with proper names, specific events, and places. One way to minimize this problem is to create a diagram with key words and names (Beach, 1995). Still, errors are inevitable, so it remains important to insist on adequate time to review edits during the publication process.

Delivery

If you decide to use only an electronic format, considerable time savings may result in the editorial process. Institutional considerations will determine how easy it is to negotiate this process. Much depends on the institutional attitude toward online publications, the currency of electronic publishing platforms, the technological expertise of staff, and the assistance that the archives can rely on when mounting the publication on its website. Generally, PDF offers an accessible option that will prove compatible with browsers, receive good indexing by search engines, and can be created easily by the printer and uploaded immediately to the institutional website. Decisions to rely solely on electronic newsletters should be planned carefully, however, because physical newsletters remain useful for such events as conferences and class visits. Important constituencies should be polled and surveyed concerning their attitudes toward electronic delivery.

Both passive and aggressive distribution options exist for newsletters (Maxymuk, 1997). Consider locations near your repository, especially if it contains genealogical research materials that may interest out-of-town visitors. You might negotiate with local civic groups and chambers of commerce to leave copies at visitor centers, hotels, and convention centers.

Delivery Options

Print: Order quantities larger than your mailing list so that you will have additional copies to hand out to visitors and distribute to nearby locations. Small batches of newsletters often may be sent out through the regular mail service of the organization, thus helping to minimize postage costs. Newsletters with eight or fewer pages also incur reduced postage costs.

Electronic: You can create PDF versions of the newsletter from desktop publishing programs, and the PDF will replicate formatting and images. You can also create an electronic version of your newsletter in HTML, but this requires additional expertise and may not replicate the formats and images that have been set by the desktop publishing program. Printers typically provide both PDF and print newsletters.

Hybrid: Creating both print and electronic versions offers you a great deal of flexibility. You can send print copies directly to your audience, and visitors can access electronic copies on the repository website.

Figure 6.6. Example of a Mailer Page and a Front Page with the Masthead and Table of Contents

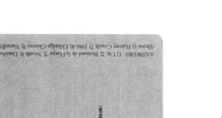

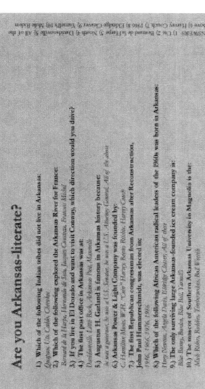

Source: Used by permission of University of Arkansas Libraries Special Collections and Archives.

Creating the Next Issue

When considering subsequent issues, the archives may conclude that the time, effort, and cost involved in preparing the newsletter did not justify the results. Did the archives receive positive feedback? Did inquiries or donations increase? The archives should not be pressured into producing regular newsletters simply because it started such an initiative (Ten Cate, 1992). Maintaining a regular publishing schedule promotes the activities and accomplishments of the archives to both stakeholders within the larger organization and constituencies outside the institution (Finch, 1994). If the initial schedule appeared too ambitious, modify it so that each issue remains a quality publication.

Realistic publication schedules remain the key element in a successful newsletter. Take into account your archives' staffing situation and staff members' available time. A more modestly funded archives should start small, creating a well-planned newsletter, and then expand its scope as staff, time, and events dictate (Beach, 1995). Time is better spent crafting a well-designed newsletter than rushing to meet unrealistic deadlines.

Create a timeline for each step when scheduling individual tasks, and create a checklist to think about where each step fits into the broader process. This does not need to be an elaborate document, but it should measure time and outline specific steps. In *Editing Your Newsletter*, Mark Beach (1995) outlined specific steps for producing a newsletter (see sidebar). Above all, always be flexible, rethinking and refining approaches as necessary.

Conclusion

Newsletters produced by repositories with large staff and ample resources may have elaborate layouts and frequent production schedules. Repositories with fewer resources may be published less frequently but still serve as effective tools to bring attention to the interesting and important work that archivists accomplish. Regardless of the publication schedule, the qualities discussed in this chapter should be part of the planning and implementation of every newsletter. An archivist who produces a great newsletter has carefully planned how the stories, text, and layout will work together. Interesting stories, strong editing, and audience appeal are universal traits of that newsletter.

Distribution flexibility is also important. Archives can elect to send out newsletters only in hard copy, in exclusively online formats, or using both distribution methods. Both an online newsletter and a hard copy newsletter may be attractive publications. Many desktop publishing software programs exist, and they usually include one-step PDF creation. Printers often create PDFs easily.

As part of a broader public relations program, newsletters are a flexible option for many archives. Well-written and well-designed newsletters can promote the collections, the personnel, and the activities of the

Checklist for Newsletter Completion

1. Brainstorm story ideas.
2. Gather content.
3. Write stories.
4. Select images.
5. Design format.
6. Lay out pages.
7. Copyedit text.
8. Proofread text.
9. Send to public relations office (if necessary).
10. Review edits and galley copies (possibly several steps).
11. Send final edits to printer.
12. Send mailing list to mail house (if using such a service).
13. Mail and post online.

Newsletter Time Frame

Create a general time frame for producing your newsletter. Use the following to help you determine a schedule:

1. How long before publication date do you want the articles completed?
2. How long will it take your editorial staff to edit the articles?
3. How long will it take to properly format articles and place them in newsletter spaces?
4. How long will it take to lay out the newsletter?
5. How long will it take to prepare the newsletter for supervisor approval?
6. How long will it take to obtain supervisor approval?
7. How long will it take to make changes suggested or mandated by your supervisor?
8. How long will copying and mailing take?

archives. By integrating the newsletter publication process into regular planning activities, you can easily incorporate the process into the repository's day-to-day activities.

THE PLAN

1. In the goals and objectives statement of your master plan, include a statement that reflects how you intend to use newsletters to support those goals and objectives. Be specific about formats. Use appropriate goals and objectives that address public relations and marketing as a key element of your marketing plan.
2. Develop a newsletter committee at your institution. Find people who can act as editors, authors, and contributors. Your master plan should spell out the committee composition and duties.
3. Set up a mailing list, in whatever format you desire, and attach a copy of the list to your marketing plan.
4. Compile newsletter writing guidelines in either checklist or narrative formats. Include such tips as these: identify your subject in the first paragraph, write only in the third person, and eliminate contractions. This will prove helpful in the editorial process.
5. If you publish your newsletter online, include a statement in the newsletter section of your marketing plan that mandates compliance with the guidelines set forth in Section 508 of the Americans with Disabilities Act.

References

Arth, Marvin, and Helen Ashmore. 1984. *The Newsletter Editor's Desk Book.* Shawnee Mission, KS: Parkway Press.

Beach, Mark. 1995. *Editing Your Newsletter.* Cincinnati, OH: Writer's Digest Books.

Finch, Elsie Freeman. 1994. *Advocating Archives: An Introduction to Public Relations for Archivists.* Lanham, MD: Society of American Archivists and Scarecrow Press.

Maxymuk, John. 1997. *Using Desktop Publishing to Create Newsletters, Handouts, and Web Pages.* New York: Neal-Schuman.

Pederson, Ann E. 1987. *Keeping Archives.* Sydney: Australian Society of Archivists.

Sandifer, Kevin W. 1996. *Public Relations Are an Asset for the Museum and Archives.* Shreveport, LA: Archival Services.

Smith, Ronald D. 2004. *Strategic Planning for Public Relations.* Mahwah, NJ: Lawrence Erlbaum.

Ten Cate, Ann. 1992. *Promoting Archives: A Handbook.* Ottawa, Canada: Association of Canadian Archivists.

U.S. Government. 2010. "Resources for Understanding and Implementing Section 508." Section508.gov. Last updated in December. http://www.section508.gov/.

Visual Materials

Stephanie Gaub

Introduction

Most archives, historical societies, museums, and other collecting institutions have rich photographic collections. Creative archivists can transform these visual materials into extraordinary corporate assets. Photographs can become integral to education programs, exhibits, partnerships with other cultural institutions, partnerships with local television/radio/newspaper outlets, the organization's own collateral publications, and sales programs.

The use of photographic collections in educational programs lends itself to many advantages. Not only is the institution able to provide quality educational materials for groups of all ages, but it also makes educators aware of the resources available to them for use in their own classroom instruction.

Photographic exhibits can take on many forms. Several institutions use images from their collection in their research rooms and hallways. In recent years, photographic exhibits have become very popular and have tremendous public relations potential. No permanent, temporary, or traveling exhibit is complete without the inclusion of historic photographs. In addition to artifacts that help illustrate an exhibit's storyline, archives, museums, and historical societies often seek permission to use images from another repository to fulfill their exhibit needs. Most institutions include information on obtaining images for use by other nonprofit institutions in their use and reproduction policies, such as those included in Figures 7.1 to 7.4 (pp. 110–111, 112–118).

With decreased budgets and other economic constraints, cultural organizations rely more on partnerships with other institutions to make collections more visible to the public. Websites have become a popular means of collaboration, allowing multiple institutions to showcase their images through online exhibits or databases.

Cultural organizations need to become partners with the local media. The media's use of historic images leads to increased visibility for the organization. The power of the media cannot be underestimated, and

Figure 7.1. Harry Ransom Humanities Research Center Policy and Guidelines for the Protection of Collection Materials during Photography, Filming, and Videotaping Sessions

HARRY RANSOM HUMANITIES RESEARCH CENTER
THE UNIVERSITY OF TEXAS AT AUSTIN
Policy and Guidelines for the Protection of Collection
Materials During Photography, Filming, and
Videotaping Sessions

Policy

To protect its collections from accidental damage during photography, filming, and videotaping sessions, the Ransom Center requires adherence to the following policy and guidelines.

1. Staff must have at least two weeks notice in advance of the session to select and/or assemble collection materials. This will permit staff to evaluate risks posed to individual items, allow for negotiations about alternative selections for problematic materials, and ensure the availability and suitability of the proposed filming site. More advance notice may be required for sessions when requests involve large numbers of items, require special preparation, such as conservation or construction of structural supports, or when personnel or facilities are unavailable to meet the terms of the request.

2. Because of the risks of high temperature, ultraviolet exposure, and light intensity to the stability of certain types of collection artifacts, quartz and mercury lamps are not permitted. HMI [Hydragyrum (mercury) Medium Iodides] are highly recommended because they produce less radiant heat in relation to their light output than other lamps. These must be fitted with ultraviolet absorbers. If tungsten lamps are to be used, thermal radiation filters are required. Lamps of all types must have wire screening shields not larger than 1/16 inch mesh. All apparatus and equipment proposed for filming is subject to Ransom Center approval, and a list of equipment to be used must be submitted at the time of the initial request.

3. A Ransom Center staff member will be assigned to attend photography, filming, and videotaping sessions to ensure that the guidelines described in this document are followed. At the discretion of the designated staff member, some variations in these guidelines may be authorized which take into consideration the nature and condition of materials being filmed, the effects of the production on the site environment, and the physical effects on the items being filmed. In all cases, the decisions of the Center's staff will be final.

4. The Ransom Center will not be responsible fiscally or otherwise for any inconvenience or liability to the schedule, deadlines, or obligations of camera and filming crews or their administration for any delays or stoppage of work caused by the decisions of Ransom Center staff authorized to enforce this policy or its guidelines.

5. Eating, drinking, and smoking are prohibited in all filming areas and elsewhere according to Ransom Center building protocols and University regulations. All building security, inspection, clearance and safety procedures must be followed.

Guidelines

Collection materials may not be used as props, stands, or supports for other items, nor may they be positioned in such as way as to cause potential or real stress or damage.

Collection materials approved for filming must be handled and positioned during the session by designated Ransom Center staff only.

Lamps must not raise the surface temperature of collection materials or the room environment beyond levels appropriate to the safety of collection materials. This is an item specific, non-quantifiable measure, and will be assessed during the session by appointed Ransom Center staff according to the response of materials during filming. Maximum duration of continuous lighting will be determined by these considerations.

(Continued)

Figure 7.1. Harry Ransom Humanities Research Center Policy and Guidelines for the Protection of Collection Materials during Photography, Filming, and Videotaping Sessions (Continued)

Lamps should be turned off when not in use. If intensity of lights can be controlled, low intensity should be used while positioning lights. Lights should be brought up to full intensity only just before shooting begins.

Precautions should be made to prevent damage to collection materials should a lamp fall or explode; this may be done either by assigning a crew member to hold the lamp stand during filming, or by placement of the lamps at a distance from collection materials which is greater than the height of the extended stand. It is for this concern that protection gratings are required for lamp fixtures.

Should power overloads or other malfunction result in erratic electrical behavior, blown building fuses, overheating cables, or other potentially dangerous situations, the session will be terminated immediately until the problem can be resolved to the satisfaction of appropriate Ransom Center, Safety Office, or Physical Plant personnel.

9/27/95

Source: Courtesy of Harry Ransom Center, University of Texas at Austin.

---

an institution should take full advantage of that. Using images from the photographic collections also contributes to special events, exhibits, and other programs sponsored by the institution. In addition, the use of historic photographs on the institution's website increases awareness of the collection, which may lead to sales and generate additional revenue for the organization.

Photographic sales include those to the general public as well as to publishers, business owners, and other institutions. A great potential exists for these images to be seen by hundreds if not thousands of individuals. When accompanied by the archives' credit line, photographs also serve as an invaluable marketing tool.

Businesses often decorate their buildings with historic images that are seen by thousands of patrons each year, offering the institution the ability to reach an untapped audience. These images often spark the ideas of the patrons and lead to additional sales at the historical institution.

Photographic collections can generate income, engage new audiences, and excite the existing clientele. All collecting institutions should promote photographic use and develop marketing plans for visual resources.

Marketing Strategies for Photograph Collections

Cultural organizations often face budgetary, staff, and space constraints that affect their abilities to reach their intended audiences. In addition, audiences increasingly rely on the Internet as a source for information. Cultural heritage organizations must continue to devise creative marketing ideas. Photographic collections can play an extremely important role in counteracting the effect of limited resources by attracting such new

(Continued p. 119)

Figure 7.2. Harry Ransom Center Materials Use Policy

HARRY RANSOM CENTER
UNIVERSITY OF TEXAS AT AUSTIN

Materials Use Policy

The Harry Ransom Center carefully regulates the use of materials in its collections. Policies governing access, photoduplication, and publication of these materials are established by the Director with the advice of the Center's Public Use Committee and the Office of General Counsel of The University of Texas System. This policy attempts to balance the needs of patrons, the exclusive rights of the copyright holder, and the Center's own rights and responsibilities toward its collections.

Access

Any patron wishing to use the Center's materials is required to complete and sign a Patron Application and give information about the subject, scope, and purpose of the research being undertaken. Patrons working onsite must show current photo identification; letters of reference are not required. We may require users of high school age or younger to be accompanied by an adult. The Ransom Center grants all patrons equal access to its collections, subject to uniformly enforced restrictions placed on materials by donor or purchase stipulation, statutory authority, or by the Ransom Center itself for preservation, processing, or other administrative purposes.

Duplication

The Center will consider requests for duplication of materials on a case-by-case basis. The Center's staff does all photoduplication, and fees are assessed on a cost-recovery basis. Rush orders are accepted at the Center's discretion and are subject to additional charges. The Center will not duplicate any materials that might be damaged by the duplication process, nor will it duplicate an entire archive. Patrons needing to use large quantities of materials should plan to conduct research onsite since the Center limits the total number of copies it will provide to any one patron for a single project. No materials may be duplicated that have had copying restrictions placed on them by purchase agreement, donors, depositors or by the Ransom Center itself for preservation, processing, or other essential purposes.

Generally, the Center provides research copies within the Fair Use and other provisions of U.S. Copyright Law, except for audio and moving-image materials. Copies in any format may not be further reproduced, sold, shared, or given to another person, company, or institution for any purpose without the written permission of the Ransom Center.

Publication

Patrons who wish to use Ransom Center original materials or images from printed material in a publication, performance, or broadcast must complete and submit the appropriate notification form. In addition to notifying the Ransom Center and (if applicable) paying a use fee, patrons also must obtain any necessary permissions from the copyright holder, which in some instances may be the Ransom Center and The University of Texas at Austin. The Center maintains the online WATCH database identifying some copyright holders, as well as a guide to locating those not listed. Patrons having questions about copyright liability should seek legal counsel.

Independent of any fees that may be assessed by a copyright holder, it is the policy of the Ransom Center to assess a fee for some uses of materials from its collections. Such fees are intended to offset a small part of the Center's costs for processing, preservation, and servicing of its collections. Fees for the use of images are determined by the print run and distribution of the intended publication. The Center also reserves the right to assess a fee to quote from or publish manuscripts when use is deemed to be significant or extensive. Fees for the use of manuscripts are negotiated on a case-by-case basis. A complete copy of any publication (in any medium) that makes use of Ransom Center materials must be given to the Ransom Center for its collections.

PATRONS WILL DEFEND, INDEMNIFY, AND HOLD HARMLESS THE RANSOM CENTER AND THE UNIVERSITY OF TEXAS SYSTEM, ITS BOARD OF REGENTS, THE UNIVERSITY OF TEXAS AT AUSTIN, ITS OFFICERS, EMPLOYEES, AND AGENTS AGAINST ALL CLAIMS, DEMANDS, COSTS, AND EXPENSES INCLUDING ATTORNEYS' FEES INCURRED BY COPYRIGHT INFRINGEMENT OR ANY OTHER LEGAL OR REGULATORY CAUSE OF ACTION ARISING FROM THE USE OF RANSOM CENTER MATERIALS.

1/08

Source: Courtesy of Harry Ransom Center, University of Texas at Austin.

Figure 7.3. Wisconsin Maritime Museum Archival Collection Research, Reproduction, and Image Use Policy

**WISCONSIN MARITIME MUSEUM ARCHIVAL COLLECTION
RESEARCH, REPRODUCTION, AND IMAGE USE POLICY**
Effective 4/18/2005

I. INTRODUCTION

The Wisconsin Maritime Museum (WMM) is a private, non-profit museum. The mission of the WMM is to engage and educate the public about the maritime history of Wisconsin and the Great Lakes, including Wisconsin's World War II submarines and USS COBIA, by collecting and preserving artifacts and archival materials, creating interactive exhibits, developing and implementing educational programs, and promoting research.

The museum is essentially of the humanities and explores the relationship between man and his historic use of the Great Lakes. Through the quality and content of its operations, the museum seeks to be one of the leading professional maritime institutions of the Great Lakes.

The WMM archival collection is housed in the Library and Archives. The holdings contain several significant collections as well as general research material concerning the history of the Great Lakes. The Library and Archives contains approximately 8,000 books and 40,000 photographs in addition to maps, blueprints, and personal & corporate memorabilia.

II. THE HENRY SCHUETTE LIBRARY AND ARCHIVES

A. The Library Reading Room

   1. Hours of Service

      a) Hours are by appointment only, during regular museum hours. A staff member or other authorized personnel must be present at all times, and appointments are subject to staff availability.

   2. The Reading and Research Room rules:

      a) Researchers must schedule an appointment and fill out a Research Request Form. A new appointment must be made and a new Research Request Form must be filed for each research project.

      b) The WMM reserves the right to refuse access to materials which:

         (1) According to the terms of the donation may not be accessed or duplicated.

         (2) Items in poor condition that would be harmed if handled or duplicated.

      c) All resource materials will be retrieved and returned by staff or other authorized personnel. The Library and Archives is noncirculating. Therefore, nothing may be removed.

      d) Laptop computers, pencils (not pen or ink) and note pads will be allowed in the Library Reading Room. All knapsacks, briefcases and other packages will be subject to inspection at the discretion of the Registrar/Collections Manager.

      e) Eating, drinking and smoking are strictly prohibited.

      f) All photocopies must be made by the Registrar/Collections Manager or other authorized personnel. Some materials may not be photocopied.

      g) Researchers may be asked to wear white gloves depending on the conditions of the materials they are researching. Gloves are required when handling photographs.

      h) In citing materials from the collections of the Wisconsin Maritime Museum, the following credit line should be used: Wisconsin Maritime Museum Collection.

B. Research Procedure

   1. On Site Research Procedure

(Continued)

Figure 7.3. Wisconsin Maritime Museum Archival Collection Research, Reproduction, and Image Use Policy *(Continued)*

a) Appointment. An appointment to do research must be made with at least one-week advance notice to the Registrar/Collections Manager.

b) Research Request Form. A Research Request Form must be completed before any research is begun.

c) Preliminary Research. Preliminary research will consist of producing a list of images, books, and other resources related to the research request. The first 15 minutes of research will be provided gratis. Additional research time will incur a research services fee. See section II.B.2 Long Distance Research Procedure.

d) Research. All research is performed by the researcher with minimal assistance of WMM staff.

e) Researchers will be required to read the researcher guidelines form and sign an agreement prior to using materials from the Library and Archives.

f) Videos. Researchers may view our video collection in the Library and Archives. Use of TV/VCR must be requested 48 hours in advance.

g) Photocopies of images. Requested photocopies will be made of images at the time of the research. All photocopies are made by WMM staff. The photocopy prices are:

   (1) $8\frac{1}{2} \times 11$ . . . .$ .25/copy

   (2) $8\frac{1}{2} \times 14$ . . . .$ .30/copy

   (3) 11×17 . . . .$ .40/copy

   * If less than 50 copies are requested, there will be no additional charge beyond the copy price. If more than 50 copies are requested, the researcher must pay the WMM $30.00 per hour to make copies. Payment for photocopies must be made at the admissions desk before leaving.

h) Orders. Images may be ordered for reproduction or use. See Section III Reproduction Of Images.

2. Long Distance Research Procedure.

a) Research Request Form. A Research Request Form must be filled out and indicate what the research is to entail. Researchers must clearly articulate the research topic (e.g. many boats have the same name and must be clearly identified.) Researchers must also indicate the scope of the research (e.g. if the researcher wishes to have pictures of topsail schooners, they must indicate the maximum amount of photocopies they wish to obtain for review). Please provide as much information as possible about the subject you would like to have researched to eliminate confusion.

b) Preliminary Research. Preliminary Research is performed by WMM staff and will consist of producing a list of images, books, and other resources related to the research request. The first 15 minutes of research will be provided gratis, along with up to 5 photocopies. Additional research time will incur a research services fee described below.

c) Research Work Order. Upon receipt of the Research Request Form and fees, research is performed by WMM staff at $37.50 per hour for non-members, and $30 per hour for museum members. The minimum charge is one hour. Staff will conduct up to two hours of research services. Before research begins, arrangements must be made for payment of fees, and the maximum research time. Pre-payment is required. The first 5 photocopies will be included; additional photocopies are available according to the prices below. Photocopies may be mailed or faxed. If no specific request is made, the photocopies will be mailed. The photocopy prices are:

   (1) $8\frac{1}{2} \times 11\frac{1}{2}$ . . . .$ .25/copy

   (2) $8\frac{1}{2} \times 14$ . . . .$ .30/copy

   (3) 11×17 . . . .$ .40/copy

   * If less than 50 copies are requested, there will be no additional charge beyond the copy price. If more than 50 copies are requested, the researcher must pay the WMM $30.00 per hour to make copies. Payment for photocopies must be received before photocopies are released.

(Continued)

Figure 7.3. Wisconsin Maritime Museum Archival Collection Research, Reproduction, and Image Use Policy *(Continued)*

d) Reproduction Order. If a reproduction of an image is requested, the patron researcher submits an order for reproduction of images and appropriate reproduction fees and shipping fees. The WMM makes reproductions. The WMM mails the order and provides a Conditions for Duplication form for use of the images.

e) Conditions for Duplication. This form must be signed and returned with appropriate fees before use of any image.

III. REPRODUCTION OF IMAGES

A. General Guidelines

1. The WMM reserves the right to refuse to reproduce images that, because of their fragile or deteriorated state, are likely to be damaged.

2. The WMM makes all reproductions.

B. Reproduction Order and Payment must be received before any reproduction takes place.

1. Ordering Images. Orders may be submitted by telephone, FAX, E-mail, in writing, or in person. All orders must include payment for the exact amount cited for both the reproductions and the shipping/handling charges. Payment can be made by check, money order or credit card, and is payable to the "Wisconsin Maritime Museum" in U.S. Dollars, or by credit card. Pre-payment is required. Members receive a 10% discount, applied to the reproduction fee.

2. Reproduction Fees by collection type:

a) Photographs. Black & white or color prints. Prices are for the first photo ordered. A 40% discount is available for each additional print ordered under the same order. Additional prints ordered after the initial order is placed do not qualify for the discount.

   (1) 4 x 5 print $35.00
   (2) 5 x 7 print $37.00
   (3) 8 x 10 print $40.00

   * Larger sizes are available by request.

b) Digital image production

   (1) Scan price per image . . . .$25.00 for 1st image

      (a) $15 for each additional image

c) Charts, Maps, Drawings, Blueprints & other structural renderings Duplication services are available for blueprints, ship plans, charts, maps, drawings and other oversized structural renderings at the following rates per sheet:

   (1) $36.50 plus $.75 per square foot

   Shipping and handling charges are $6.50 per order. Additional charges may be added for originals that are not paper. Members receive a 10% discount, applied to the reproduction fee.

3. Normal reproduction time is four weeks. Faster service is available at additional cost. Please contact the Museum if you need faster service and/or have a specific date the order is needed by.

4. Rush Reproduction Services. If a patron researcher wishes reproduction on a schedule that is earlier than the anticipated reproduction time the WMM will ascertain the ability to do so. If rush service is possible, the researcher pays any additional costs including reproduction fees and a $50 rush service fee. Payment for rush service must be received before the service begins. Credit card payment is acceptable.

(Continued)

Figure 7.3. Wisconsin Maritime Museum Archival Collection Research, Reproduction, and Image Use Policy *(Continued)*

5. Shipping. Shipping/handling charges must be added to the price of all reproductions ordered, unless the patron intends to pick up the order at the Museum. Shipment will be made via the U.S. Postal Service unless other arrangements have been made. Payment of shipping charges must be made prior to shipping.

Shipping/Handling Charges (per item)
a) 4 x 5 or 5 x 7 print $3.50
b) 8 x 10 print $4.00
c) Blueprint $6.50
d) Digital Image—disk or CD $5.00

IV. USE OF IMAGES

COPYRIGHT WARNING: Purchase of images from the WMM archives collection does not imply authority to publish, reproduce, or otherwise use. Written permission must be obtained from the copyright owner. Use of image is not authorized until both written permission is obtained from copyright owner AND a use fee is paid to the WMM.

A. A researcher who wishes to use or publish an image must sign the Conditions for Duplication Form contract to use any item from the WMM Collection. Use fees and the Conditions for Duplication form apply only to those images for which the WMM has copyright or reproduction rights.

B. Use Fees by type of use

1. Black & White Publication
   a) For-profit entities $50.00
   b) Non-profit entities $15.00

2. Color Publication
   a) For-profit entities $100.00
   b) Non-profit entities $25.00

3. Book Jackets/Covers
   a) For-profit entities $150.00
   b) Non-profit entities $50.00

4. Exhibition Use
   a) For-profit entities $50.00
   b) Non-profit entities $15.00

5. Electronic Use
   a) CD ROM ....
      (1) For-profit ....$200 per image
      (2) Non-profit ....$50 per image
   b) Internet display
      (1) For profit ....$200 per image
      (2) Non-profit ....$50 per image

6. Television/Video Use of Still Images $100 per image

7. Film/Video Footage Use (Image Use Fees in 30 Second Increments)
   a) TV World Wide $400
   b) TV Network (National Broadcast) $250
   c) TV Network (Local Broadcast) $125
   d) TV Public (National Broadcast) $125
   e) TV Public (Local Broadcast) $75
   f) TV Foreign Broadcast $250
   g) Home Video Market $250
   h) Theatrical Market $500
   i) Film Festivals $75
   j) Non-profit Educational Use $25
   k) For-profit Educational Use $50
   l) Corporate Presentations & Exhibits ..$150
   m) Amateur productions for private use ..$25

   * The above prices are for 30-second increments. Any part of a 30-second increment will result in a charge for that 30-second increment.

C. Non-profit eligibility

Non-profit fees are available to organizations that prove not-for-profit status. Tax-exempt certificates or letters of identification are acceptable methods of proof.

Source: Courtesy of the Wisconsin Maritime Museum.

Figure 7.4. Maymont Mansion Photograph Policy

**Maymont Mansion
Photograph Policy**

Ordering

Upon receiving a request, Maymont Mansion will send a copy of the Photography Policy, permission form, and invoice. All orders should be prepaid. While some images are on file, special orders may require 6 to 8 weeks for delivery.

Maymont Mansion reserves the right to limit the number of photographic copies; to restrict use/reproduction of rare or valuable materials; to make special price quotations for materials involving unusual difficulty in copying and/or photographing; and to charge a higher fee than standard fee.

Maymont Mansion will allow individuals to photograph an object in the collection or interiors of the house museum. Individual photographers must first complete the use permission form. A staff member must be present at all times during photography sessions.

Use

Images are to be used only once for the purpose listed on the permission form. Any subsequent or different use constitutes a re-use and must be applied for in writing and is subject to applicable fees.

If the borrower intends to publish the photograph(s) requested, Maymont Mansion may authorize publication of the image or decline to give permission. The borrower will be informed by return of the competed permission form with "not approved" or "approved" indicated on the form.

The borrower may not permit others to reproduce the photographic copy or any facsimile of it.

The borrower may not use photographs for resale without an agreement with Maymont Mansion.

Credit Line

For each image that is published from the collections of the Maymont Mansion, appropriate credit line, Maymont Mansion, Richmond, Va., must accompany that image. For some photographs, a photographer's name may be required in addition to the name of the museum.

The borrower will assume all responsibility for questions of copyright and invasion of privacy that may arise in copying and in the use made of the photographic copy.

Fees and Other Considerations

Standard Photograph/Image Use Fee: $25.00 per item
Shipping and handling charges will be added to every order, as appropriate.

Maymont Mansion will make special price quotations for materials involving unusual difficulty in copying and/or photographing. A higher fee may be quoted for use as a cover image.

If the image is to be published, the borrower will notify the Maymont Mansion of publisher and publication date. Maymont Mansion requests one copy, free of charge, of any published work in which the photograph appears.

Maymont Mansion

Application for Permission to Photograph or to Reproduce an Image

Permission to photograph or to reproduce images from the collections of Maymont Mansion is provided for a fee. Please provide a description or name of image(s) requested. Include photocopies if possible.

Name: _____ Company: _____

Address: _____

City: _____ State: _____ Zip Code: _____

(Continued)

Figure 7.4. Maymont Mansion Photograph Policy *(Continued)*

I/we hereby apply to Maymont Mansion for permission to photograph or to reproduce the image of the following object(s), interior(s) or archival item. Use separate sheet or back, if necessary:

For Published and Video Works: (all information below must be included for publication permission to be granted)

Title:_____

Publisher/Producer:_____

Social Security# or Federal Identification # (required): _____

Type (circle one):   Non-Profit/Educational Institution   Commercial

Circle One:

Book	Periodical	Editorial-Other	Advertising
Cover Use	Video-Broadcast	Video-VHS	Video-DVD
Video-Other	CD-ROM	Exhibition Catalogue	

For Exhibition: (all information below must be included for exhibition permission to be granted)

Title:_____

Institution: _____

Period: _____

I hereby agree to accept the conditions in the Photograph Policy and to use the credit line Maymont Mansion, Richmond, Va. I agree to furnish one copy of the publication or work, free of charge. I assume full responsibility in regard to questions of copyright and invasion of privacy. It is understood that only one-time rights for the use stated above are granted in all cases.

_____

Name and Title (please print)   Signature   Date

_____

Address   State/Zip Code

_____

Telephone   FAX   Email

Image Use/Photograph Permission

_____ Approved

_____ Not Approved

Comments & Special Conditions: _____

_____

Signature & Title of Maymont Mansion Representative   Date

Return completed form to:

Maymont
Manager of Historical Collections
1700 Hampton Street
Richmond, VA 23220

Internal Use: Copy Director, Maymont Mansion

Source: Courtesy of Maymont Foundation, Richmond, Virginia.

audiences as tourists, journalists, historians, publishers, and students. A good marketing plan will aid in raising the public profile of an organization and its photographic collections in addition to attracting users from previously untapped sources (Ritzenthaler and Vogt-O'Connor, 2006).

Marketing plans are multifaceted and involve the creation of audience surveys and marketing strategies aimed directly at the target audience for each endeavor. Audience surveys involve analyzing potential audience, understanding user trends, and gathering information on the best type of communication to reach the intended audience. Marketing strategies should describe the existing and potential audiences, articulate the necessary resources to achieve the goal, explain the roles for each person participating in the project, and delineate the institution's goals. The following tasks can aid an organization in creating a marketing plan:

1. Compile a list of services offered to aid in the creation of articles, brochures, press releases, and so on.
2. Offer customer relations and publicity training for staff to enhance current skills.
3. Determine potential target audiences, and compile relevant contact information.
4. Identify the features that make your collections unique.

However, if yours is a smaller institution, you may want to tackle tasks 1, 3, and 4 before embarking on a full-fledged plan (Ritzenthaler and Vogt-O'Connor, 2006).

Archives offer more than research opportunities for their patrons. You and other staff members should brainstorm and list all of the services your archives offers to the public. Following are some examples of services:

- Research opportunities
- Community education
- Preservation advice
- Photo reproductions

Training staff on customer relations and publicity will better enable them to serve their patrons and understand the needs of their visitors. Good customer service is imperative in any business and should also be considered a top priority for archival repositories. Helpful and courteous staff members can make the difference when working with the public. Having a professional demeanor and good communications skills are also important. A satisfied customer will not only be more apt to return to your organization, but they will also be more likely to purchase memberships and support the institution in other ways in the future.

Target Audience

Determining the institution's target audience is critical in reaching new and established patrons. Your institution can craft the most wonderful and creative exhibits and programs, but if those efforts miss your target audience, attendance will lag. For this reason, it is important to understand

Target Audience Considerations

- What are their interests, and how do your collections fit with these interests?
  - General history
  - Niche groups
- What are the age groups you wish to reach?
  - Senior citizens
  - Families
  - School groups
  - Adolescents
  - Teens
  - Young adults
- Where do they live?
  - Local
  - Tourists
  - Statewide

the needs of your audience and know who you want to attract. You may appeal to several audiences, each with its own interests, but until you carefully research audience needs, you may continue to market to the same people and achieve the same disappointing results—poorly attended exhibits and events. Focus groups can help you to understand the needs of your target audience as well as determine if this audience has a special interest in your institution. Understanding the dichotomy between your audiences and your institution will help you to cultivate successful relationships.

Finally, it is important to understand what makes your collection unique and special. Your peculiar strengths will interest people and bring them to your institution. Several archives within your area may have photographs of the downtown area, but yours may be the only one that has photographs taken during parades and other public events. Or your institution may hold the oldest known photographs of your city or the only photographs by a particular photographer. Consider who donated their photographic collections to your organization. Did the head of a local organization donate all of the club's photographs to your archives? These are important questions to consider. Use the following points as a guide to determine the significance of your photographic collections and what makes your collection unique:

- Subjects covered in the collection
- Types of photographs included
  - Daguerreotypes
  - Ambrotypes
  - Tintypes
  - Carte de vistas
  - Polaroid photographs
  - Color slides
  - Black-and-white photographs
- Age of photographs in collection
- Number of photographs in collection
- Local, regional, national, and international importance

Many websites can prove beneficial when conducting research on how other organizations market their institutions and holdings. The following websites offer marketing tips as well as examples of marketing efforts undertaken by various cultural institutions:

Getting Attention
http://www.gettingattention.org/
    This blog, created for nonprofit organizations, serves as a source for ideas and tips to help those responsible for their marketing.

Indianapolis Museum of Art
http://www.imamuseum.org/blog/category/marketing/
    The Indianapolis Museum of Art's blog offers several great entries related to its marketing strategies.

Museum Marketing Blog
http://www.MuseumMarketing.info
   Dimitry van den Berg, a Dutch museum marketing professional, created this blog to discuss basic museum marketing theory through book reviews and personal experience.

National Arts Marketing Project
http://artsmarketing.org/
   The National Arts Marketing Project is a program of Americans for the Arts. The program's website contains practical information as well as case studies on arts marketing success.

Network for Good
http://www.fundraising123.org/nonprofit-marketing
   Network for Good operates a website that contains marketing tips for nonprofits.

Nonprofit Marketing & Fundraising Zone
http://www.nonprofitmarketingzone.com/
   The Nonprofit Marketing & Fundraising Zone's website offers a compilation of online resources to assist those charged with marketing nonprofit organizations.

Implications for Copyright, Fair Use, and Creative Commons

When selecting photographs from the collection to use in various programs, it is important to determine if the copyright is still active or if the item has fallen into the public domain. Figure 7.5 summarizes guidelines for determining if a photograph is still under copyright and, if so, when copyright should expire. In addition, it is also important to determine if the intended use of the image falls under the guidelines for fair use. These two topics can be tricky to understand, especially because copyright laws change regularly. Despite this, understanding copyright and fair use and following the guidelines can save the institution embarrassment and costly legal fees.

   U.S. laws provide protection to "the authors of 'original works of authorship,' including literary, dramatic, musical, artistic, and certain other intellectual works" (U.S. Copyright Office, 2008: 1). This law gives the copyright holder exclusive rights to reproduction, distribution, and display of the work in question. Photographs were eligible for copyright protection as early as 1865, so it is important to keep in mind that simply because your organization owns a photograph does not mean that it holds the copyright (Shapiro and Miller, 1999). Consider whether or not the owner transferred copyright to the institution at the time of donation or if that person ever had the authority to do so. A review of the copyright durations will help to establish whether photographs are still under copyright. If they are, the next step is to determine when the copyright will expire and who currently holds the copyright. While these steps may be time consuming, they ensure that the repository has permission to freely disseminate the photographs.

Figure 7.5. Summary of Copyright Protection, by Date

Works Published or Registered Before 1978	
Publication Date	**Copyright Status or Duration**
Prior to January 1, 1923	Public Domain
January 1, 1923–December 31, 1963	Protected for 28 years from the date of the first publication or registration in unpublished form making it in the Public Domain unless: • Timely renewal application was filed at the conclusion of the initial 28 year term with the US Copyright Office. The work is then protected for 95 years from the first publication or registration in unpublished form • The work is of foreign origin. It is then protected for 95 years from the first publication or date of registration in unpublished form
January 1, 1964–December 31, 1977	95 years from the date of first publication or registration in unpublished form
Works Unpublished and Unregistered as of January 1, 1978	
Works by a single creator	Life plus 70 years unless: • If published between 1978 and 2002, copyright will not expire earlier than December 31, 2047
Works by two or more creators	Life of last surviving creator plus 70 years unless: • If published between 1978 and 2002, copyright will not expire earlier than December 31, 2047
Made-for-Hire or anonymous works	120 years from the date of creation or 95 years from date of first publication, whichever is shorter
Works Created after January 1, 1978	
Works by a single creator	Life plus 70 years
Works by two or more creators	Life of last surviving creator plus 70 years
Made-for-Hire of anonymous works	120 years from date of creation or 95 years from date of first publication, whichever is shorter

How long copyrights last depend on when the work was created and/or published (made available to the public by the creator on an unrestricted basis). It is also important to note that copyright expires on December 31 of the year in which it is set to end. All works published before 1923 are in the public domain, while works published between 1923 and 1977 remain copyrighted for 95 years following their publication. If a work was created before 1978 but never published, its copyright does not expire until 70 years after the creator's death. For any works published after 1977, the copyright expires 70 years after the creator's death. If the work is the result of an individual's employment at a company, the copyright can last for 95 or 120 years, depending on the publication date. Figure 7.5 is useful in determining the duration of copyrighted materials (Stanford University Libraries, 2007). For more detailed information, see the U.S. Copyright Office's website (http://www.copyright.gov/).

There are many other issues concerning copyright that you need to consider, including such things as fair use, and they are far too complicated to discuss here. Consult the following standard works when determining the level of risk that you are willing to assume at your institution: Menzi L. Behrnd-Klodt, *Navigating Legal Issues in Archives* (Chicago: Society of American Archivists, 2008); Peter Hirtle, Emily Hudson, and Andrew T. Kenyon, *Copyright and Cultural Institutions: Guidelines for Digitization for U.S. Libraries, Archives, and Museums* (Ithaca: Cornell University Press, 2009); and Kenneth D. Crews, *Copyright Law for Librarians and Educators*, 2nd ed. (Chicago: American Library Association, 2006).

Creative Commons was created in 2001 because "people have long since concluded that all-out copyright doesn't help them gain the exposure and widespread distribution they want. . . . [I]t is clear that many citizens of the Internet want to share their work . . . with others on generous terms" (Creative Commons, 2011). An artist who agrees to have his or her works governed by a Creative Commons license gives up rights as copyright holder and allows free access to his or her work, thus placing the work in the public domain. Several companies, including Flickr, Google, Wikipedia, and Whitehouse.gov, currently utilize Creative Commons licenses for materials on their websites (Creative Commons, 2010).

While Creative Commons has made it easier for people to use images in publications and other works without obtaining permission, it remains controversial. Some artists have complained that their works were mislabeled as having a Creative Commons license when this was not the case. In addition, photographs of copyrighted works such as Walt Disney World's Big Thunder Mountain Railroad attraction have been listed under a Creative Common license. The problem is that the attraction itself is copyrighted; thus images of the ride are not allowed to be distributed or used without Disney's permission.

Always be careful when using images to which you do not own the copyright. Whenever there is doubt regarding the ability to use an image, seek the proper contacts to determine if copyright exists. The following websites offer practical advice on copyright and rights and reproduction rules and regulations:

> Coalition for Network Information
> http://www-ninch.cni.org/forums/cni-copyright/cni-copyright.html
> The Coalition for Network Information hosts a copyright forum that discusses issues related to copyright, intellectual property rights, and public access to information.

> Copyright and the Public Domain in the United States
> http://copyright.cornell.edu/resources/publicdomain.cfm
> This Cornell University site summarizes U.S. copyright, including copyright term and dates of publication for never published works, works first published in the United States,

works first published outside the United States, sound recordings, and architectural works.

Rights and Reproduction Information Network (R.A.R.I.N.)
http://www.panix.com/~squigle/rarin/01rcsite.html
R.A.R.I.N. is a task force of the Registrars Committee of the American Association of Museums, which provides a website to aid in researching copyright, intellectual property, and rights and reproduction services at museums.

Stanford University Libraries
http://fairuse.stanford.edu/
Stanford University Libraries hosts a website on copyright and fair use.

U.S. Copyright Office
http://www.copyright.gov/
The U.S. Copyright Office's website has the most up-to-date information regarding copyright law and expiration dates.

Creation of Use and Reproduction Policies

Cultural institutions need to have policies in place for use and reproduction of photographs in their collections. When an archives sells reproductions of archival photographs, it is important to consider if the archives has the permission to grant reproduction and whether special cautions need to be addressed. It is also important to recognize intellectual property rights and the terms of any agreements made with donors regarding the use and access of such collections (Malaro, 1998). By looking at policies created by other institutions and considering the following information, you can write a policy that will meet the needs of your institution:

- Statement of purpose: Language should balance the needs of patrons with the organization's responsibilities toward the care and protection of its collections
- Research rules
  - Amount of time needed by staff to fulfill requests
  - Onsite research procedures
  - Distance research procedures (via e-mail or postal service)
  - Handling of photographic images
- Photo reproduction guidelines
  - Associated reproduction fees
  - Use fees: include cautionary clause regarding copyrights in this section
    - For-profit or nonprofit use
    - Publications
    - Web use
    - Exhibits and commercial displays
    - Advertising
    - Presentations

○ Credit line information
○ Any other requirements, such as approval by the archives of publications or other products utilizing the image before production

Photographic reproduction policies should not be carbon copies of those utilized by other institutions but should be specific to the institution for which they are created. Also, maintaining complete and organized records of each donation ensures that an institution will be able to find original deeds of gift from photograph donors quickly, streamlining the process of finding the copyright status of each photograph. For further information on intellectual property rights, consult the following websites:

Canadian Heritage Information Network
http://www.chin.gc.ca/English/Intellectual_Property/Developing_Policies/index.html
  The Canadian Heritage Information Network's website contains detailed information on creating intellectual property policies.

Cultural Resources Management
http://crm.cr.nps.gov/archives/23-05/23-05-18.pdf
  The National Park Service's Cultural Resources Management website contains a great article by Diane Vogt-O'Connor on collections access and intellectual property rights.

"Exploring New Models for Administering Intellectual Property: The Museum Educational Site Licensing (MESL) Project" by J. Trant
http://www.archimuse.com/papers/jt.illinois.html
  This paper appears on the Archives & Museum Informatics website. Though it was written in 1996, it contains a lot of great information for those who deal with Intellectual Property Rights.

Focus on International Property Rights
http://www.america.gov/media/pdf/books/iprbook.pdf
  The America.gov website features an online version of the publication *Focus on International Property Rights* by Thomas G. Field Jr.

"Safeguarding Cultural Heritage, Protecting Intellectual Property and Respecting the Rights and Interests of Indigenous Communities: What Role for Museums, Archives and Libraries?" by Wend Wendland
http://icme.icom.museum/fileadmin/user_upload/pdf/2005/wendland.pdf
  The author presented this article at the conference "Can Oral History Make Objects Speak?" in Nafplion, Greece, in 2005.

U.S. Patent Office
http://www.uspto.gov/web/offices/ac/ahrpa/opa/museum/1intell.htm

The U.S. Patent Office's website contains information on intellectual property rights.

"World Intellectual Property Organization (WIPO) Guide on Managing Intellectual Property for Museums" by Rina Elster Pantalony
http://www.wipo.int/copyright/en/museums_ip/guide.html
The WIPO website contains an article by Rina Elster Pantalony on intellectual property rights for cultural organizations.

Educational Programs

Archival repositories foster life-long learning, and many programs cater to the young and old alike. Whether the staff is venturing into the schools, training teachers, hosting workshops, or using other educational methods, photographs can play an important role in teaching about the past as well as providing visual representations of historical topics. When exposed to images from the collections, learners become more aware of the available resources. Such programs also can instill curiosity and an appreciation for these materials.

School Tours

Giving tours of the archives to schoolchildren is an excellent way to utilize images from the collection. Copies of photographs can be used during onsite tours to enhance student learning by allowing them to view primary source materials and ask questions directly related to the photographs. This also allows them to compare and contrast historical photographs with their current surroundings.

Teacher Training Programs

Many archival repositories are involved in educating teachers on how to use primary sources in their lesson plans through curriculum planning and development. Photographs are a wonderful primary source to include in these sessions. Teachers can use these photographs when teaching about local history, the Civil War, World Wars I and II, civil rights, and so on. Teachers need to be made aware of the various ways in which photographs from archival collections can be utilized. By creating a list of topics and subtopics, along with a sampling of images, archivists can highlight valuable resources held by their collections and entice teachers to use these images in their classrooms. Several organizations have excellent examples of the use of photographs on their online education pages:

Chicago History Museum
http://www.greatchicagostories.com/
The Chicago History Museum's *Great Chicago Stories* are historical fiction stories that highlight various aspects of the city's history and showcase photographs and artifacts from the

museum's collection. The stories are broken into age groups and include classroom activities.

Getty Museum

http://www.getty.edu/education/for_kids/

The Getty's education website contains links to several great online resources for kids that use photographs from the institution's collections.

Exhibits

Michael Belcher (1991: 135) argued that "Photographs have an advantage over illustrations and other graphic representations because for the majority of visitors they represent the truth, and are a faithful reproduction of how something actually appeared. No other non-electronic medium can claim this, for, in the opinion of most visitors, the camera does not lie." In addition, exhibits are one of the easiest ways to utilize photographic collections. Exhibits can be as simple as a small display of photographs from the collections with little interpretation to large-scale, permanent exhibits that are the result of years of research. Within exhibits, photographs show objects in use, represent an object when an item is not available for display, and place subjects in context.

There are additional benefits to using photographic collections in exhibits. With all exhibits, it is important to require that the institution's copyright acknowledgement appears with all images. This tells the viewer where he or she can obtain a copy of the image. Using these images also enables the staff to have better intellectual control over the images held within their collections. This not only aids in creating quality exhibits but helps with assisting researchers with their photographic needs. For additional information, see the exhibits checklist on page xx.

Most archives have research rooms with blank wall space. A great way to showcase images from the collection is to frame reproductions of the archival originals and place them on these blank walls. Researchers often seek photographs of a specific area. Once they enter the research room and see the variety of other potential topics, they may expand their topics and vision. Had these images not been on display, researchers may have simply purchased typical downtown street images that often dominate history publications.

It is important to use care and consideration when choosing images for research rooms. Unique and stimulating images will help to engage the researcher. This is one opportunity to showcase collection strengths. A good practice is to select images that will create conversations. If you work with photographs on a daily basis, bring the photographs you deem to be unique and interesting out of storage. Patrons often enjoy street scenes, landscapes, interesting architectural elements, people, animals, and parades. Be sure to look for photographs that are clearly focused and show interesting points of view, as well as for those that have a historic feel to them. People enjoy seeing photographs of the way things "used to be" and comparing them to the way an area looks today.

Temporary Exhibits

Temporary exhibits are another effective way to showcase photographic collections. These exhibits are usually on display for a short period of time and thus feature many different photographs throughout the year. Temporary exhibits can include copies (Figures 7.6 and 7.7) or original photographs (Figure 7.8) and often require very little interpretation.

When mounting temporary exhibits, choose simple topics that will showcase photographs that might surprise and stimulate visitors. Possibilities include nature scenes, famous people, local businesses, travel, and oddities. Images should evoke a "wow" from visitors and cause them to think "I didn't know that was here," or "who knew these images existed!" Exhibits should educate visitors and create a connection between them and the images, causing them to want to learn more about the archives' holdings. By changing exhibits regularly, you will also entice visitors to repeatedly visit your institution.

Permanent Exhibits

Many cultural institutions have permanent exhibits that highlight their sites. Using images from the organization's permanent collections is a

Figure 7.6. Photographs Used in Temporary Exhibit Text Panels

Source: Photograph by Stephanie Gaub.

Figure 7.7. Several Photographs Reproduced and Enlarged for Use in a Temporary Exhibit

Source: Photograph by Stephanie Gaub.

Figure 7.8. Original Photographs Displayed with Artifacts in a Temporary Exhibit

Source: Photograph by Stephanie Gaub.

great way to showcase those images and illustrate the exhibit story (Figures 7.9 and 7.10). Many visitors do not read exhibit text, but photographs always attract attention. By including several photographs in the exhibit, you will better engage visitors. In addition, using images from the collection can keep the cost of exhibit design low.

Traveling Exhibits

Traveling exhibits are created by one institution and then rented to other institutions for a small fee. This type of exhibit has become increasingly popular, as it enables organizations with limited staff to change exhibits without having to create them. Traveling exhibits also allow museums to showcase topics and collections to which they may not have access. Traveling exhibits can be one of the best ways of reaching people who most likely would not visit your institution to see images

Figure 7.9. Reproductions of Photographs Used in Permanent Exhibit Text Panels (Example 1)

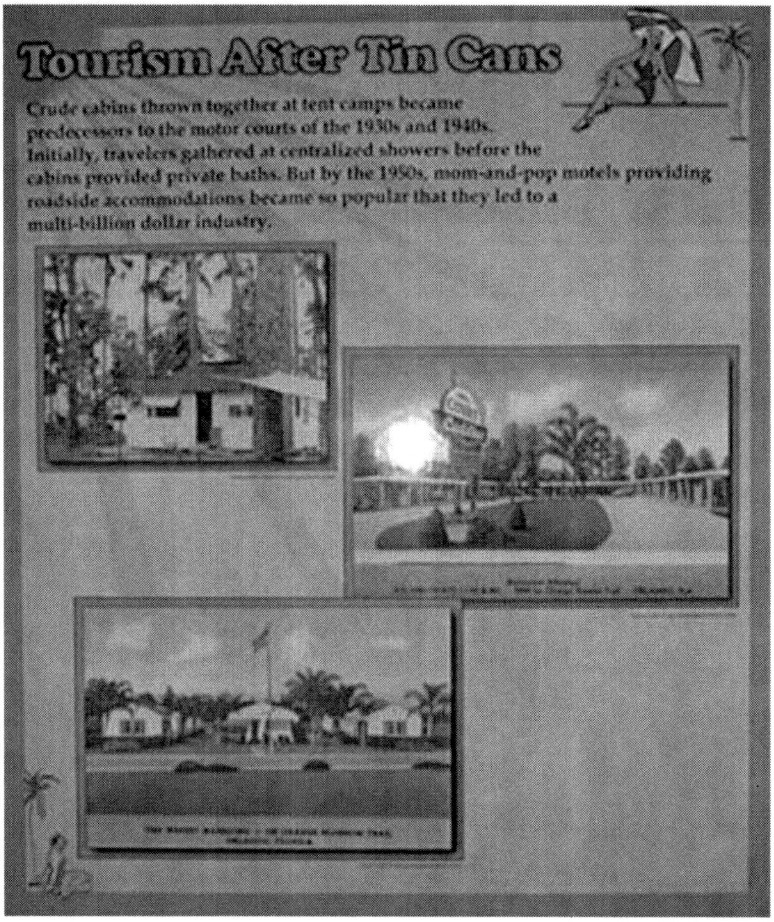

Source: Photograph by Stephanie Gaub.

Figure 7.10. Reproductions of Photographs Used in Permanent Exhibit Text Panels (Example 2)

Source: Photograph by Stephanie Gaub.

from your collections. These exhibits are seen by audiences other than regular patrons, thereby generating additional revenue and promoting the institution.

Before deciding on the creation of a traveling exhibit, it is important to determine the feasibility of the intended display. Important questions include these: Does the topic lend itself to traveling outside of the organization? What are the costs involved? How much staff time is needed? Is there sufficient information to include?

No matter what type of exhibit an organization plans to create, the archivist must keep in mind budgetary needs and resources, exhibit goals, schedule, preservation risks, safety and security, staff involvement and duties, and theme (Ritzenthaler and Vogt-O'Connor, 2006). Create an exhibit checklist to aid in the selection, duplication, fabrication, and installation processes. The sidebar includes a list of tasks to complete for an exhibition; related tasks are grouped together for convenience and are not necessarily in the order of completion. Keep in mind that you can adjust an exhibit to fit the needs of the institution, and it need not be excessively detailed.

Many organizations have online exhibits that utilize photographs from their collections. These websites are good examples:

Tasks for Creating an Exhibition

- Decisions to be made before creating the exhibit
  - Create exhibit title
  - Determine exhibit dates
  - Identify key staff
- Exhibit design
  - Decide on scope
  - Determine size of space
  - Create layout
- Photographic activities, deadlines, responsible staff
  - Identify photographs for inclusion
  - Identify any copyright issues
  - Research photographs for exhibit labels
  - Determine use of photographs (copies, originals, etc.)
  - Arrange for any photo replication
  - Write photographic exhibit labels
  - Record all photographs used in exhibit and file documentation appropriately
- Fabrication of all exhibit materials and text panels
- Installation of exhibit materials and photographs

National Archives

http://www.archives.gov/exhibits/

The National Archives has several wonderful online exhibits featuring materials from its collections.

National Park Service Museum Handbook

http://www.nps.gov/history/museum/publications/MHIII/mh3ch7.pdf

The National Park Service Museum Handbook, Part II, contains a checklist for using objects in exhibits that you can use as a model for creating your own checklist.

New York State Archives

http://www.archives.nysed.gov/a/research/res_webexhibits.shtml

The New York State Archives' online exhibits highlight images from its collection.

Special Events and Internal Marketing

Another creative way to utilize photographic collections includes special events and internal marketing programs. Some of the most common uses include invitations, websites, rack cards, and brochures. Readily available images are more cost-efficient than pricey graphics, adding a bit of nostalgia while promoting the organization's holdings.

Invitations

Most organizations have holiday parties, volunteer celebrations, exhibit openings, and public programs that are by invitation only. If your organization is hosting a Christmas party, why not use a Christmas image from the collections on the invitation? You can use Valentine's Day, Halloween, and Thanksgiving photographs in the same manner. Invitations to exhibit openings should include an image featured in the exhibit. Use images from the collections related to the event to create unique invitations that not only express the intended purpose but also promote the vast photographs owned by the institution.

Websites

Today almost every institution has its own website (see Chapter 1). With the unlimited potential for website visitation, you should use photographs to their fullest extent throughout the site. If your collections contain photographs of schoolchildren, place these on pages that discuss educational programs. If your collections contain photographs of people volunteering for the Red Cross or other organizations, place these on pages that discuss such opportunities. Think creatively and use collections-related images where they will fit on the website. Not only will the images add character to the pages, but they will also highlight the varied types of photographs contained within the collections.

Hints on Using Photographs on Websites

- Consider the topic(s) to be covered on the webpage; look for photographs from the collection that match the topic(s).
- Is the photograph of good quality?
  - Photographs that are out of focus or faded will not reproduce well.
  - Very small photographs, such as those that are 2" x 2" or similar size, may not reproduce at a high quality.
  - Stained, torn, or repaired photographs also pose a problem when reproduced.
- Does the photograph look "busy," or are the subjects far away?
  - When using photographs of people, use those that show individuals or small groups rather than those of large groups of people.
  - Photographs of objects should be clear enough that viewers understand what they are looking at.
  - Subjects within the photograph should not appear in the distance. If necessary, crop the photograph to bring the subject closer to the viewer.
- Is the photograph in the public domain, does your organization own copyright, or is copyright still maintained by the creator? To avoid potential legal ramifications, it is best to use photographs for which copyright is not in question.

Guidelines for Image Digitization

There are several formats in which you can save a scanned image. Two of the more common formats are called *tagged image file format* (TIFF) and *joint photographic experts group* (JPEG). Be sure you understand the differences between TIFF and JPEG files as well as the implication of image size for each format.

The filename of a TIFF file includes the extension .tif. TIFF files are large, uncompressed files that are best used when creating high-quality images that will be used to create professional reprints, exhibit backgrounds, and other items that require a great amount of detail. Because TIFF files are so large, they use a lot of memory (Carey, 2008a). Unless you are making the image available on your website for the general public to download, you should not use TIFF images.

The JPEG format is the industry standard for delivering digital images over the Internet; it has the file extension .jpg. The compression size (amount of space the file takes up) of a JPEG image is reduced to 5 percent of the image's normal size as a result of the destruction of information each time the file is changed and saved. JPEG files can easily be made from TIFF files, so save files first as TIFFs and then as JPEGs (Carey, 2008a).

Rack Cards and Brochures

Rack cards and brochures are the perfect way to advertise exhibits, special events, and archival holdings to the general public. Using photographic images on these types of materials is a great way to spread the word about holdings. An excellent way to advertise photographic collections is by creating a brochure or rack card dedicated solely to these collections (Figures 7.11 and 7.12). The information should highlight important collections and themes within the archives. Using photographs not only makes a brochure more visually appealing but also allows the viewer a glimpse into the collections.

Web-Based Tools

In addition to organization websites, many cultural institutions are taking advantage of sites such as Facebook and Flickr to promote their photographic collections. These sites offer the advantage of a free hosting service that is especially beneficial to organizations with little funding available for such projects. See Chapter 2 of this book for information on choosing the site that works best for your archives.

As well as understanding the needs of your organization, it is also important to determine the intended use of the photographs before putting them online. Will they be merely for educational purposes, or are they to be downloadable by visitors to the website? Determining the intended use will help you decide the size and type of file you will place online. Also be aware of the potential threat for copyright infringement by visitors to your archives or your site. Having a grasp on these factors

---

Important Aspects of Image Digitization

- Determine whether you want the viewer to be able to download the photograph.
  - If no, save the image as a JPEG file that is small enough that the printed image will be of undesirable quality.
    - The dimensions should be no larger than 750 x 499 pixels with a JPEG quality of 6 (Carey, 2008b).
    - The user is given quality options ranging from 0 to 12 when saving a JPEG file, 6 is the mid-range in quality output.
  - If yes, save the image as a JPEG file at least 700 KB in size; for highest quality photos, save as a TIFF file.
- Watermark all digital image files that you place online to help prevent unauthorized publication (watermarking methods vary depending on the software used).

How to Create a Brochure

- Determine the content.
  - Will the brochure focus on the collections as a whole, or will there be different brochures created for manuscript, photographic, and other collections?
  - Determine the format of the text; usually a brief paragraph about the archives and its holdings followed by bulleted lists of various collections works best.
- Choose photographs that reflect the overall content of the collection as well as those that are unique or have an interesting subject.
- Be sure that the photographs will be easy to view once reproduced in a smaller format.
- Always include contact information and photo credit lines.

Figure 7.11. Front Cover of a Brochure Created for the Joseph L. Brechner Research Center at the Orange County Regional History Center

ORANGE COUNTY REGIONAL
HISTORY CENTER

Orlando

FLORIDA

"The City Beautiful"

JOSEPH L. BRECHNER
RESEARCH CENTER

ORLANDO, FLORIDA

Source: Courtesy of the Orange County Regional History Center.

will enable you to create a website that fits not only your needs but those of your visitors as well.

Types of Sites

Some of the top photo-hosting sites on the Internet are Funtigo, Kodak Smugmug, Webshots, PhotoWorks, Shutterfly, Snapfish, and Flickr. Following is a list of the pros and cons of each:

- Funtigo, http://www.funtigo.com, allows you to create a website and photo slideshows.
  - Pro: easy to use
  - Con: fee to use
- Kodak, http://www.kodakgallery.com, allows you to organize photos into albums that can be shared with anyone online or via password access.
  - Pros: free service, quick photo upload, offers ability to purchase prints
  - Con: does not offer the ability to create a customized website
- Smugmug, http://www.smugmug.com, allows you to upload and share photos and videos with unlimited photo storage.
  - Pros: free, offers external linking capabilities, offers the ability to password protect images, and tracks number of visitors
  - Con: does not offer the ability to create a customized website
- Webshots, http://www.webshots.com, offers free desktop software to create photo albums, slideshows, wallpapers, and screensavers.
  - Pros: free, offers the ability to keep track of all activity from the desktop, easy to upload photos, and offers the ability to create a photo album website and the ability to password protect photos
  - Con: must download the software for the site to work
- PhotoWorks, http://www.photoworks.com, offers photos albums with captions.
  - Pros: free, easy-to-order reproductions
  - Con: does not offer the ability to create customized websites

Figure 7.12. Interior of the Brochure Created for the Joseph L. Brechner Research Center at the Orange County Regional History Center

ARCHIVAL COLLECTION

266 linear feet (272 cubic feet) of primary source archival materials including:

- *Scott Family Papers and Photographs, 1824–1993*
  Records of Dr. Stanley Scott, a Scottish immigrant, and his son Colonel Stanley Hill Scott concerning their large citrus grove, Kelso Grove, in Windermere

- *J.M. Cheney Papers, 1880–1960*
  Personal and business papers of Cheney, a federal judge and politician, who came to Orlando in 1855 and purchased the Orlando Water Company, which later became Orlando Utilities Commission

- *Henschen Family Papers, 1870–1965*
  Records of several generations of this influential immigrant family who settled near Sanford and their involvement in citrus, railroading, and government

PHOTOGRAPH COLLECTION

More than 16,000 photographs and postcards including:
- T. P. Robinson Collection, 1915–1955
  One of Orlando's first commercial photographers
- Dr. Phillips Collection, 1935–1945
  Documenting one of Central Florida's most important citrus producers
- Central Florida Fair Collection, 1925–1975
  An extensive collection of one of the area's longest-running fairs

- *William (Bill) McCollum Naval Training Center Closure Papers, 1991–1995*
  Records from U.S. Representative Bill McCollum's efforts to keep Orlando's Naval Training Center open

- *Great Oaks Village, 1920–1989*
  Records of the foster care facility and juvenile court system

- *Mayor Robert Carr Collection, 1956–1967*

- *Mayor Carl T. Langford Collection, 1967–1980*

- *Orange County Commissioner Mary Johnson Collection, 1992–2004*

- *Orange County Commissioner Ted Edwards Papers, 1996–2004*

Source: Courtesy of the Orange County Regional History Center.

- Shutterfly, http://www.shutterfly.com, offers users customized websites to share their photos.
  ○ Pros: free, unlimited photo storage, customized website creation, features editing photos with effects
  ○ Cons: none
- Snapfish, http://www.snapfish.com, offers free photo software that allows you to edit, organize, and upload images from your desktop.
  ○ Pro: free software
  ○ Con: does not have the ability to create customized websites
- Flickr, http://www.flickr.com, is an image- and video-hosting site that also offers an online community.
  ○ Pros: offers free and paid services; offers the ability to tag images and organize them by these tags, public and private image access, and ability to tag images as "all rights reserved" and to search by licensing options
  ○ Con: free version allows uploading of only 100 MB and two videos each month

In addition to the sites listed earlier, the Internet enables many historical organizations to display their photographic collections throughout their websites. Here are some of the most notable examples:

Historical Society of Palm Beach County
http://www.historicalsocietypbc.org/
The Historical Society of Palm Beach County's website not only uses its photographic collections on the site's various pages but it also sells very creative products with their images.

Kentucky Historical Society
http://history.ky.gov/
The Kentucky Historical Society's website makes wonderful use of its photographic collections.

Lake County Discovery Museum
http://www.lcfpd.org/teich_archives/
The Lake County Discovery Museum north of Chicago houses the Curt Teich Postcard Archives, one of its many permanent collections. A page on the museum's website is dedicated to this incredible collection and has many useful links related to Curt Teich postcards.

National Park Service *Conserve O Gram*
http://www.nps.gov/history/museum/publications/conserve ogram/22-02.pdf
http://www.nps.gov/history/museum/publications/conserve ogram/22-03.pdf
In 2008 the National Park Service published two *Conserve O Grams* related to the use of digital images.

National Park Service *Digital Image Guide for Media Production*
http://hfc.nps.gov/hfc/pdf/digital-image-guide-dec06.pdf
The National Park Service published these guidelines "for selecting or preparing digital image files for use by Harpers

Ferry Center or by parks for media production." The guide, revised in March 2010, includes definitions and steps for working with digital photography and other media.

Smithsonian Institution's Flickr Site
http://www.flickr.com/photos/smithosonian
    The Smithsonian Institution has a Flickr site on which it has placed thousands of images scanned from its collections.

Smithsonian Institution's Photography Initiative
http://photography.si.edu/
    The Smithsonian Institution's Photography Initiative is a collection of essays and stories that discuss how photography shapes our culture and lives, illustrated by photographs from the Smithsonian's collections.

Victoria and Albert Museum
http://www.vam.ac.uk/collections/photography/index.html
    The Victoria and Albert Museum's website has a section devoted to its photographic collections.

Wisconsin Center for Film and Theater Research
http://www.wcftr.commarts.wisc.edu/index.html
    The Wisconsin Center for Film and Theater Research's website is a wonderful resource that illustrates how photographs can be used online.

Publications

Journals, newsletters, and books are an excellent way to use photographs to promote photographic collections. As with all other forms of marketing, publications reach a wide audience and often lead to additional photographic sales. It is not uncommon for an individual or business to see a photograph in a book and contact the credited institution to obtain copies of that photograph as well as copies of other photographs in the collection.

Organizational Publications

Most organizations produce some type of publication, either for members or for the general public. Often these publications include a section devoted to the collections (Figure 7.13), as well as articles based on scholarly research (Figure 7.14). These are great avenues to educate readers about the organization's photographic collections, as the audience already has a vested interest in the organization and its collections (Figures 7.15, 7.16, and 7.17).

Books

Books are a great way for organizations to promote their photographic collections, and these can often be published with little or no upfront cost. Companies such as Arcadia Publishing, Historical Publishing

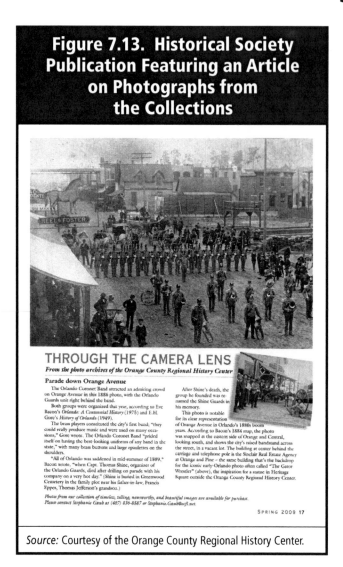

Figure 7.13. Historical Society Publication Featuring an Article on Photographs from the Collections

Source: Courtesy of the Orange County Regional History Center.

Figure 7.14. Scholarly Article Published in a Historical Society Publication Utilizing Photographs from the Collection

Source: Courtesy of the Orange County Regional History Center.

Network, and The History Press publish local history books rich with photographic illustrations. Coffee table–type books have become increasingly popular, and tourists often buy these types of publications as souvenirs of their travels. The books can contain narratives with photographs to enhance the stories, or they can focus on the photographs themselves with captions that describe the images. Arcadia features both types of publications, while Historical Publishing Network and The History Press focus on the first. No matter which your organization chooses, books are a great way to educate the public and showcase collections at the same time. In addition, the sale from publications can generate additional revenue for the organization. Before embarking on the publishing journey, it is important to determine which type of book will work best for your organization. If your book will contain a considerable amount of text, choose an author and determine his or her compensation. Often, archival staff author such a book because they are usually the most familiar with research services. In addition, the staff will know which photographs best tell the story. If you take on such a

Figure 7.15. Annual Report Highlighting Photographs from the Institution's Collection

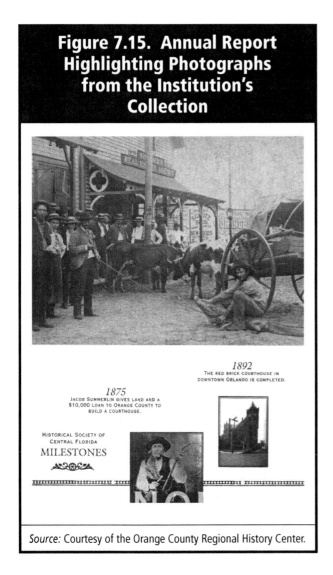

Source: Courtesy of the Orange County Regional History Center.

Figure 7.16. Article in Membership Letter Focusing on Wedding Gown Preservation and Showcasing Wedding Photograph from the Collection

Source: Courtesy of the Orange County Regional History Center.

project, be aware that it may take at least 18 months to complete, and you should be prepared to spend a considerable amount of time working on the manuscript. Plan ahead and leave adequate time to work on the book. Most important, make sure you clear copyright for any images that will be used in such publications.

Policies and Forms

Outside authors will also want to use your images in their upcoming works. For this reason, it is important to have use policies in place, along with forms to guide this process, such as those in Figures 7.18 and 7.19.

Many publishers focus on the creation of illustrated historical publications. Following are examples of these publishers:

Arcadia Publishing
http://www.arcadiapublishing.com/
Arcadia Publishing has published more than 5,000 local history titles.

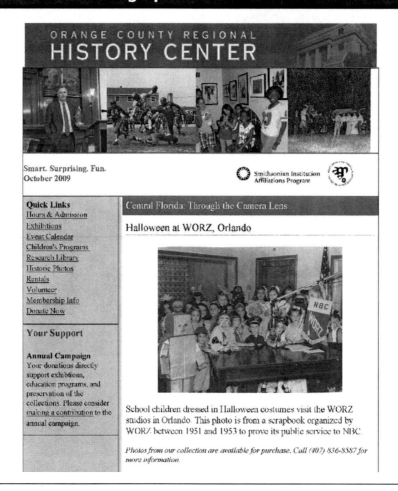

Figure 7.17. Organization's Electronic Newsletter Featuring a Photograph from the Collection

Source: Courtesy of the Orange County Regional History Center.

Historical Publishing Network
http://www.lammertinc.com/HPNhome.html

Historical Publishing Network produces pictorial history books designed as fundraisers for sponsoring organizations.

History Press
https://historypress.net/indexsecure.php

The History Press publishes local history books at no charge to the author and even offers a commission on each book sold.

Sales

Sales of reproductions from the archives' holdings can generate income for the organization. Think outside the box when it comes to marketing

(Continued p. 145)

Figure 7.18. Harry Ransom Center Publication Fees

HARRY RANSOM CENTER
THE UNIVERSITY OF TEXAS AT AUSTIN
Publication Fees

Publication of images of Harry Ransom Humanities Research Center materials is subject to approval and fees may be charged for such use. "Publication" includes the following media: print, electronic/digital, videotape, film, or microform. Permission to use images must be obtained in advance and in writing from the Ransom Center by completing the appropriate "Notification of Intent" form. These fees are separate from any which might be assigned/assessed by the copyright holder.

Fees are assessed in addition to photoduplication costs, are for non-exclusive use, and must be paid in advance of publication. Only those images actually used in publication are subject to these fees. If a request covers more than one publication or project, then additional fees will apply. Publication fees are waived for theses, dissertations, student projects, and for University of Texas at Austin faculty, staff, and students (up to $750).

STILL IMAGES				
Books	FEES			
	TEXT ILLUSTRATIONS			
	One-time use One-language One country	One-time use One-language Worldwide	One-time use All languages Worldwide	All editions & all uses
2,000 copies or less	$ 20	$ 30	$ 40	$ 50
2,001–10,000 copies	40	60	80	100
10,001 or more copies	80	120	160	200
	JACKET/COVER ILLUSTRATIONS			
2,000 copies or less	$100	$150	$200	$250
2,001–10,000 copies	200	300	400	500
10,001 or more copies	300	450	600	750
Periodicals	FEES			
	TEXT ILLUSTRATIONS			
Circ. 1,000 or less	no fee	no fee	no fee	no fee
Circ. 1,001–10,000	$ 20	$ 30	$ 40	$ 50
Circ. 10,001–99,999	40	60	80	100
Circ. 100,000 or more	80	120	160	200
	JACKET/COVER ILLUSTRATIONS			
Circ. 1,000 or less	no fee	no fee	no fee	no fee
Circ. 1,001–10,000	$100	$150	$200	$250
Circ. 10,001–99,999	200	300	400	500
Circ. 100,000 or more	300	450	600	750

(Continued)

Figure 7.18. Harry Ransom Center Publication Fees *(Continued)*	

Other Print Products	FEES
Calendars, posters, greeting cards, postcards, novelty items, etc.	
Printing: 1,000 or less	$200
Printing: 1,001–9,999	300
Printing: more than 10,000	500

Electronic Formats	FEES	
	TEXT ILLUS	PACKAGING/COVER
2,000 copies or less	$ 20	$100
2,001–10,000 copies	40	200
10,001 or more copies	80	300

Note: Above fees for non-exclusive, one-time, single-language, single-country rights only. Fees for additional rights are the same as those for books.

INTERNET/ONLINE: $100 per image (commercial); $25 (nonprofit; no charge for UT-Austin)

Broadcast	FEES
One country use, single language only	$ 50
World use, single language only	100
World use, all languages	200

Note: For home video format add $50 per image in addition to the broadcast fees.

Feature Films	FEES
U.S. distribution	$500
World distribution	1000

Note: For home video format add $100 per image in addition to the distribution fees.

Special Uses	FEES
Advertisements for television/film	$500
Other promotional	200
Exhibition (personal)	25
Exhibition (non-profit)	50
Exhibition (commercial)	200

MOVING IMAGES	

Broadcast/Home Video	FEES
World use, all languages (includes home video rights)	$60/second with $350 minimum
Note: For feature films add 100% to above fees.	
Broadcast/Home Audio	FEES
World use, all languages (includes home format rights)	$30/second with $200 minimum

08/07

Source: Courtesy of Harry Ransom Center, University of Texas at Austin.

Figure 7.19. Harry Ransom Center Notification of Intent to Publish Photographic Images

THE UNIVERSITY OF TEXAS AT AUSTIN

NOTIFICATION OF INTENT TO PUBLISH PHOTOGRAPHIC IMAGES

Name (please print): _____

Phone: _____ Fax: _____ E-mail: _____

Address: _____

I hereby notify the Harry Ransom Humanities Research Center of my intent to publish the following images that are part of the Ransom Center's collections: (Please state specifically and in detail the images you intend to publish.)

Please provide publication information below:

Author/editor: _____

Title: _____

Publisher: _____

Projected publication date: _____

Print run (number of copies): _____

Projected retail price: _____

Intended audience: _____

Rights requested:	One country	One language	One-time use
	Worldwide	All languages	All editions

PAGE 1 of 2: PLEASE READ AND COMPLETE ALL PAGES

(Continued)

Figure 7.19. Harry Ransom Center Notification of Intent to Publish Photographic Images *(Continued)*

Conditions Governing Use of Ransom Center Images:

1. All requests for use of Ransom Center materials, whether in publications, motion pictures, videos, or performances will be considered on a case-by-case basis.

2. It is the responsibility of the patron to obtain any required copyright permissions from the copyright holder, which in some instances may be the Ransom Center and The University of Texas at Austin.

3. It is the policy of the Ransom Center to assess a fee for some uses of materials from its collections. Such fees are assessed on a case-by-case basis and are intended to offset a small part of the Center's costs associated with processing, preserving, and servicing of its collections.

4. Use fees cover non-exclusive, one-time use only unless otherwise indicated and are to be paid in advance. They are assessed in addition to any duplication costs.

5. The proposed publication must result in a suitable presentation of the original image. Superimposition of text, cropping, bleeding, the addition of color, or other alterations are not allowed.

6. The following credit line must be used:

   Harry Ransom Humanities Research Center
   The University of Texas at Austin

7. The Ransom Center requires that a complete copy of any publication (in any medium) that makes use of its materials be given to the Center for its collections.

8. Publication-ready images are not to be further reproduced, sold, shared, or given to another person, company, or institution for any purpose, without the written permission of the Center.

9. THE APPLICANT WILL DEFEND AND HOLD HARMLESS THE RANSOM CENTER AND THE UNIVERSITY OF TEXAS SYSTEM, ITS BOARD OF REGENTS, THE UNIVERSITY OF TEXAS AT AUSTIN, ITS OFFICERS, EMPLOYEES AND AGENTS AGAINST ALL CLAIMS, DEMANDS, COSTS, AND EXPENSES INCLUDING ATTORNEYS' FEES INCURRED BY COPYRIGHT INFRINGEMENTS OR ANY OTHER LEGAL OR REGULATORY CAUSE OF ACTION ARISING FROM USE OF RANSOM CENTER MATERIALS.

AGREEMENT: I certify that the information provided by me herein is correct. Further, I have read, understand, and by my signature below, agree to abide by the rules, regulations and obligations as set forth by the Harry Ransom Humanities Research Center in "Conditions Governing Use of Ransom Center Images." (A signed copy of this form will be returned to the applicant in acknowledgment of this agreement.)

Signature: _____ Date: _____

To be completed by Ransom Center staff:

Publication of Ransom Center images is approved, subject to payment of use fee of _____ PDC: _____

Curator/Librarian: _____ Assoc.Director: _____ Date: _____

PAGE 2 OF 2: PLEASE READ AND COMPLETE ALL PAGES

11/07

Source: Courtesy of Harry Ransom Center, University of Texas at Austin.

these types of sales. Visitors often enjoy keepsakes of their vacation, business owners like to showcase historic images in restaurants and hotels, and authors use photographs in books and articles. Individual images can be sold in organization gift shops (Figure 7.20), through Internet stores, or directly to researchers.

Product creation is another way to promote photographic collections and generate additional funds. You can use photographs that are in the public domain, or that the archives owns copyright to, on T-shirts, tote bags, postcards, note cards, magnets, mouse pads, and any other potential product. Before using images of individuals, be sure that your use is not infringing on any content-related rights. This includes any image that represents an individual in a negative light. However, the right to privacy generally dies with the individual, so most images held by archival repositories should not be affected. Once you have obtained all of these clearances, the sky is the limit for product creation!

When creating a form that grants permission to reproduce photographs, include a cautionary clause that places responsibility for obtaining

Figure 7.20. Museum Store Display of Photographs from the Institution's Collection for Sale to the General Public

Source: Courtesy of the Orange County Regional History Center.

all copyright clearance on the requesting party. By doing so, this individual is on notice that the organization may not have full rights to the image and that it may be necessary to look further to determine who holds copyright to the photograph in question. Statements such as "permission is granted by XYZ Archives to the extent of its ownership of rights related to the photograph" or "purchasing images from XYZ Archives does not grant copyright permission" should be included in any forms related to the sale of reproductions of photographic materials. Examples of the types of information to include on these forms include:

- Intended use of reproduced photograph
- Name and contact information of requestor
- Statement of agreement of one-time use of image
- Credit line information
- Title of requested image
- Signature of requestor and archival representative
- Total cost, including reproduction and use fees

When determining reproduction and use fees, it is important to consult with similar-sized organizations. Reproduction fees will depend on how much it costs for the institution to replicate images from its collections. Because most archives rely on outside companies for reproduction, it is important to recoup any fees associated with reproduction while including an additional amount to cover staff time. For example, it may cost $15 to reproduce an 8" × 10" image. An additional $10 might cover staff time, which will bring the total price for an 8" × 10" image to $25. On the other hand, use fees are less easy to calculate, and it will be advantageous to look at those charged by similar-sized repositories when determining charges. For sample policies and forms, see Figures 7.21 through 7.26 (pp. 147, 148–158).

In addition to selling online through your organization's website, you can sell photographs through the following Internet sites:

1000|Museums
http://www.1000museums.com/
1000|Museums makes available reproductions of images from museums throughout the world. Partner museums include the Guggenheim, Detroit Institute of Arts, and the LA County Museum of Art.

Boca Raton Historical Society
http://www.bocahistory.org/photo_archives/photo_archives
.asp
The Boca Raton Historical Society's site includes a page dedicated to photo sales.

Cafepress
http://www.cafepress.com
Cafepress allows registered users to create an online store and personalized products by uploading their own images.

Figure 7.21. Pensacola Historical Society Resource Center Fee Schedule

(Taxes are included in the fees.)

RESEARCH FEE:

| Members/Students | $0.00 | Florida's Historic Passport | $0.00 |
| Local academic faculty | $0.00 | Non-Members | $5.50 |

PHOTOCOPIES:

Black and White		Color Copies	
8½" x 11" and 8½" x 14"		8½" x 11" and 8 ½" x 14"	
Members/Students	$.20/page	Members/Students	$.30/page
Non-Members	$.25/page	Non-Members	$.35/page
11" x 17"		11" x 17"	
Members/Students	$.30/page	Members/Students	$.45/page
Non-Members	$.35/page	Non-Members	$.50/page

DIGITAL IMAGING SERVICES (300 dpi):		POSTAGE AND HANDLING FEE	
Members/Students	$4.00		$5.00
Non-Members	$6.00		

PHOTOGRAPHIC REPRODUCTIONS:

	5" x 7"	8" x 10"	11" x 14"	16" x 20"	20" x 30"
Members/Students	$12.50	$18.00	$25.00	$35.00	$70.00
Non-Members	$15.00	$20.00	$30.00	$45.00	$80.00

There is an extra charge for images used for commercial purposes.
Any materials used in publications or other commercial purposes must be properly credited.

Source: Courtesy of Pensacola Historical Society, a division of West Florida Historic Preservation, Inc.

George Eastman House
http://www.eastmanhouse.org/inc/collections/rights.php
    George Eastman House sells photographs online, with a link to its policies and order forms on the same page.

RequestAPrint
http://requestaprint.com/
    RequestAPrint, operated by Rudinec & Associates, offers reproductions of museum images for sale to the public. Partner institutions include The Butler Museum of Art, Detroit Historical Society, George Peabody House Museum, and the White House Historical Association.

(Continued p. 159)

Figure 7.22. Wisconsin Maritime Museum Photographic Reproduction Order Form

Wisconsin Maritime Museum
Photographic Reproduction Order Form

Date: _____

Name: _____   Phone: _____

Address: _____   City/State/Zip: _____

Email: _____

Accession # & Description	Size	Unit Price	Shipping/Handling
	Subtotals		
	Member Discount 10%		N/A
	Tax (WI residents only) 5%		N/A
	Reproduction & Shipping/Handling Subtotals		

Payment for Order: TOTAL:
_____ check _____ credit card _____ money order

Check or money order, payable to Wisconsin Maritime Museum, in U.S. Dollars, or by credit card (VISA, MasterCard, American Express)

CC#: _____   Exp. Date: _____

Name on card: _____

Source: Courtesy of the Wisconsin Maritime Museum.

Figure 7.23. Orange County Regional History Center Library and Archives Reproduction and Use Fees

Historical Society of Central Florida
Library & Archives
Reproduction and Use Fees

All reproduction requests are on a case-by-case basis. Costs for reproduction of materials from the Historical Society of Central Florida's collection are the sum of two fees and are per image: reproduction and use (if applicable). Rates for uses not listed below will be quoted upon request. All fees listed are subject to change.

REPRODUCTION FEES

Black and White/Color Prints:

5 x 7	$35.00	20 x 24	$85.00	30 x 40	$145.00
8 x 10	$40.00	24 x 30	$110.00	30 x 50	$175.00
11 x 14	$45.00	30 x 30	$130.00	30 x 60	$195.00
16 x 20	$60.00				

Negatives:
Color $20.00
Black and White $18.00

Scans:
300–600 dpi JPEG or TIFF $10.00

Burning Images to CD: $2.00/CD

Video/Digital Camera (no flash):
At the discretion of the staff, users may film or videotape the Society's materials.
Staff requires 48 hours advance notice and the applicable use fees will be charged.

USE FEES

Use fees are assessed in addition to photoduplication costs for one-time, one use, non-exclusive, single language, publication rights for images for which the Historical Society of Central Florida has ownership rights. All requests for reuse of images or a change in use must be applied for in writing. Permission to use images must be obtained in advance and in writing by completing the appropriate "Permission to Publish or Use Reproductions of Materials" form. These fees are separate from any which might be assigned/assessed by the copyright holder. "Commercial Display" includes display in public areas of buildings and businesses. This does not include display in private residences or personal offices.

Books	FEES	
	For-Profit	**Non-Profit**
4,999 copies or less	$75.00	$25.00
5,000–9,999 copies	$100.00	$45.00
10,000–24,999 copies	$150.00	$65.00
25,000–49,999 copies	$200.00	$85.00
50,000 or more copies	Quoted upon Request	
Worldwide Rights	Quoted upon Request	

(Continued)

Figure 7.23. Orange County Regional History Center Library and Archives Reproduction and Use Fees *(Continued)*

Periodicals (Magazines, Newspapers, etc.)	FEES	
	For-Profit	Non-Profit
	$75.00	$25.00
Video and Film Production	**FEES**	
	For-Profit	Non-Profit
	$100.00	$25.00
Special Uses	**FEES**	
	For-Profit	Non-Profit
Advertising	$150.00	$50.00
Commercial Display	$75.00	N/A
Exhibition	N/A	$25.00
Internet Use	$250.00	$150.00

ORDERS AND DELIVERY

High volume orders may require a deposit. Normal orders will be processed in two to four weeks. Rush service is available at the discretion of the staff and additional charges will be assessed.

CREDIT LINE GUIDELINES

- Credit line: "Courtesy of the Orange County Regional History Center."
- For published materials, the credit line should appear on the same page or the page facing the illustration. Individual images must be credited separately.
- For films and video presentations, include the credit line in the credits section or "Sources for Illustrations" section of the production.
- Images used in exhibitions should have the credit line directly below or adjacent to the original copy.
- When used with the Web, credit should appear adjacent to the image in a "Sources or Illustration" section.

08/2008

Source: Courtesy of the Orange County Regional History Center.

Figure 7.24. Harry Ransom Center Photoduplication Fees

HARRY RANSOM CENTER
THE UNIVERSITY OF TEXAS AT AUSTIN
PHOTODUPLICATION FEES
Effective 1/5/09

Acceptance of all orders is subject to administrative approval. Besides the fees below there is a service charge of $8.00, in addition to postage, for orders delivered by mail, email, or FTP. Fees are subject to change without notice. Order size limitations per six-month period: High-resolution digital images: 50 items; low-resolution (JPEG) digital images: 50 items; low-resolution (PDF) digital images: 350.

Mastercard and Visa are the preferred forms of payment. Payment is always required before orders can be initiated. Turnaround times vary depending on the type of product; we can provide a current estimate on request. Rush orders are accepted at the Ransom Center's discretion and are subject to a doubling of the service and per-image fees.

If you plan to publish any materials copied from Ransom Center collections, you must complete the appropriate "Notification of Intent to Publish" form, available on the web site.

****

Digital Scans

Unless otherwise specified, scans will be in color and will include the color scale.

For encapsulated and oversize (over 24x36 inches) materials, foldouts, tightly bound volumes, extremely fragile items, and other materials requiring special handling (including sculpture, furniture, costumes, bindings, and other three-dimensional objects), as well as extremely high-resolution scans, there will be an additional charge based on the labor involved. In the case of mail orders involving fewer than ten copies of unbound manuscripts, we may supply these as conventional photocopies at a flat fee of $8.00.

High-resolution scans and large orders of low-resolution scans are generally supplied on CD-ROMs. Requests for fewer than 25 low-resolution scans will be emailed if possible.

Low-resolution (72 dpi) scans:	
PDF reference copies or printouts, per image	$.60
JPEGs suitable for reference or PowerPoint purposes, per image	$5.00
High-resolution (300 dpi) scans:	
TIFFs or JPEGs suitable for publication, per image	$25.00
High-quality inkjet prints from above, additional per image	$15.00
Panoramic photographs: low-resolution scans for reference, per image	$15.00
Panoramic photographs: high-resolution scans, per image	$40.00
High-quality inkjet prints from above, additional per image	$30.00
CD-ROM or DVD (media), per disc required	$3.00

Copies from Microfilm

Reader-printer copies, per image	$.25
Duplicate microfilm, per reel, from existing master	$45.00

Conventional (Film) Photographs

All conventional photographic copies, other than slides and transparencies, are outsourced. In addition to the **lab cost plus 50%**, a **$16.00** charge will be added whenever it is necessary to produce a useable negative.

Color slides (35mm), per slide	$10.00
Color transparencies, 4x5, per image	$36.00
Color transparencies, 4x5, from existing transparency, per image	$45.00

Audio, Film or Video: Audio is normally delivered as audio CD, moving images as DVD. Some duplication can only be done by commercial laboratories. There is a one-hour minimum fee.

Reproduction from existing master	**$30.00 per disc**
Reproduction (in-house)	**Cost of Media Plus $25.00/hr.**
Reproduction (commercial)	**Lab Costs Plus 50%**

1/09

Source: Courtesy of Harry Ransom Center, University of Texas at Austin.

Figure 7.25. Sheldon Swope Art Museum, Inc., Image Reproduction Request and Invoice Form

SHELDON SWOPE ART MUSEUM, INC.

Image Reproduction Request & Invoice Form

REQUESTED BY: _____ DATE: _____

Address: Street _____ City _____ State _____ Country _____ Zip/postal code _____
      (FedEx will not deliver to P.O. boxes)

Phone: _____ Fax: _____ Email: _____

Name of Individual Contact: _____

USE TO BE MADE OF IMAGE: (Include publishers, author, editor, title, date, print run and distribution)

IMAGE(S) REQUESTED:

—see page 2 for Swope credit line.

FEES per item

PURCHASE	Commercial	$ 15
Color Slide:	Non-Profit	$ 15
(Not for reproduction)	Scholar	$ 15
Black & White Photograph:	Commercial	$ 30
(8x10 glossy print)	Non-Profit	$ 20
	Scholar	$ 20
RENTAL (for reproduction)		
Color Transparency (4" x 5")	Commercial	$ 75
Or digital CD: (indicate format)	Non-Profit	$ 60
	Scholar	$ 60
PUBLICATION/REPRODUCTION:	Commercial	$ 175
	Non-Profit	$ 100
	Scholar	$ 75

SUBTOTAL $____

Waiver of pre-payment (add 50% of sub total fees) $____

HANDLING/POSTAGE   3 day U.S. Mail $5.00

                  U.S. Urgent-Fed Ex $ 20 or your shipping Account # & info.

                                                       _____

                  International Fed Ex,   Fees vary $____ or your shipping Account # & info.

                                                         _____

TOTAL AMOUNT DUE $____

We accept **Visa /MasterCard**   Name: _____

Address:_____

Phone: _____, Acct. #: _____, Exp. Date: _____

I hereby agree to the conditions above and on page two of this form, and agree to pay all applicable fees. Signed
_____ Date _____

Return signed form with payment to Registrar. (Material will be sent and contract will commence when payment is received.)

25 S. 7th Street, Terre Haute, IN 47807
Phone: 812/238-1676   Fax: 812/238-1677   Page 1 of 2

(Continued)

Figure 7.25. Sheldon Swope Art Museum, Inc., Image Reproduction Request and Invoice Form *(Continued)*

SWOPE

REPRODUCTION CONDITIONS

REQUESTS	All requests must be received in writing. Transparencies and digital CDs are rented for three months, and are not sold.
FEES	Pre-payment is required. Fees are based on specific application, not on previous applications. Any waiver or change in fees is solely at the Museum's discretion. All fees are non-refundable. Foreign payments must draw on a US bank using US dollars.
LATE FEES	for nonreturned transparencies are $50 per month. After 3 months, unless a new request is made, nonreturned transparencies will be considered lost and a replacement fee will be charged.
REPLACEMENT FEE	for damaged or lost transparency is $150 per.
PERMISSION	Permission must be granted in writing. Permission (if applicable) is granted for only one usage in one publication, one edition and one language. Additional language editions and subsequent editions will be considered upon application. Permission terminates upon publication. Permission is valid for one year from date of authorization. If publication has not appeared at the end of that time, permission is revoked and must be requested again.
	Duplicates may not be made of photographic material supplied by the Museum.
	No image may be in any way distorted or manipulated.
RE-USE	Any new reproduction other than that covered in the original request requires a new application.
CREDIT LINE	Credit line must read: "Artists name (dates) Title date, medium, Swope Art Museum, Terre Haute, Indiana." If image is cropped, credit line must additionally read "Detail."
DISCLAIMER	Certain works of art may be protected by copyright not owned by the Museum. The responsibility for ascertaining whether any such rights exist and for obtaining all other necessary permissions, remains with the applicant. The Sheldon Swope Art Museum assumes no responsibility or liability for applicant against claims from artist, agent or anyone else because of reproduction.
COPIES OF PUBLICATION	Two copies of material featuring the requested image should be forwarded to the Museum upon publication.
CD-ROM	Permission will be granted for electronic formats, such as CD-ROM, that are sufficiently secure to prevent unauthorized downloading, transferring, copying, and manipulation of content. The resource file must be hidden from view so that the file names and icons do not appear in windows or on the desktop. Permission will not be authorized for floppy disks or other formats that do not meet the criteria stated above.
ELECTRONIC MEDIA	Permission is granted for the right to use the image in the production and distribution of the series, as noted, in domestic and foreign markets. This is to include videocassette, laser disk and any analogous home-viewing medium. Permission is granted for the life of the copyright series.

25 S. 7th Street, Terre Haute, IN 47807
Phone: 812/238-1676   Fax: 812/238-1677   Page 2 of 2

Source: Image Reproduction from Swope Art Museum, 25 South 7th Street, Terre Haute, IN 47807.

Figure 7.26. The Henry Ford Photograph Order Form and Use Agreement

PHOTOGRAPH   ORDER   FORM
AND USE AGREEMENT

| Reference No. |
| Date Received: |
| Staff Initials: |

Please read, supply the requested information, and return all four (4) pages of this form - with payment - to: Benson Ford Research Center, The Henry Ford, 20900 Oakwood Blvd., P.O. Box 1970, Dearborn, MI 48121-1970

Name:

Institution or Company:

Address:

City: State: Zip:

Phone: Fax: e-mail:

Type of User/Purpose of Use (check one):

A. (   ) Individual or student for private or educational purposes
B. (   ) Print Publication
C. (   ) Television or Home Video/DVD
D. (   ) Feature Film
E. (   ) Exhibit
F. ( ) Internet/WWW
G. (   ) Advertising

For types B-G, please complete the following:

Proposed Title:

Publisher/Producer:

Publisher/Producer's Address:

Tentative Publishing/Release Date:

For web use, describe how the image(s) will be used: URL:

PLEASE NOTE

The copyright status of photographs and audiovisual material is often difficult to determine, because it is affected by such things as the employment status of the photographer, the date material was created, the date material was first published, and what information accompanied the first publication. The Henry Ford has not determined copyright status for many of the photographs and audiovisual materials in our collection. Therefore, The Henry Ford is acting only as an owner of the physical original:

- The Henry Ford is not responsible for either determining the copyright status of the image(s) or for securing copyright permission.
- Possession of a photograph from The Henry Ford does not constitute permission to use it.
- Users of materials are required to complete and return this permission form.

The Henry Ford charges individual, non-profit and commercial users fees in order to support the maintenance of the collections. Use fees will be determined from the information on the permission form.

TURN AROUND

- NORMAL turn around for an order of up to twenty images for which no new studio photography is required is ONE TO TWO WEEKS from the receipt of the completed and signed permission form.
- FIVE WORKING DAY turn around is available for orders of up to ten images for which no new studio photography is required. Add 50% to the appropriate use fee.
- TWO WORKING DAY turn around is available for orders of up to five images for which no new studio photography is required. A high resolution (600 dpi or better) scan, shipped on CD-ROM or via e-mail, AND NOT A PHOTOGRAPHIC PRINT can be provided. Add 100% to the appropriate use fee.

The Henry Ford Photograph Order Form and Use Agreement - Page 1 of 4
Updated 2/10/09

(Continued)

Figure 7.26. The Henry Ford Photograph Order Form and Use Agreement *(Continued)*

PHOTOGRAPH ORDER FORM
AND USE AGREEMENT

FEES FOR REPRODUCTION AND USE

as of January 2009

| Reference No. |
| Date Received: |
| Staff Initials: |

Fees include reproduction, unless New Photography is required.
All fees are per image for one-time use in one project unless stipulated otherwise.

A. Individual or Student for private or educational purposes

( ) Private Study; ( ) School Paper; ( ) School Multimedia Project: $15.00 (low res); $30.00 (high res or 8x10 photographic print)

( ) Personal, Non-Commercial Website: $30.00 (low res)

( ) Other:

B. Print Publication	Print run under 1,000	Print run under 5,000	Print run under 50,000	Print run over 50,000
( ) Book, North American Distribution	$30.00	$60.00	$90.00	$120.00
( ) Book, Worldwide Distribution	$60.00	$120.00	$240.00	$240.00
( ) Periodical	$30.00	$60.00	$90.00	$120.00
( ) CD-ROM	$30.00	$60.00	$90.00	$120.00
( ) Media Bundle - includes Print, CD-ROM or other supplement, and Internet	$90.00	$180.00	$270.00	$360.00
( ) Cover, image as main illustration	$120.00	$240.00	$360.00	$480.00
( ) Cover, image as secondary illustration	$60.00	$120.00	$180.00	$240.00

C. Television or Home Video/DVD	Non-Profit/ Educational/Local	Commercial, North American distribution	Commercial, Worldwide distribution
( ) Television Broadcast	$60.00	$180.00	$360.00
( ) Home Video or DVD	$60.00	$180.00	$360.00
( ) Media Bundle - includes Television, Home Video/DVD, Internet, and Promotional Use	$120.00	$360.00	$360.00

D. Feature Film ( ) Commercial, Worldwide distribution: $360.00   ( ) Media Bundle - includes Film, Home Video/DVD, Internet and Promotional Use: $720.00

E. Exhibit	Temporary Exhibit (12 months or less)	Traveling Exhibit	Permanent Exhibit
( ) Exhibit (Non-Profit/Educational)	$60.00	$90.00	$120.00
( ) Media Bundle - includes Exhibit, Internet, and Promotional Use	$180.00	$270.00	$360.00
( ) Exhibit (Commercial)	$120.00	$120.00	$120.00

F. Internet/WWW ( ) Website (Non-Profit/Educational): $60.00   ( ) Website (Commercial): $120.00

( ) E-Book: $60.00 + book fee

G. Advertising ( ) Print Advertising: $600.00   ( ) Internet Advertising: $600.00   ( ) Television Advertising: $600.00

NEW PHOTOGRAPHY FEES: Three-dimensional objects: $125.00 first item; $50.00 each additional, similar item.
Additional Conservation fees, determined on a case-by-case basis, may apply.

The Henry Ford Photograph Order Form and Use Agreement - Page 2 of 4
Updated 2/10/09

(Continued)

Figure 7.26. The Henry Ford Photograph Order Form and Use Agreement (Continued)

PHOTOGRAPH ORDER FORM
AND USE AGREEMENT

| Reference No. |
| Date Received: |
| Staff Initials: |

TERMS AND CONDITIONS

PLEASE NOTE: Permission requests must be submitted on this form. No other permission or licensing forms will be accepted nor may the wording of this form be altered in any way.

1. Rights: The Henry Ford does not claim exclusive ownership of the rights to all the images in our collection. We are simply granting permission to use images in our collections. This permission is nonexclusive, and nontransferable.

2. Use: Permission is for one-time use worldwide and in all languages for the life of the work, but only for the purpose stated in this document. The images may be used in the direct promotion of the work, but wider use or use in subsequent editions will require renegotiation. This includes all current and future forms of media.

3. Use fees: The Henry Ford charges use fees to support the preservation and maintenance of our collections. Use fees must be paid in full when the order is submitted.

4. Credit Line: The credit line must read "From the Collections of The Henry Ford." For web site use the statement must read "From the Collections of The Henry Ford, Copy and Reuse Restrictions Apply" and must be placed near the image and linked to our web use policy at http://www.TheHenryFord.org/copyright.html. If a negative number and/or photographer name exists for an image, this information must also appear on the credit line, unless a specific waiver is received from the Head of Access Services.

5. Indemnification: The user agrees to defend, indemnify, save, and hold harmless The Henry Ford, its employees, officers or designates, from any and all costs, expense, damage and liability arising because of any claim whatsoever which may be presented by anyone for loss or damage or other relief occasioned or caused by the release of said negatives, prints, photographs, and audio-visual materials to the undersigned and their use in any manner, including their inspection, publication, reproduction, broadcast, duplication or printing by anyone for any purpose whatsoever.

6. Image Manipulation: The Henry Ford's primary interest is to protect the integrity of the original. The Henry Ford will not allow the inversion of the original or the removal (except for allowable cropping) or addition of content. We will allow adjustments to contrast and sharpness, and minor adjustments of color. Images may be cropped at the edges or a portion may be selected from within a photograph. An explanatory statement—e.g., "Detail from…."--must be added describing any changes. Any manipulation of the materials beyond that stated in the policy must be approved by the Head of Access Services.

7. Endorsement: Use of materials from The Henry Ford does not imply that The Henry Ford endorses any product, enterprise, opinions, or confirms the accuracy of any content on the site, in publication, and broadcast.

8. Web Site Use: Images may be distributed via the World-Wide Web, as part of a single online display, exhibit, site, or online collection. Any additional or different use of the image(s) will require renegotiation. Resolution: The Henry Ford normally will not allow an image higher than 100 dpi to be placed on a web site. Arrangements for higher resolution must be made with the Head of Access Services.

9. Museum Copy: One copy of the published work, including motion pictures and videotapes, in which the photographic copy appears, will be donated to The Henry Ford for its collections.

10. Noncompliance: The Henry Ford reserves the right to refuse to grant permission and/or provide photo reproduction and audio-visual services to anyone who has not complied with our policies.

I understand that I am responsible for conforming with the laws of libel, publicity rights, and copyright which may be involved in the use of these materials.

I have read, accept, and agree to abide by the conditions listed above for the one time use and specific purpose(s) stated in this document.

Requested by (Signature):   Date:

Name (Please Print):

Title, if applicable:

Approved by (The Henry Ford rep):   Date:

Title (The Henry Ford rep):

The Henry Ford Photograph Order Form and Use Agreement - Page 3 of 4
Updated 2/10/09

(Continued)

Figure 7.26. The Henry Ford Photograph Order Form and Use Agreement (Continued)

America's Greatest History Attraction

PHOTOGRAPH ORDER FORM
AND USE AGREEMENT

INVOICE

| Invoice No. |
| Date Received: |
| Staff Initials: |

Benson Ford Research Center
The Henry Ford
20900 Oakwood Blvd.
P.O. Box 1970
Dearborn, MI 48121-1970
P: 313.982.6100 ext. 2517
F: 313.982.6244

THIS IS THE ONLY FORMAL INVOICE YOU WILL RECEIVE

Payment must be included with this invoice before processing will begin.
Please itemize each image. Include the item number and a brief description of each image.
Refer to the Fee Schedule included in this agreement. Use fees will not be refunded.

Name: _____   Used For: _____

	Object ID	Image ID (if different)	Title/Caption/Description	Location (Ace, Box, etc.)	Fees	Office Use Only
1						
2						
3						
4						
5						
6						
7						
8						
9						
10						

More than 10 images - continue on Addendum

Subtotal	
New Photography Fees	
10% Member Discount	
Rush Fee	
6% MI Sales Tax*	
Shipping Charges**	
Total	

Type of Reproduction

( ) Permission Only

( ) 8x10 Photographic Print

( ) Digital File   File Format: ( ) JPEG or ( ) TIFF

        Delivery: ( ) CD-ROM or ( ) e-mail (JPEG format only)

        Digital Files are 600 dpi, 5x7" unless specified below.

Special Instructions: _____

Method of Payment

( ) Cash (in-person orders only)

( ) Check or Money Order payable to "The Henry Ford"
      Payment Company Name (if different from yours):

( ) Credit Card (Mastercard, Visa, Discover, or American Express)
      Credit Card #: _____   Expiration Date: _____

The Henry Ford Federal ID # 381359513-N

* If tax exempt, enter number here: _____

** No additional shipping charge for items sent First Class Mail in U.S. and Canada. Other shipping destinations and services available, charges vary by destination, service, and size of order. Please ask.
Or, provide your shipping account #: _____

The Henry Ford Photograph Order Form and Use Agreement - Page 4 of 4
Updated 2/10/09

(Continued)

Figure 7.26. The Henry Ford Photograph Order Form and Use Agreement *(Continued)*

PHOTOGRAPH ORDER FORM
AND USE AGREEMENT

ADDENDUM

America's Greatest History Attraction

| Invoice No. |
| Date Received: |
| Staff Initials: |

Name: Used For:

	Object ID	Image ID (if different)	Title/Caption/Description	Location (Ace, Box, etc.)	Fees	Office Use Only
11						
12						
13						
14						
15						
16						
17						
18						
19						
20						
21						
22						
23						
24						
25						
26						
27						
28						
29						
30						

Type of Reproduction	
( ) Permission Only	
( ) 8x10 Photographic Print	
( ) Digital File File Format: ( ) JPEG or ( ) TIFF	
Delivery: ( ) CD-ROM or ( ) e-mail (JPEG format only)	
Digital Files are 600 dpi, 5x7" unless specified below.	
Special Instructions:	

Subtotal	
New Photography Fees	
10% Member Discount	
Rush Fee	
6% MI Sales Tax*	
Shipping Charges**	
Total	

The Henry Ford Photograph Order Form and Use Agreement - Page 4a
Updated 2/10/09

Source: From the Collections of The Henry Ford Museum.

VStore
http://www.vstore.ca
    VStore offers a fully customizable online store that allows users to keep 100 percent of the profit from sales.

Conclusion

Because most people enjoy photographs and can relate to them, photos constitute an effective medium to connect institutions to their audiences. It is important to know your collections thoroughly to identify appropriate images. The next step is to match the right images to your targeted marketing campaign. Remember to choose images with a wide appeal that will catch the visitors' attention. Photographic collections often have the most appeal to visitors and should be employed to their fullest extent in any promotional materials.

Any time you use an image from your collection, you are marketing your archives. Credit lines are the most effective tool in making a reader or visitor aware of a photograph's provenance. Exhibits, educational programs, and photographic sales can showcase your photographic collections to a broad and diverse audience.

Be creative, and constantly consider how your photographs can best be used to promote your archives. The end result will be increased recognition of the uniqueness and importance of your collection by your community and peers, increased visitation, and perhaps a few extra dollars in your revenue stream.

THE PLAN

1. Using the examples presented in this chapter, create your own policies and include them in your marketing plan.
2. Create a boilerplate copyright or Creative Commons statement, granting permission for use of your photographs, that will accompany all of your images, whether they are used in house or by other institutions. Put these statements in your plan.
3. Create digitization guidelines for your photographs that include such things as format, size, dpi, and color variation. Include these with your plan.
4. Create guidelines for publishing photographs on websites and put these in your plan.

References

Belcher, Michael. 1991. *Exhibitions in Museums.* Washington, DC: Smithsonian Institution Press.

Carey, James L. 2008a. "Understanding Digital Image Formats." *National Park Service Conserve O Gram* 22, no. 2. http://www.nps.gov/history/museum/publications/conserveogram/22-02.pdf.

———. 2008b. "Understanding PPI (Pixels Per Inch), DPI (Dots Per Inch, And Digital Display." *National Park Service Conserve O Gram* 22, no. 3. http://www.nps.gov/history/museum/publications/conserveogram/22-03.pdf.

Creative Commons. 2010. "Who Uses CC?" http://creativecommons.org/about/who-uses-cc/.

———. 2011. "FAQs." http://creativecommons.org/about/who-uses-cc/.

Malaro, Marie. 1998. *A Legal Primer on Managing Museum Collections.* Washington, DC: Smithsonian Books.

Ritzenthaler, Mary Lynn, and Diane Vogt-O'Connor. 2006. *Photographs: Archival Care and Management.* Chicago: Society of American Archivists.

Shapiro, Michael S., and Brett Miller. 1999. *A Museum Guide to Copyright and Trademark.* Washington, DC: American Association of Museums.

Stanford University Libraries. 2007. "Copyright and Fair Use." http://fairuse.stanford.edu/Copyright_and_Fair_Use_Overview/chapter0/0-a.html.

U.S. Copyright Office. 2008. "Copyright Basics." 2008. *Circular 1.* Washington, DC: U.S. Copyright Office. Revised in July. http://www.copyright.gov/circs/circ1.pdf.

Audiences

Educational Programming

Maria Mazzenga

Introduction

While archivists are aware of the treasures they guard in their repositories, key constituencies who might benefit from knowledge and use of such collections are often not aware of those same treasures. Educating potential user groups on collections of special interest benefits both the archives and the interest group. In this way, various constituencies gain knowledge of archival collections and of possible uses for archival materials, while archivists gain the opportunity to publicize their materials, solicit donations, and educate researchers and other stakeholders on those materials. In identifying areas where marketing principles and educational functions intersect, archivists can develop effective educational outreach programs, such as document-based learning, online resource creation, and in-house instruction, and pair them with marketing strategies, such as constituency targeting and positioning of an archives and its collections among its peer institutions in the field.

The practice of keeping records is thousands of years old, but the establishment of the concept of making archives accessible to the public has a relatively recent history, dating back to eighteenth-century France. When legislation passed in the wake of the French Revolution specified that archives be opened to the public, it ended the general practice of maintaining them exclusively for private use (Posner, 1984). With openly accessible archives came the necessity of interaction between archival staff and the broader community. Public archives have evolved since then, though only more recently has attention been given to the ways that archival materials can be marketed to various publics, and the idea that the marketing of collection materials can take place through education is newer still. The marketing of archival materials, however, naturally lends itself to an educational mode, as these materials require historical contextualization for full appreciation. This educational mode becomes an effective one through which to inform a range of constituencies on one's archival collections and programs and for promoting those materials among groups that may not otherwise know of a repository's collections.

Knowing Your Patrons

Educating patrons entails first knowing exactly who those patrons are so that you can tailor programs to meet the needs of specific communities. The variety of groups that you can educate on archival holdings is potentially wide ranging, depending on staff ambitions, available resources, and collection content. Ideas about who comprises an archives' constituency have changed over time, particularly with the growth of the Internet. The archival patron base has evolved from a largely scholarly and, to an extent, genealogical-researcher community to encompass the following groups:

- Academics benefiting from greater knowledge of collection materials they might use for scholarly research
- Genealogists in need of education on using archives and which collections might be most useful in family history research
- Students interested in archives-based educational programs
- Teacher and student users of virtual archival materials for educational purposes
- Virtual users seeking web-based archival materials, from finding aids to digital exhibits
- Patrons interested in archives-sponsored lectures, exhibits, or film events
- Donors/potential donors of collection materials who would benefit from education on the archives' mission and holdings

Individuals in these discrete categories may also fit into multiple communities at the same time. Educational programs can and should target multiple audiences. Elsie Freeman Finch and Paul Conway (1994) see archival constituencies as "interlocking" and "interchangeable." Archival programs should be marketed in terms of the specific audiences they are intended to serve but with the recognition that audiences expand and contract depending on the particular program offered (Chute, 2008). Users of virtual materials can easily become in-house researchers; lecture attendees might become collection donors; and different educational programs and the way they are publicized can draw groups of patrons from one event to another, thereby increasing general support for your archives.

Approaching Your Educational Marketing Program: Key Questions

An effective archival education marketing program begins with an assessment of staff and institutional resources, goals, and strategies involved in creating and maintaining such a program. For this assessment, several questions should be addressed at the outset:

1. What are your educational program goals?
2. What skills and talents can archives staff contribute to an educational program?

3. How much time is archives staff able to devote to educational programs?

4. What monetary costs are involved in your education outreach agenda?

5. Which constituencies are you targeting with your educational program?

6. Who are your institutional stakeholders?

7. How do you plan to evaluate your educational program?

What Are Your Educational Program Goals?

While developing an educational program for your archives, think about the key reasons you want to start such a program in the first place. Certainly, a chief goal is to raise the general profile of your archives. How you measure whether this occurred to your satisfaction should inform your goals. Are you looking for a measurable rise in the number of visitors to your archives or in users of particular collections? For an increase in media coverage of your materials? Some combination of these? Second, it is useful to think of second-tier objectives that fit into larger ones. Are there specific collections you would like to highlight in your program? Do you want to focus more on in-house programs or virtual programs? Are there underserved groups of patrons you are especially interested in attracting? Which kinds of programs will attract the constituencies you wish to target? Answering such basic questions will assist you in setting out achievable goals for your institution.

What Skills and Talents Can Archives Staff Contribute to an Educational Program?

And now, a warning against putting the cart before the horse: it is easy for archivists to envision an educational agenda that will raise the profile of an archives without first considering whether staff skills and talents are compatible with that agenda. If your goal is to create a more substantial web presence through digitized collections or educational websites, have you looked at the staff to determine if you have information technology staff with the proper skill set to ensure that the site is maintained in a timely and professional manner? Does the staff have the time to update the site on a regular basis? Are there staff available to write high-quality text supporting digitized educational materials? For in-house educational programs, are there staff with the specialized knowledge needed for lectures or workshops on particular topics? If not, are there funds available to bring in outside lecturers or workshop organizers for such events?

Knowing your staff is very important; it allows you to move forward toward your institution's goals without worrying that you won't have the necessary personnel to achieve those goals. One way to ensure that you do is to include detailed skills and expertise sets in the biographies you insert in the press kits discussed in Chapter 5. Those press kits will be a great help to you when you plan educational programs.

Educational Goals Checklist

When deciding on your educational outreach program, answer the following questions:

- How will I measure the impact of the outreach program?
- Do I want to attract new patrons to my archives? How many?
  - Current main constituencies
  - Underserved groups
  - Targeted group(s)
- Are there specific collections to which I would like to attract patrons?
  - Which collections?
  - How many patrons?
- Are there specific programs to which I would like to attract patrons?
  - Which programs?
  - How many patrons?
- Do I want to attract more publicity to my archives?
  - Which programs/collections would I like the public to know more about?
  - Which media would most effectively enable me to publicize my collections/programs?

How Much Time Can Archives Staff Devote to Educational Programs?

Most archives do not have funds to hire an entire staff for education and outreach programs. Educational programs are usually conducted by staff hired for other archival duties. Coming up with a general estimate of staff time needed for educational programs will help you plan an efficient program and ensure that such conflicts in staff commitments do not cause conflict later.

What Monetary Costs Are Involved in Your Education Outreach Agenda?

In addition to staff time costs, you may need funds for various aspects of a planned educational program, which you should estimate and prepare for before the event. If you are planning a lecture or exhibit, how much will speakers, exhibit cases, and other materials cost? If you need brochures, fliers, or invitations, how much will each cost? Do planned events involve space rental? Gather your costs, prepare your budget, and get approval well ahead of time.

Types of Educational Programs

The events constituting your educational outreach agenda will of course reflect your broader program goals, the skills and talents of your staff, the amount of time your staff can devote to such programs, costs, the needs of your stakeholders, and, finally, the interests of the patrons you wish to attract to your archives. As you read through the following types of educational programs, keep in mind your answers to the previous key questions.

Tour Presentations

The range of presentation possibilities depends on your archives' collections and staff talents. After pinpointing the ways that staff strengths and collection emphases intersect, you can create a "menu" to circulate, both in hard copy and on the web.

At the most basic level, it is a good idea to prepare a 20- to 30-minute tour of your facility for general researchers, donors, stakeholders, and others who might benefit from an overview of your operation. Such a tour should feature highlights from your collection that help illuminate your history, collection strengths, and reason for existing. For example, a local historical society might feature documents related to the establishment of its town or city or objects related to a prominent family or local industry.

After preparing a general presentation, you and other staff members can work out a more specific menu of choices depending on knowledge and interests. An archives with a large labor history collection most likely has an archivist who is knowledgeable on that subject and therefore ready to present a talk featuring strong documents or objects from the repository's collections. You can couple a focused presentation with a short general tour, thereby educating a particular constituency on both the general and specific value of your archives. Use every opportunity to educate in-house patrons on the worth of your repository.

You can offer visitors a simple way to schedule tour presentations by providing a reservation form on your website. This offers convenience and is a simple way to publicize the fact that your repository is more than a place to house collections and researchers. Figure 8.1 shows the

Figure 8.1. Tour Menu from the American Catholic History Research Center and University Archives

Visiting the Archives: A Resource for the University Community

The American Catholic History Research Center and University Archives is here to serve the University as well as the broader academic community. We are happy to offer a range of tours for University faculty, staff, and classes.

1. **Guidelines for visits to the Archives:**
   - Professor must be present with students on any instructional tour.
   - Please plan ahead: staff needs three weeks notification prior to a visit.

2. **Request Form:** Please submit the following completed form to request a tour. Your request will be confirmed when you receive a response from an Archives staff member.

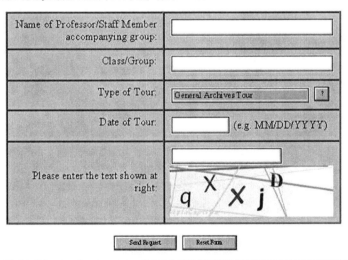

Source: Reprinted courtesy of the Catholic University of America.

American Catholic History Research Center and University Archives' online form for an in-house visit. Finally, you can post a staff-directed tour online, create an illustrated tour specifically for an online audience, and/or post videos of presentations related to your repository.

Lectures and Public Events

Lectures, panels, and workshops can publicize the educational mission of the archives, as well as a newly digitized collection, finding aid, or anniversary. You can post a new digital collection or finding aid on your website that has the potential to generate innovative scholarship and public interest in a field, but if the materials are not situated in a comprehensible framework for a broader audience, the value of the collection will remain unknown, and it will be used far less than if it is rolled out with an event or series of events. The voluminous mass of information available on the web makes such accompanying interpretive activities tremendously helpful for the public and for the reputation of the archives making those materials available online (Robyns, 2001).

Archival education is an excellent tool for publicizing anniversaries. Indeed, activities accompanying anniversaries can temper the overly nostalgic tone that sometimes characterizes such events while serving to utilize the publicity potential. A centennial celebration of an organization whose records are housed in an archives can entail an exhibit featuring key collection documents, objects, and photographs illuminative of that organization's history and connection to the broader society. Such an exhibit can accompany any ceremonial event sponsored by the organization, if it still exists. For manuscript collections associated with a particular individual, the individual's birthday presents an opportunity to host a lecture or panel on his or her significance in time or an exhibit or film on his or her life (Ericson, 1994).

Evaluating Your Archival Educational Programs

A useful evaluation can answer the question about whether the specific events and the broader programs met the goals set out for the program. If your aim in holding a lecture and distributing informative e-fliers was to increase site visits by a targeted group, was there a measureable increase in new site visits by members of that group? Did a presentation on the life and work of a particular person result in greater awareness of the significance of that individual's papers or of that person's role in local education? Did a series of press releases outlining a recently processed finding aid find its way into the local newspaper, the regional archival newsletter, or scholarly history journal? All programs have potentially measurable effects; if those effects match goals, the program is on track. If not, you can modify, reassess, or rework such programs into the broader educational plan.

Most archivists, in fact, are natural educators who might not think about how their educational skills can be put to use for outreach. As authorities on the collections in their repositories, they engage individuals in a variety of communities toward illuminating the value of their materials. They develop an exceptional capacity to link scholarly researchers, teachers, students, genealogists, and others who may not have a clear concept of what they are looking for with materials that are often buried deep in collections. Creating an effective educational outreach agenda entails becoming more aware of these skills and strategically linking them to a goal-oriented program that best serves the archives and its patrons.

To form a general appraisal of its success in achieving the goals you've set for a program, you should evaluate it at each level of implementation. You can conduct evaluations most easily through traditional hard-copy handouts created by staff for presentations, lectures, films, exhibits, and in-house events, although you can also use appropriate electronic surveys, such as those offered by SurveyMonkey.com (http://www.surveymonkey.com/). Google Analytics (http://www.google.com/analytics/) offers a free tool for assessing a range of aspects of website usage.

Conclusion

Educational programs are an invaluable tool for archivists who are seeking to bring new visitors, researchers, and donors into their archives. Following the steps of defining the targeted audience, carefully planning each event, and following up with an evaluation will keep programs fresh and viable. This chapter presented various techniques and processes for the archivist to use in developing educational programs. In addition, taking advantage of new technologies, including the archives' website, in this outreach effort gives you limitless possibilities for educating your audience about the value of your archives and its collections.

THE PLAN

1. Develop a list of staff expertise and skills and include it as an addendum to your marketing plan.
2. If you use the same handouts for tours and lectures, include copies of these with your marketing plan so you always have a master copy available for duplication.
3. Copy the evaluation checklist in this chapter, modify it to fit your needs, and include it as a section in your plan. It can work for all types of public relations programming, not just educational programs.

References

Chute, Tamar G. 2008. "Perspectives on Outreach at College and University Archives." In *College and University Archives: Readings in Theory and Practice*, edited by Christopher J. Prom and Ellen D. Swain, 137–154. Chicago: Society of American Archivists.

How to Evaluate Education Outreach Programs

- Before individual program implementation
  - Have I defined the audience for this particular event (or website)?
  - How does the event content match the interests of the targeted audience?
  - Do I have a plan for reaching this audience with information about my event?
  - What information do I want the targeted audience to take away?
    - About my archives generally
    - About my archival collection(s)
    - About my archival educational efforts
- After individual program implementation
  - Did the intended audience materialize for the event?
  - How did the audience members learn of the event?
  - Did the content match audience interests?
  - How did the event affect the audience's view of
    - My archives generally
    - A specific collection(s) addressed within the event
    - My archives as an educational institution
- Evaluating the entire program
  - Did the education outreach program reach its intended audiences?
  - Did the education outreach program affect perceptions of the archives?
  - Did the education outreach program raise the visibility of the targeted collections?
  - Did the education outreach program increase knowledge on collection-related subjects?

Ericson, Timothy. 1994. "Anniversaries: A Framework for Planning Public Programs." In *Advocating Archives: An Introduction to Public Relations for Archivists*, edited by Elsie Freeman Finch. Metuchen, NJ: Society of American Archivists and Scarecrow Press.

Finch, Elsie Freeman, and Paul Conway. 1994. "Talking to the Angel: Beginning Your Public Relations Program." In *Advocating Archives: An Introduction to Public Relations for Archivists*, edited by Elsie Freeman Finch, 5–22. Metuchen, NJ: Society of American Archivists and Scarecrow Press.

Posner, Ernst. 1984. "Some Aspects of Archival Development Since the French Revolution." In *A Modern Archives Reader: Basic Readings on Archival Theory and Practice*, edited by Maygene F. Daniels and Timothy Walch, 3–14. Washington, DC: National Archives and Records Services, U.S. General Services Administration.

Robyns, Marcus C. 2001. "The Archivist as Educator: Integrating Critical Thinking Skills into Historical Research Methods Instruction." *American Archivist* 64 (Fall/Winter): 363–384.

Additional Resources

American Catholic History Research Center and University Archives. 2011. http://libraries.cua.edu/achrcua/index.html.

Archival Education and Research Institutes (Focused on archival studies). 2011. http://aeri.gseis.ucla.edu/aeri.htm.

Daniels, Maygene, and Timothy Walch. 1984. *A Modern Archives Reader*. Washington, DC: National Archives and Records Administration.

Google Analytics. 2011. http://www.google.com/analytics/.

Hendry, Julia. 2007. "Primary Sources in K–12 Education: Opportunities for Archives." *American Archivist* 70 (Spring/Summer): 114–129.

SurveyMonkey. 2011. http://www.surveymonkey.com/Default.asp.

UCLA Institute on Primary Resources. 1999. http://ipr.ues.gseis.ucla.edu/info/definition.html.

Public Presentations

Elizabeth A. Myers

Introduction

Many people are afraid of public speaking; thoughts of standing alone in front of a crowd and staring into a sea of blank faces prevent them from ever giving a presentation. Luckily, most people's jobs do not require them to speak publicly. For many decades, most archivists were not required to do a lot of public speaking. In fact, the old, largely inaccurate caricature of an archivist was that of a lone purveyor sitting on boxes, hunched over some dusty old tome, hoarding documents rather than sharing them willingly. Engaging the public through outreach did not fit any part of that stereotype. Yet, archivists have always communicated with the public, even if that consisted of talking with researchers. Now with innovations in technology and shifting user, institutional, and donor expectations, archivists must connect more often and in more complex ways with the nonarchival world. One method involves thinking in much bigger, broader ways about presenting to diverse communities.

How do you get started speaking to audiences about your archives? First, acknowledge that there is a plurality in the term *public presentation*— not all audiences and environments are the same. Second, understand that although your goal is to meet your own list of objectives, it is just as important—if not more so—to help your audience meet their goals as well.

The Oxford English Dictionary defines the term *public* in several ways, including, "open to general observation, view, or knowledge; existing, performed." Further, it also means "the community or people as a whole; the members of the community collectively" (*Oxford English Dictionary*, 2009). Working within this framework, public presentations are by definition performances that engage a community. However, you must rethink what constitutes *public* and *community*. Not every presentation will take place in a room of 100 anonymous people. Far more common is the reality that you also must connect with your immediate public—researchers, donors, and administrators—to promote the collections, raise visibility and usage, and reinforce your archives' intellectual, social, educational, and economic value. Each conversation, workshop, and formal presentation is an opportunity to open a dialogue about your archives. Indeed, the more diverse the public, the better, because chances are higher that entirely new constituencies will be exposed to the archival world. These chance encounters can and often do produce unanticipated benefits, such as new professional contacts, new donors, or access to new resources and partnerships.

At the same time, presentations are too often driven solely by the needs of the speaker. There are practical reasons for this, of course. Each presentation is dictated by the event theme or purpose, such as announcing a project launch, opening a new collection, publicizing a successful grant application, reaching out to a new constituency of researchers, starting a conversation with potential donors, or even giving a status report to upper administration. The speaker's goal is always focused on meeting or perhaps exceeding the purpose for giving the presentation in the first place. In this typical model, there is an immediate need to push as much information as possible—to make the case, inform, define, or report as necessary. Yet, in all of these cases, the best presentations are those that put the unique needs of the audience on the same level as the goals of the speaker. As such, archivists must adopt a new form that puts as much emphasis on needs of the varied community—in this case the audience—as it does on meeting the need of the speaker. Therein lies the real challenge of putting together vibrant, dynamic, and engaging presentations: understanding diverse audiences.

The Speaker–Audience Dynamic

In the course of a single day, you deal with several types of audiences or communities. Presenting yourself or promoting your archives' collections is never a one-size-fits-all scenario. Rather, the most successful presentations depend on how well you know the audience, can anticipate their needs, and can combine those needs with your own objectives. Typically you will deal with three primary types of audiences: donors, administrators, and the general public. These categories are not exclusive. Donors of materials and money can easily overlap but do not always do so. At the same time, dealing with the general public naturally implies a diverse group, while the category of administrators implies a finite group. At the start of a presentation, you never know exactly who is there to listen and what they expect to get out of what they hear. However, these three general categories offer an opportunity to talk more broadly about audience dynamics.

It is impossible to rank any one audience type above or below another, but understanding donors is in many ways the bread and butter of the archivist's job. Though we have all received those out-of-the-blue phone calls that result in a fascinating addition to the collection, such occurrences do not happen every day. Rather, we must rely on our instincts, knowledge, skills, and understanding of the donation process to facilitate collection growth. Yet to fully understand the donation process beyond mechanical execution means to think more holistically about the donor. Ask yourself: What motivates a donor? What do donors hope to receive as a result of donating? What do they need? What was the catalyst for the donor to turn to donation, fiscal or otherwise? Often donors and their collections emerge as a consequence of some substantive change in their lives: retirement, relocation, death, or other major life transitions are all basic reasons. Change is not the same as motivation, however, when it comes to the underlying purpose of a donation. Donors may be motivated by altruism or egotism, profit, legacy building, or simply cleaning out the basement. In all cases, archivists have to possess great sensitivity to each particular situation and in doing so will better understand the donor's needs to respond or, if necessary, navigate through them.

Presentations to Donors

It is imperative that you think more broadly about what a presentation means in the context of donors. Each conversation is in fact a presentation of what you and the archives can offer in direct response to the donor's needs (explicitly expressed or otherwise). Obviously, when you speak to fiscal donors, you should not offer the exact same information as you would offer to collections donors. The principal difference between the two is the broader context of the donor's intent. Collections donors are typically, though not always, emotionally invested in their papers or the records of their organization. Thus the act of donating often works within a framework of equal trust between the parties involved. The intimacy created by that trust naturally changes the tenor of the conversations, if not the content. With potential fiscal donors, you must strike a balance between the needs of the archives and the ability of the donor. In addition, conversations about fiscal donations often speak not only to what the archives is presently but what it can become with additional support. Collections donors may or may not be interested in future outreach programs or new digitization programs, but fiscal donors certainly are.

Ultimately, collection donors can also be fiscal donors, but the center of the conversation should not address both wants at the same time: muddling the want of materials with the need of fiscal support runs the danger of conveying multiple agendas, each of which competes against the other for preeminence. Ultimately, you must treat both types of donors as partners in the noble endeavor of preserving valuable history, a concept too often buried in the back of a presentation. Indeed, when dealing with donors, you can never assume they appreciate archival value or relevancy. However, a lack of knowledge about archives is also an opportunity to engender support—be it materially or monetarily. A donor who is a proverbial blank slate is actually a great opportunity to advocate for the practice and profession of archives. Within this context, you have tremendous power to shape a donor's core knowledge about archives in general but also to engage with him or her in a joint effort to preserve history. This type of conversation or presentation is much more personal and often creates a partnership between you and the donor that ideally fosters a great amount of trust between the two. (For more information on donors, see Chapter 11.)

Primary Issues to Consider When Dealing with Donors

- **Motivation:** The impulse that brought the donor to the archives
- **Intent:** What the donor hopes to accomplish by donating
- **Broader context:** The catalyst for donating (e.g., life change)
- **History of the relationship:** Between the archivist and donor

Having Conversations with Donors

- **Be ethical:** Foster trust, be patient, and understand the donor's needs.
- **Be practical:** Review (or build) the case file, and research the donor as necessary.
- **Separate needs:** Be clear, concise, and responsive to the exact type of conversation most relative to each donor.

Administrators as an Audience

When presenting to an administrative group, your approach should function in much the same way. Though internal audiences may be more familiar to you and might seem easier to communicate with, this is in fact a false assumption. Even sympathetic administrators may not have a clear sense of what you do as an archivist, why you do it, or what the complexities of your day-to-day professional life entail. Rather than relying on such oblique sympathies, you must understand how the administration's decision-making process affects the archives. What information do they need about the archives that they do not already have? What are their expectations of the archives, if any? How can this opportunity be used to underscore the value of the archives? A common mistake in presenting to upper management is relying solely on the data: surveys and statistics of users and donors. Although this information is invaluable for stating the case of archival value, overreliance on statistics can also dehumanize the archives. In addition to statistics, try also to cast the archives as a vibrant place of learning: highlight a new collection, a new (online or physical) exhibit, and any efforts to increase accessibility and outreach. As with donors, remind administrators whenever possible that you are in a joint venture of fostering a living legacy, not just housing dusty documents. Stress value internally and externally to the institution whenever possible.

Remember, the challenge is to be able to read the needs of the administration. When you describe how you comply with these needs, you have an opportunity to sway opinion about your job. With internal audiences, your own unique knowledge of, and experience at, your institution is the best building block for identifying potential audiences and formatting presentations to the needs of the workplace environment.

Another aspect of presenting to administrators is that you must deftly understand the larger structure of your institution. Clearly this is easier at smaller organizations than at larger ones, but in both cases understanding the structure is invaluable for understanding (and preparing for) administrators-as-audience members. All institutions have some degree of organizational hierarchy, and the design is most commonly reflected as a pyramid. This is not helpful in preparing presentations. Thinking only of presenting upward will create more stress and ignore potential allies within the institution. Instead, think about an administrator's archival knowledge as concentric circles (Figure 9.1).

Those administrators closest to the center have the most detailed knowledge about archives. Conversely, the circles furthest away are administrators who have the least knowledge about archives. Just as with presenting or communicating with donors, the truly priceless skill of any speaker is to address the audience at its knowledge level.

Speaking with the General Public

Unlike donors and internal administrators, understanding the general public as an audience is more difficult. For the first two categories, there

Keys to Administrative Presentations

- Determine an administrator's level of knowledge.
- Understand the purpose of the presentation from the administrator's point of view.
- Identify opportunities to enlarge the conversation.
- Remember to humanize the archives, not just rely on statistics.

Figure 9.1. Levels of Archival Knowledge

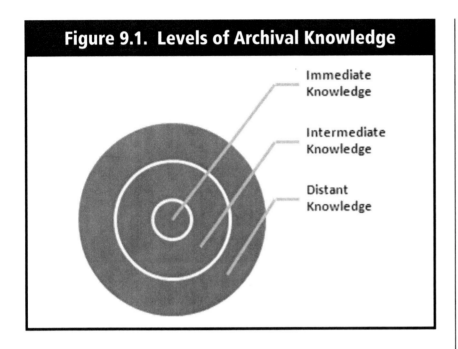

Immediate Knowledge

Intermediate Knowledge

Distant Knowledge

is at least some comprehension about what an archives is, even if that idea is not very complex or accurate. In contrast, the general public possesses even less of an understanding of what an archives is, let alone what an archivist does. Altering that perception is a large part of many archival outreach and educational efforts. For archivists, working with the public and presenting the archives is often an extraordinary opportunity to educate someone new about the archivist's job. Presentations can result in new researchers and new communities of donors. They can raise awareness about new collections, digital initiatives, or publications.

Inherently, a public audience is going to be the most diverse group you deal with. Even a talk with a very specific topic will likely draw an incredibly diverse population in terms of age, race, gender, education, and, of course, interest level. Through this challenging dynamic emerges a great opportunity to connect with whole new populations. At the same time, the diversity in a public group presents its own unique set of difficulties. For example, how can a speaker reasonably learn about—and thereby better understand—an audience if it is such a diverse community of people? Can you speak to an 18-year-old and an 80-year-old and keep the attention of both at the same time with the same topic? With any public presentation, members of a diverse audience can be fickle and unforgiving of a speaker who fails to address the needs of an audience segment. Thus any rigid, one-size-fits-all approach will simply not work. Following are several suggestions for how to tackle even the most complicated presentations and the most diverse audiences:

- **Location**: Identify the audience as much as possible by considering where the presentation is taking place, the sponsoring organization's typical audience, and the declared intent of the

Knowing Your Audience

1. How many people will be at the presentation?
2. What are the demographics of the group (ages, gender, ethnicity and race, religion, education level)?
3. Does your audience know the basics of the topic you are presenting?
4. Are there members of your audience who have more expertise on the topic than you do?
5. Does anyone in the audience have special needs (hearing, sight, mobility issues)?
6. How long will your presentation be, and should you offer breaks?

presentation. This will help you speak with, rather than at, the audience.

- **Diversity**: Identify the audience diversity as much as possible by considering qualifiers such as age, race, ethnicity, education, and interest. The audience's collective identity should always affect both the format and the content of the presentation. There is never a one-size-fits-all presentation for the public.

- **Opportunity**: Most importantly, see a diverse public group as an opportunity rather than a challenge.

Great Start, Fantastic Middle, Perfect Finish

Without question, a critical understanding of audience dynamics is the foundation of every great presentation. This solid foundation will help any speaker be a success, but it is not a foolproof toolbox. As any experienced speaker can attest that no amount of good intention and audience research will save every presentation from falling flat. The first step in avoiding such a calamity is to recognize that no matter how skillful the presenter, a certain level of redundancy surfaces again and again in most archival presentations. As such, it can be helpful to create a basic template about your particular archives that you can adapt to the specific needs of each audience. This template should include the basic information about the archives, including location, contact information, access policies, fees, institutional history, up-to-date collection strengths, collection statistics, growth potential, exhibits, digital content/web presence, user statistics, and any larger institutional affiliations or partnerships. Some people may prefer to think of the presentation template more as a pull sheet of information that can be expanded on or edited down, depending on the audience and the purpose of the talk. Indeed, the real value in having a standard data sheet of information is that it saves you time in the long run. If you keep your sheet updated, especially the statistics, the template will be a great resource.

The key, however, is not to mistake the template for a presentation; by design, templates are inherently limited. As a speaker, you must understand and adapt quickly to each particular situation. Using a template without regard to event specifics often results in forcing a square peg into a round hole. Worse yet, the audience always knows this. Further, each event has particular time and space limitations that impair the use of a template. Consider the problem of putting together a long, detailed, boilerplate presentation. Now imagine presenting that template to an elderly audience at a local library, to high school students in a classroom, and to advanced scholars in a small workshop. Therein lies the danger of the one-size-fits-all approach. Your goal is to promote the use of the collections, but your over-reliance on a template means you will ignore the audience's needs. In all cases,

Archives Information Template

I. Basic
   1. Location
   2. Contact information
   3. Access policies
   4. Fees

II. History
   1. Institutional background

III. Current
   1. Collection strengths
   2. Growth areas/new acquisitions
   3. Recent/planned exhibits
   4. Digital content
   5. Web presence
   6. Outreach/programming
   7. Staff projects
   8. Other access points: catalog records or database partnerships

thoughtfulness, flexibility, and adaptation are the keys to a successful presentation.

Language Usage in Presentations

Other considerations in presenting are the dangers of assumption, jargon, and level of detail. By default, the audience is present because they either want or have to be. One rightly presumes that the theme of the presentation is drawing the audience, but presuming too much is often a mistake. Whenever possible, learn more about your audience and its particular type of composition. If there is an event coordinator or group representative, speak with him or her about the audience. If the audience primarily comprises students, ask the teacher or professor about the class dynamic. By maintaining a dialogue with the instructor, you will be able to better judge each class on its own unique composition. Further, the class may be required to attend or have a specific assignment or task required of them as a result of the presentation. If you know this ahead of time, then you can design the presentation to be relevant to the students' immediate needs. Each group is going to be different, so the particular mood or group composition will dictate the level of attention and reception of the presentation. Use earlier conversations, the case file, and the web (if applicable) to assess information, interest, and need as much as possible beforehand. However, if it is a cold presentation—spontaneous with little context or time to collect information—then use the Internet, your communications networks, and other archivists to find out as much as possible about your audience.

Underestimating or overestimating the audience's knowledge about the subject matter in the presentation can also be a major problem. There are several levels of knowledge about archives, ranging from the most basic (none) to the most advanced (professional archivists). One of the worst assumptions you can make is that the audience deeply values history and the role of archives in preserving it. Especially in this digital age when the assumption of universal accessibility through the web continues to grow among researchers—especially the young ones—continually restating the why and how of archival value even in the most basic terms is essential. Further, you must be wary of the fact that working as a professional in the archival field can create a kind of perception cocoon that in turn creates a distorted understanding of how nonarchivists (and even nonresearchers) view the archival world. Speakers who are aware of these potential pitfalls will go a long way in being able to communicate well with their audience.

Equally serious is the problem of jargon: does the average citizen know the basic difference between the terms *manuscript* and *monograph*? When archivists talk about format migration or Encoded Archival Description (EAD) does that have any substantive meaning for the general public? Further, and perhaps more controversially, does it have to? A great deal is lost in a presentation that speaks above, rather than to, the audience. The obvious danger is to use words that create barriers between the speaker and audience rather than a shared place of open

Dangers to Look Out for in Your Presentation
- Over-reliance on templates or boilerplate presentations
- Assumptions of audience interest or knowledge
- Archival jargon
- Unbalanced presentations (e.g., too little or too much detail)

dialogue. Worse is that jargon further leads to the continued estericism of the archives profession. As aptly noted by one student of the profession, insularity means failure for the future of archives (Moore, 1998). Instead, reserving the use of jargon and anachronisms for professional conferences saves the general public audience from unnecessary confusion and frustration. Ultimately, finding common language between the audience and speaker builds an instant community through the presentation, where knowledge is accessible and shared.

The importance of the choice of words for the presentation is only part of the language issue. Just as important is the amount of information offered during the talk. Luckily, a time limit naturally helps to narrow down the length and depth of a presentation. However, a presentation fails if you pack too much into too short a time or, even worse, you give too little information to satisfy the needs of the audience. But, how do you know what is the optimum amount of information? Inherently, there is trial and error involved in the process. Sometimes the answer comes too late to affect the immediate presentation but might be very helpful in the future. One possible clue is the question-and-answer session. If the audience asks a number of clarifying questions, then you

TRANSLATING COMMON JARGON FOR GENERAL AUDIENCES: A BRIEF GUIDE

Jargon	Alternate
Accession record	Inventory record
Acquisition	Donation
Arrangement	Organizing
Accrual	Addition
Addendum	Addition
Catalog record	Library record
Conservation	Care of the records or repair
Duplication	Copies, scans
Digitization	Making digital copies, scanning
Electronic management system	Database
Electronic mail	E-mail
Enduring value	Value
Expunge	Remove or destroy
Final disposition	Disposal or destruction
Humidification	Add moisture, humidify
Inclusive dates	Date range, date span, dates
Metadata	Information, identifying information
Mylar	Polyester, sheeting, cover
ND	Undated
OCR	Key word searchable
pH	Acidity, level of acid
Processing	Arrangement
Provenance	Origins, original state
Redaction	Restriction, to conceal
Vellum	Calfskin, animal skin

did not provide enough information or provide the information clearly enough. An example of a prime clarifying question is: What did you mean when you said...? Getting several of these is a red flag. To avoid this snag, take a critical look at what the audience needs and decipher the best possible method of delivery. If, for example, you have 15 minutes to talk to a potential donor, then the information you offer must be as succinct, clear, and precise as possible. In contrast, if you have 45 minutes to an hour to address a mixed audience of archives novices, then the situation merits the use of examples to illustrate more abstract concepts. Ultimately, how much information to provide is going to be unique to each situation, which is another effect of your understanding the audience. As a general rule, the less the audience knows about archives, the more basic and illustrated the information should be.

Handouts: A Bygone Era?

In the age of PowerPoint presentations, handouts and show-and-tell items have fallen out of favor. Yet, these tools can be just as effective and perhaps even more so, depending on the audience. Not so long ago, the use of representative physical items in a presentation meant that the location of the presentation had to be in the archives, but with the wide-scale availability and affordability of quality scanners and printers, taking facsimile examples of letters, diary entries, photographs, transcriptions, and other similar material is possible. Even though institutional brochures remain a steadfast and incomparable handout for the public, inexpensive technology also enables the creation of presentation-specific handouts. Perhaps even better than a PowerPoint, creating event-specific take-aways helps to convey to audience members the time, energy, and effort put into the presentation while speaking directly to their needs (Figure 9.2).

Brochures can accomplish the general introduction, but specific handouts, even if only a single page, help to continue the conversation. However, just as with event-specific presentations, the greatest effect of a handout is in its uniqueness. Typically every handout includes some standard information, such as name of the archives, location, and hours, but the key is tailoring each handout to the community it is supposed to serve. When partnered with a presentation, the handout often functions as an extension of the presentation but should not attempt to repeat the same exact content. Brevity is essential. Just as in PowerPoint presentations, however, there is an opportunity here for you to visually brand your archives. Branding in part centers on creating a memorable logo or using an image over and over again. Thus, over time the public will begin to associate the name of the archives with the image or logo.

The standout features of the handouts included here are the repeated use of the same image, the university logo, and the banner/logo of the archives itself. That is the end of the similarity. Compare the full-page handout (Figure 9.2), which targeted potential materials donors, and the bookmark (Figure 9.3), which was used at an alumnae event. In both cases the goal was to give each audience something to reference in

Figure 9.2. Basic Template Plus Event-Specific Information

Women and Leadership
ARCHIVES

Preparing people to lead extraordinary lives

Celebrating and Documenting
Women Artists

The Women and Leadership Archives (WLA) holds over 120 manuscript collections representing women from all vocations and walks of life. Our collection strengths include women activists, second wave feminism, radical Catholic women, and women as community builders, business owners, politicians, educators, and academics. We hope to expand our collections to include more women artists whether local, regional, or national. Women's important contributions to artistic creation, imagination, and women's art as expression and activism must be preserved as part of our collective cultural and social history.

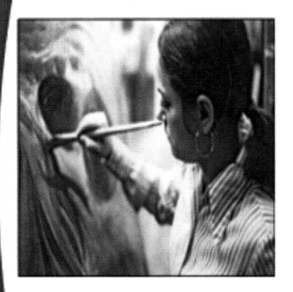

Our mission is simple: The WLA collects, preserves, organizes, describes, and makes available materials of enduring value to researchers studying women's activities. The WLA strives to promote knowledge and understanding of women's many diverse and important contributions to society through active collection development, research, and the facilitation of learning about women's history.

Help support this goal by considering the WLA as a respository for your own papers!

For more information about archives, donating a collection, or scheduling a visit, please contact:

Women and Leadership Archives
Beth Myers, PhD, Director
Loyola University Chicago – Piper Hall
1032 W. Sheridan Road – Chicago, IL 60660
Phone: 773-508-8837
E-mail: WLArchives@luc.edu
Hours: Monday–Friday 8:30 AM to 4:30 PM
Visit us at our website: http://www.luc.edu/wla

the moment but refer to later. Both are simple, offer visual interest, and provide crucial information. In every case, the usefulness of show-and-tell items has not changed—people still *love* to see the stuff—but, thanks to technology, the method of delivery has been irrevocably altered to the archivist's advantage.

Brochures offer the opportunity for the speaker to interact with the audience. However, there is no substitute for the question-and-answer session. Too often this part of the presentation is seen as an afterthought. In reality, it is a great chance to connect directly with the audience. If, for example, you have not addressed the group's specific needs, you can make the extra effort in the Q&A. One major pitfall to avoid, however, is the ratio of too-few-questions to too-many-answers. In other words, the Q&A is a chance for the audience members to have their specific, even individual, needs met. It is not an opportunity for you to expound at length or provide a demonstration of your cleverness. If any one question

Standard Types of Handouts

- **Single-page reference sheet:** The most basic and useful of handouts, the single-page reference sheet is most successfully employed with general or public audiences. The sheet is not meant to convey detailed information, but to be effective as a quick-glance document.

- **Multipage reference sheet:** For more advanced audiences, multipage handouts (e.g., listing collections in detail, collection scope, donation policies) work best with those audiences who want or require more information than the general public. This is especially true for donors who wish to move the discussion beyond the brochure level of information.

- **Brochure:** The go-to handout, brochures can be glossy, heavily designed, and expensively produced trifold documents or single-sided in-house-printed giveaways. The type and quality of brochures varies widely. Though it is always advisable to have brochures at the ready for every event, it should not substitute for an event-specific handout. Rather, the two items should work in cooperation with one another.

- **Bookmark:** The greatest appeal of a bookmark is its simplicity. Typically the smallest of handouts, the type and amount of information must be succinct. Very often the design challenges of such a small area can turn into design successes through imagination.

- **Facsimiles of images/artifacts:** With the advance of technology, you can now produce beautiful reproductions of items in the collections. This type of handout is generally used with a very specific audience who is less interested in the archival process than in the stuff in the archives. Facsimiles may also be useful as a design addition to any other type of handout.

Figure 9.3. Example of a Bookmark

Experiment with the Archives!

The Women and Leadership Archives' Mundelein College Record Collection has many online tools for you to use to bring back memories and share with friends. Did you know:
- the entire run of the *Skyscraper* is digitized? Take a stroll down memory lane!
- the Mundelein College Timeline includes a decade by decade pictorial?

Over 14,000 people have visited the Archives site – have you visited yet?

Quick Links:
WLA Webpage: http://www.luc.edu/wla/

Mundelein College Records page:
http://www.luc.edu/wla/mcarchives.shtml

Mundelein Alumni page: Find us at luc.edu under Resources/Alumni Association/Special Interest Groups/Mundelein Alumni

WOMEN AND LEADERSHIP
ARCHIVES

Note: Similar to handouts, bookmarks are easy to create, inexpensive to produce, and great take-aways for the audience.

demands an at-length answer, there are diplomatic ways to offer more discussion after the session is over or to provide contact information to pick the dialogue up at another time.

Another function of the Q&A session is to indicate to the speaker places where the presentation might need editing. If, for example, an audience has several questions about a subject that you thought you covered thoroughly, this is a good indication that the presentation did not work to meet the audience's needs.

When the presentation is in a more intimate setting, there is not always a formal Q&A session. In such an environment it is much more fluid to answer questions during the presentation rather than afterward. A smaller group allows for a less formal exchange and, as time allows, more specific questions and, by extension, better answers. In the end, the Q&A session—as well as conversations with those who linger afterward—are the last opportunities to leave the audience with the best impression.

Although it has been said often in this chapter, it bears repeating here that at the core of any presentation is the audience. To dispel any lingering and negative stereotypes of the archives profession, to underscore the value of our collections and repositories, to increase use, promote collections, and connect to the next generation of archival users, you

---

PRESENTATION CHECKLIST

- **Pre-event**
  - Research the audience. This is especially important if the group or person(s) is totally unknown to you, but it is also necessary for presenting to administrative groups.
  - Speak with the event organizers, if any, to determine the goals for the presentation. If there are no organizers, double-check with a member of the group to whom you are speaking about the purpose of the presentation. Once the topic is decided, do not deviate.
  - Determine the location, physical limitations of the space, and available technology.
  - Construct the presentation.
    - Create an outline of speaker's notes. Unless you are speaking at an academic conference, do not read your presentations to the audience. Speak from notes, which allows for eye contact.
    - Use PowerPoint. Always create a PowerPoint file from your notes, not vice versa.
    - Create handouts. Decide now what handouts (e.g., brochure, specifically created one-page take-away, and appropriate tchotchkes), if any, would be most appropriate.
  - Practice by yourself and in front of another person, if possible.

- **Event**
  - At least one hour before the presentation, double-check all of the technology, including a dry run of the PowerPoint file. Not all projectors project at the same brightness, so stand at the back of the room and make sure the text, background, or other items are 100 percent visible. Likewise, the projector will likely provide a slightly different screen size than your computer terminal, which may require adjustment.
  - Timing. Make sure you have a watch, phone, clock, or friendly audience member in your line of sight to keep you on time. No one will appreciate a presentation that runs over.
  - Bring water or mints, especially if the environment is particularly dry.

- **Post-event**
  - Allow time for the question-and-answer session.
  - Point out where your handouts, contact information, or other materials are located in the room.

must be able to communicate effectively. More static and passive methods of the past—waiting to do show and tells in the reading room—must be put aside in favor of the more labor-intensive, but ultimately more effective, outreach. At the core of any outreach program is communicating the archives' needs and meet the needs of its users. That may mean traveling offsite, adapting to each group's needs, making a study of the audience to best determine how to communicate, and putting forth the best presentation possible.

Conclusion

Compared to politicians or other major public figures, archivists are a quiet and reserved professional group. The monastic quality of an archives contributes to the seriousness of the research enterprise, for archivists and researchers alike. At the same time, recent technological advances and shifted user expectations have fundamentally altered the actual practice of the profession. Rather than the traditional ebbs and flows of paper finding aids, appointment-only access, and outreach that consisted of a handshake, archivists have increasingly adopted practices of direct advocacy and organized, targeted outreach. Whether in the archives or out in the community, the archivist's role is vastly more publicly engaged than it once was and continues to grow as such. Chief among the new outreach practices is developing the skills to connect regularly with diverse audiences.

Beginning with the recognition that audiences are inherently more complex than speakers often credit through the practical application of handouts, this chapter sought to advise professionals on how to be better speakers. The top three principles of presenting—knowing the audience dynamic, being prepared for anything, and using technology to the best advantage—will help any speaker become better at the task. To become a truly great speaker, however, an archivist must also embrace the role of spokesperson willingly and enthusiastically. Recognizing presenting as an everyday part of the job will normalize it and help those archival professionals more reluctant to become a presenter. In the end, archivists have to effect change in the diverse audiences with which they interact, and that change begins, always, with a single conversation.

THE PLAN

1. Develop a template for your presentations, and include this in your marketing plan.
2. If you give handouts with your presentations, develop a policy that will govern handouts, such as boilerplate information that should be included, and put this in your plan.
3. If you regularly use terminology that may be confusing to different audiences, create a handout that defines and explains the terminology and put it with your plan.

References

Moore, Ilana Brown. 1998. "Archival Outreach: Strategies for Success." Master's thesis, Western Washington University.
Oxford English Dictionary. 2009. "Public." http://www.oed.com/.

Additional Resources

Arant, Wendi, and Pixie Anne Mosely. 2000. *Library Outreach, Partnerships, and Distance Education: Reference Librarians at the Gateway.* New York: Haworth Information Press.

Blais, Gabrielle, and David Enns. 1990–1991. "From Paper Archives to People Archives: Public Programming in the Management of Archives." *Archivaria* 31 (Winter): 101–113.

Cook, Terry. 1990–1991. "Viewing the World Upside Down: Reflections on the Theoretical Underpinnings of Archival Public Programming." *Archivaria* 31 (Winter): 123–132.

Craig, Barbara. 1990–1991. "What Are Clients? Who Are the Products? The Future of Archival Public Services in Perspective." *Archivaria* 31 (Winter): 135–141.

Dingwall, Glenn. 2004. "Trusting Archivists: The Role of Archival Ethics Codes in Establishing Public Faith." *American Archivist* 67 (Spring/Summer): 11–30.

Ericson, Timothy L. 1990–1991. "Preoccupied with Our Own Gardens: Outreach and Archivists." *Archivaria* 31 (Winter): 114–122.

Finch, Elise Freedman, ed. 1994. *Advocating Archives: An Introduction to Public Relations for Archivists.* Metuchen, NJ: Society of American Archivists and Scarecrow Press.

Grabowski, John. 1992. "Keepers, Users, and Funders: Building an Awareness of Archival Value." *American Archivist* 55 (Summer): 464–472.

Gracy, David B. 1989. "Archivists, You Are What People Think You Keep." *American Archivist* 52 (Winter): 72–78.

Hoff, Ron. 1988. *I Can See You Naked: A Fearless Guide to Making Great Presentations.* Kansas City: Andrews and McMeel.

Jimmerson, Randall C. 2006. "Embracing the Power of Archives." *American Archivist* 69 (Spring/Summer): 19–32.

Nesmith, Tom. 2002. "Seeing Archives: Postmodernism and the Changing Intellectual Place of Archives." *American Archivist* 65 (Spring/Summer): 24–41.

Pederson, Ann E., and Gail E. Farr. 1982. *Archives & Manuscripts: Public Programming.* Chicago: Society of American Archivists.

Schuyler, Leslie. 2008. "The Wonderful World of Archives: American Archives and Their Quest for Public Support." Master's thesis, Western Washington University.

Ten Cate, Ann. 1992. *Promoting Archives: A Handbook.* Ottawa, Canada: Association of Canadian Archivists.

Historical Societies, Genealogists, and Volunteers

Suzanne Campbell

Introduction

Archives have many publics. These include researchers, volunteers, donors, and the community in general. Another potential public and source of support for archives are local and regional historical and genealogical societies. Experience and tracking have shown both groups are among the best supporters of archives and special historical collections. These groups can be your best friends or worst enemies, so handle with care.

In *Advocating Archives*, Elsie Freeman Finch and Paul Conway state (1994: 5): "The public relations of an institution is no better than the quality of its management decisions and its service to the public." This is certainly true of an archives' relationship to historical and genealogical societies.

Included in the category of historical societies are lineage societies. In your area, these organizations may include the Daughters of the American Revolution, the Sons of the American Revolution, the Colonial Dames of the XVII Century, and the Mayflower Society, to name a few. Many of these groups date their origins to the late 1800s. Other societies are more concerned about local and regional history.

Preservation societies have come about more recently as citizens have begun to realize that they were losing their historical resources. These groups tend to focus on state and local preservation. Communities see the benefit of showcasing historic buildings and the revitalization of downtown areas. Preservation and heritage tourism give archives a highly visible community presence. Local chambers of commerce are also important archives' collaborators and can be important archival supporters.

Building Relationships with Outside Groups

Historical, genealogical, and other related groups are a natural fit for your archives. They are also important to the long-term viability of your

Public Relations and Marketing for Archives

organization. It is a great idea to include members of these groups when planning events, displays, and programs. They have wonderful ideas, they often help support activities with manpower and money, and they make great volunteers. These are the supporters who will solicit new materials for your archives. They are like-minded individuals and groups who will donate funds and are likely to make up a large portion of your patron group.

This leads to a tried-and-true method designed to include groups such as these: ask their opinion on a number of topics. How can you improve access to the archives? What can you as an archivist do to better meet their needs? It's important for your organization that these groups buy into your program. Pay attention to their ideas. When the staff implements a suggestion made by a member of one of the groups, do not fail to call attention to this change. That means you and the archives staff were responsive to them.

Genealogical and Historical Societies

Genealogists love to find information and make it available to fellow genealogists. That alone makes them excellent volunteers. Do you have newspapers that need to be indexed? One community had a group of interested individuals come together for the purpose of indexing the local paper. The local academic library assisted by providing a microfilm reader, a computer, and a place to work. This material is extremely important to all researchers. Make sure you appoint a leader to this type of project; you need someone who can keep the project moving forward and who is committed.

Genealogists in particular like to share their knowledge and expertise. Ask your local or regional society to provide volunteers to assist novice genealogists who come to your archives. Set aside a day each week, or whatever timeframe works best for the society, when a volunteer will be present, and then advertise their availability. You will gain new patrons in the process.

Friends Organizations

Friends groups can also be a wonderful source of support for your archives; they are great workers and encouragers of archives. If you are part of a larger institution, check the legal process necessary to start the program. Such an organization should be set up as a 501(c) tax organization; this IRS designation will allow you and your supporters to apply for grants. Once the group is organized, determine what projects you want to consider. Unless the group has someone who is familiar with the work, you will need to provide a great deal of support and education. You must be on hand to keep the organization going until it is up and running with only minimal help from your staff.

Following are the steps for starting a friends group. Keep in mind that this is a simple list but that the process can become complex. More information on friends groups can be found in Herring (1993) and Thompson and Smith (1999).

- If you are a part of a larger institution, check with the administration to determine if the group can be authorized.
- Find five to seven supporters of your archives, and invite them to attend your organizational meeting.
- Your best sources for group members are the local historical and genealogical organizations.
- Explain what you want to do—organize a group who will be your representatives in the community. Keep that in mind when selecting your organization's board.
- Before you can do anything, elect officers. It is important that you allow the group to do this; after all, this will be their organization.
- The group will need to write bylaws that include the following sections:
  - Name of organization
  - Purpose
  - Membership (dues, voting privileges, removal)
  - Meetings (how often, notice, quorum)
  - Board of Directors (authority, terms of office, nominating committee, vacancies, meetings, quorum)
  - Officers (how many officers, duties)
  - Executive Committee (makeup, duties, and actions)
  - Committees
  - General Funds and Liability (audits, where money will be held, how the money can and cannot be used)
  - Amendments (how the bylaws can be changed)
  - Dissolution (In the event the group is dissolved, what happens to the money and property belonging to the group?)
- Check with your state government to determine what is needed to start your friends group. For example, in Texas, you go to the Secretary of State website for the information you need to proceed.
- You will need an Employee Identification Number.
- Apply in your state to be a nonprofit organization.
- To find out how to apply for tax-exempt status, go to the IRS website: http://www.irs.gov/charities/charitable/index.html
- Write Articles of Incorporation that include these sections:
  - Name
  - Duration
  - Purposes and Powers
  - Directors
  - Membership
  - Principal and Registered Office
  - Bylaws
  - Registered Agent
  - Distribution of Assets on Dissolution
  - Amendment

Book Fairs

Book fairs are a terrific method of collaborating with others in your community, such as bookstores and libraries. To host a book fair, try these tips:

- Have one person or committee be in charge of the event, which requires a great deal of organization.
- Ask for support from book dealers, bookstores, libraries, and archives in your area or community.
- Schedule the fair for a time when the weather is warm enough to hold it outside. Otherwise, find a large indoor area.
- If outside, provide tables and chairs for the vendors. You might use this as a fundraising opportunity and charge a fee for vendor tables.
- Ask societies and organizations that work with you to help with the event. They may want to plan a children's event, such as a reading time, or host an author of children's books.
- You may want to include the public schools in the event. Teachers usually have creative ideas for encouraging young people to read.
- At the end of the event, assess what needs to be changed for next year and gather new ideas for improving the event and including more people.

- Once you have been granted tax-exempt status, remember to file a Form 990 with the IRS each year.

Encourage the friends group to initiate activities that promote books and encourage reading. You may want to begin with the more obvious and later go to the more creative activities (see following sections for examples).

Book Fairs

Book fairs are great projects for friends groups. This type of event can "kick off" a new organization. If you do a book fair, invite local and regional authors to attend, sell, and autograph books. One twist to this is an edible book contest, which an academic library sponsored in conjunction with a book fair. People were asked to design a book in which everything was edible. The competition included categories for different age groups, and the entries were very creative. Winners received gift certificates to a bookstore.

Book Sales and Signings

Your friends group may want to do something on a slightly smaller scale and sponsor a book sale or book signing. Events such as these are also great advertisements for your archives and for your friends organization. If your archives is part of a larger institution—a museum, college, or university with its own bookstore—you will need to follow the rules regarding hosting such an event. Check with the bookstore for rules about book signings; you may find it easier to host the book sale in another location. Also, there is a difference between a public library and an academic library in contributing books for a sale. A public library can most likely cull its books and put them in the sale, whereas an academic library, if state supported, cannot place withdrawn books in the sale; everything must be donated from outside the campus.

Collecting from Outside Groups

Remember that these organizations' members often have collections of their own, and as the members grow older, they begin to look for a safe place to house those collections. Many realize their children will not be interested in the collections, and they do not want their work and material tossed. At the same time, the archives must have a collection development or acquisitions policy in place to give the staff a gracious way of refusing certain unwanted collections without offending donors. As an archivist, you are governed by this policy, which gives specific criteria for acquiring and appraising items and working with a donor according to the specific collection needs and desires of the archives. Many donors will bring you collections that contain materials they simply did not have the heart to dispose of themselves. Have a clear understanding with your donors about items you do not wish to add to your permanent collection. Simply ask if you should toss the unwanted items or return them to the donor.

It is important to have written procedures for your collection development plan. This document will help you answer all queries about accepting donations from collectors. See the sidebar for a sample set of procedures.

Housing Organizational Records

Some archivists do not recommend housing records from organizations such as historical and genealogical societies. Those archives that do take organizational records take only records that are no longer used by the group so that the archivist does not spend a lot of time retrieving material for the group. Before accepting records from one of these groups, check your collection policy and get input from your superiors.

If you do accept materials, you will find that housing organizational records for your target groups will prove to be a good marketing tool for your archives. Members see it as a validation of their organization's worth to the archives. To continue the good will, you can let the organizations know that they can bring you each year's records at the end of that year.

Despite having a policy that states the archives will accept only records that are no longer current, an archivist may find that on occasion a group will need something from the collection—say, a scrapbook—for a special event. The archives can then ask a designated officer of the group to sign out the material; the archivist will then sign the sheet when the material is returned. This policy has worked well for a number of archives and has created much goodwill with organizations.

Several archives in our area have successfully worked with historical, lineage, and genealogical societies to house their collections. During special group events, a designated individual signs out materials such as scrapbooks. The individual gives a date of return. When returned, the items are checked back into the archive; the form is kept in the organization's file as a record. Use the Release Form for this type of removal (see Figure 10.1). If you allow the group to keep material for an extended period of time, you may want to use the Loan Agreement (see Figure 10.2).

Process the organizational records as you would other collections. Make a finding tool for researchers, and give the group a copy so you and they can find what they need. As you provide a safe place to store the group's records, you will find that members feel invested in your archives and are then encouraged to donate personal collections and money.

Volunteer Programs

Volunteers can often make the difference in your ability to process collections in your facility and make them available to researchers. These individuals come to archives from all walks of life and occupations, giving an archives a wealth of experience and expertise. With tight

Procedures for Collection Development

Purpose: A collection development policy gives focus and direction to the acquisition of new collections for your archives.

Step 1: List your archives' main areas of interest as well as examples of suitable items.

Step 2: If you are part of a larger institution, include a statement to the effect that your archives supports the mission or curriculum of your institution.

Step 3: In addition, state that your archives will accept, on a case-by-case basis, items and material relating to the general history of your state.

Step 4: Check with your state laws and your institution's policies, if part of a larger establishment, guiding the use of appraisals. The IRS has very specific guidelines for appraisals: http://www.irs.gov/publications/p561/ar02.html. Include that information in your policy document.

Figure 10.1. Sample Release Form

Release Form

The following has been removed from the existing collection of _____.

Name

Accession Number _____

Description of materials: _____

By: _____

Signature of Donor or Authorized Representative   Date

Address: _____

_____

Phone: _____

Witnessed by: _____

YOUR REPRESENTATIVE

Materials due back by: _____

Figure 10.2. Sample Loan Agreement

[YOUR ARCHIVES]

Loan Agreement

DATE:

On this date _____ borrowed the following items:

_____

_____	_____
Borrower	[YOUR ARCHIVES PERSONNEL]
_____	_____
Date	Date

Item Returned:

_____	_____
Borrower	[YOUR ARCHIVES PERSONNEL]
_____	_____
Date	Date

budgets, volunteers can be life savers, and many volunteers can be recruited from historical and genealogical societies.

Procedures Manual

Before starting a volunteer program, check with the legal department, because there may be liability issues to consider. Check with other entities that have successful volunteer programs and get ideas. At this starting point, it is a good idea to compose and write down procedures for volunteers. A procedures manual will be of value to you, the archivist, to your volunteers, and, if you are a part of an academic institution, for your student assistants. Sections for your procedure manual include the following:

- Collection Development or Acquisitions Policy
- Mission Statement
- Processing New Collections
- Arrangement and Description of Collections
- Care of Rare Books
- Inventorying New Collection
- Processing Newspapers and Maps
- Processing Photographs
- Registering Patrons
- Taking Queries by Phone
- Answering E-mail Queries
- Requests for Photographs
- Processing Genealogical Quarterlies
- Vertical Files
- Copying Materials
- Deposits
- Labeling Books without Archival Slips
- Labeling Books with Archival Slips
- Definitions

Formal Training

Prepare a training session for your volunteers just as you would for new employees. Consider how in-depth the training should be. As you compose your training guidelines, be sure to include a statement of expectations. Make the statement clear but reasonable.

You will need approximately a week's worth of time for training. This can be divided into ten half-day sessions or five full-day classes. You may also want to tailor your sessions to fit the interests of the volunteers. Remember, not all volunteers are computer literate.

Necessary Forms

Next, it is important to continue formalizing the volunteer program by creating several forms for prospective volunteers:

- Volunteer Registration Form
- Volunteer Job Performance Evaluation (archives with smaller volunteer groups may find this form unnecessary)
- Monthly Time Report

Figures 10.3 through 10.5 provide examples of these forms that you can revise for your archives; customize them to match your needs.

Figure 10.3. Volunteer Registration Form

VOLUNTEER REGISTRATION FORM
[NAME OF ARCHIVES]

Date _____

Name _____

Address _____

City/State _____ Zip Code _____

Phone (Home) _____ Phone (Office) _____ Birthday (MM/DD) _____

Employed _____ Retired _____ Business_____

Student _____ School _____

Education _____

How referred _____
_____

Experience _____
_____

Special interests and skills _____
_____

Languages other than English, degree of proficiency _____
_____

Person to contact in case of emergency _____
Phone (Home) _____ Phone (Office) _____

Circle choice of volunteer duty: Archives   Genealogy   Reference/Documents   Unknown

Write specific hours when you are available for volunteer work each day.
Genealogy schedule is Tuesday–Saturday, 8 a.m.–5 p.m.
Archives and Reference/Documents schedule is Monday–Friday, 8 a.m.–5 p.m.

	Monday	Tuesday	Wednesday	Thursday	Friday	Saturday
Morning						
Afternoon						

Comments: _____
_____
_____
_____
_____

Figure 10.4. Volunteer Job Performance Evaluation

VOLUNTEER JOB PERFORMANCE EVALUATION

Name _____

Date of this review _____ Date of last review _____

Supervisor _____ Collection assignment _____

_____

Use the following measures to assess the quality of the volunteer's performance: 5 outstanding, 4 more than adequate, 3 adequate, 2 less than adequate, 1 not satisfactory.

1. Works well with staff	5	4	3	2	1
2. Keeps designated hours and appointments	5	4	3	2	1
3. Appearance is appropriate for job situation	5	4	3	2	1
4. Shows initiative and creativity	5	4	3	2	1
5. Works well without supervision	5	4	3	2	1
6. Effective carrying out assignments	5	4	3	2	1
7. Makes substantial contribution to Archives	5	4	3	2	1

Questions for discussion:

1. What do you do that satisfies you the most?

_____

_____

2. What do you do that satisfies you the least?

_____

_____

3. Are there any specific problems you would like to discuss?

_____

_____

4. What suggestions do you have for improving the volunteer program?

_____

_____

5. Actions to be taken as result of performance evaluation:

_____

_____

Comments: _____

_____

_____

_____

_____

Figure 10.5. Monthly Time Report

MONTHLY TIME REPORT

Submit the completed form to your supervisor on the last working day of the month.

VOLUNTEER _____

MONTH/YEAR _____

Day	Start Time	End Time	# of Hours	General Description of Activity
1			:	
2			:	
3			:	
4			:	
5			:	
6			:	
7			:	
8			:	
9			:	
10			:	
11			:	
12			:	
13			:	
14			:	
15			:	
16			:	
17			:	
18			:	
19			:	
20			:	
21			:	
22			:	
23			:	
24			:	
25			:	
26			:	
27			:	
28			:	
29			:	
30			:	
31			:	

TOTAL HOURS WORKED: _____

Working with and Training Volunteers

Once you have everything in place, survey your local historical and genealogical groups to determine individuals' interests. Make every effort to tailor their jobs to what they enjoy and what interests them; otherwise, they will lose interest and you will lose volunteers. Following are some practical ideas for working with and training volunteers in your archives.

Projects Involving Computers

- Sort and index collections within your archives, such as
  - Court cases and county records
  - Court books that are not indexed
  - Newspapers
  - Funeral home records
  - Genealogical collections
- Create databases of material.
- Scan/digitize various records in your collection.

Projects That Do Not Involve Computers

- Answer the telephone at the reception desk.
- Look up queries for researchers.
- Look up obituaries.
- Re-shelve books.
- Retrieve and return archival material and collections.
- Organize fundraisers.
- Assist genealogists.
- Assist researchers interested in joining lineage societies.
- Stamp and process books and periodicals.
- Sort and identify photographs.

Computer Skills and Workshops

Members of the organizations with which you will work, as well as your archives' patrons, have a wide range of computer skills; some don't have a computer while others are quite technically savvy. Determine the level of computer knowledge among your patrons and volunteers by visiting with them. To improve their computer skills, you can offer a computer workshop.

In planning the computer workshop for volunteers, patrons, and friends, you will most likely find that you need to offer workshops at two levels: beginner and advanced. If you feel it is needed, plan for an intermediate-level workshop as well. If you do not feel comfortable leading the workshop yourself, hire an individual who knows computers but also has the ability and patience to teach, especially beginners. These workshops might be sponsored by the archives or by the friends group and could focus on a variety of computer skills, from using Word or Excel

How to Prepare for a Computer Workshop

1. Determine the skill level for the workshop.
2. Find a location for the workshop. Ideally, there would be enough computers for each attendee to have a computer. This may limit the number of workshop attendees.
3. Select a trainer. Your patrons will be more successful if the individual conducting the workshop gives them handouts to take home.
4. Advertise the workshop. Make it clear that you have limited seating.
5. Prepare handouts for the attendees. You may want to compile a notebook of some sort for each individual.
6. If allowed, have snacks and a location for a break time that is away from the computers.
7. Prepare an evaluation form for those who attend. Their comments will give you an idea of how successful the workshop was, what needs to be changed, and suggestions to consider.

to using e-mail. Emphasize to your beginners that the Internet is not always a reliable source of information; they need to check their sources.

For an intermediate or advanced computer workshop, you need an instructor who can explain how to conduct research on the computer. A number of archives teach genealogy classes in their area or collaborate with the local genealogical society to teach classes. This is a wonderful method of getting genealogists into your area. In turn, they become supporters, and some become volunteers. In addition to teaching skills, this will give you an opportunity to both show off the databases and websites available in your institution and to find out what the patrons really want.

To train your volunteers, hold a computer class just for this group. Patrons will often ask volunteers for help with basic computer functions, so volunteers need to have some knowledge to share. Be careful not to make them feel ill at ease, but use this as an opportunity to assess the skills of your volunteers. This will help you place them in a job or project they feel comfortable doing and will let you know the best method of communicating with them as well.

Communication with Volunteers and Patrons

The use of computers will ease your communication with volunteers and patrons. Newsletters are a wonderful way to communicate with supporters and you can send them electronically. If, however, you have individuals who are not computer literate, print and mail copies to them. If you have a volunteer or a staff member who especially enjoys this type of work, allow them to design and send a newsletter about your archives, but check it before it goes out. Many state genealogical organizations give prizes for the best newsletter; if applicable to your archives, encourage your group to enter the competition. Or volunteer to write a column in the genealogical society's newsletter about your archives, such as new collections, new books received, or historical information from the past that is not widely known. (See Chapter 6 for more information about newsletters.)

Activities to Connect Your Archives to Historical/Genealogical Societies

You can take on certain activities to publicize the archives to historical and genealogical societies. The activities discussed here are not a complete listing, of course, but many archivists have found them to be most beneficial in fulfilling the goals and objectives of an archives' public relations campaign. Each has its own unusual aspects, but all have a dual purpose: helping the archives publicize itself and helping the historical/genealogical societies fulfill their missions.

Let these groups know what you and your archives can do to help them by creating a simple, computer-generated brochure, fact sheet, or bookmark listing information about your facility. You can include a calendar, times of operation, and any other important information. In addition, let them know how they can help you as well: as donors, patrons, and volunteers. Go that extra mile to help them; they will return the favor many times over.

Helping Historical/Genealogical Societies with Their Publicity

Always be willing to help the historical and genealogical societies with publicity. For example, many archives depend almost solely on donations for books, and historical and genealogical groups frequently donate books to archives and libraries. To recognize and celebrate these donations, you can do some of the following:

- When a person or group donates a book or collection, take a photograph of the donor giving you the book or collection.
- Write a press release about the donation and send it to the local newspaper. Most newspapers look for items to include. It is wise to go visit your local paper and get the name of a contact to whom you will send the information.
- If a book will go in your regular stacks, insert a bookplate saying it was donated by the organization. If the book is to go in closed stacks or is a rare book, use an archival book slip and type the donation information on the slip. *Never* put indelible marks on rare books.

Media Day

Sponsor a media day and also invite members of the historical and genealogical societies to attend. This gives you the opportunity to describe your archives, its mission, and its collections to the media, and it allows the societies to describe themselves and their work. You can spotlight your archives as well as introduce volunteers, the friends board, and so on. Consider the following before hosting a media day at your facility:

- To avoid losing the media to another event, check the community's calendar before setting the date.
- Select a date on or near to a particular event—perhaps the kickoff of a new friends group or a new display.
- Sponsor a media day only for special events pertaining to the historical or genealogical societies. If you plan too many such days, the event will become commonplace and the media will not come.
- Send invitations to various media outlets, including the local newspaper and television and radio stations in the area.
- Serve refreshments.
- Prepare a handout about your archives and what you are showcasing. It helps to provide them with information they can use later.

Brochures
- If you have the budget, write and print full-color brochures about your archives. If this is cost-prohibitive, design a simple trifold brochure on your computer. If possible, use a higher grade of paper than simple copy paper; however, even a brochure on copy paper is better than not having anything to hand to visitors to your archives.
- Include your contact information and a statement about the archives being a resource to the various historical and genealogical societies.
- If your archives has an area of specialization, create a separate brochure describing that area and how the material can be accessed.
- Consider making a separate brochure for genealogists explaining what you have available for them to use on a specific topic. For example, if you have books and information on Jewish genealogy, make a brochure on "How to Conduct Jewish Genealogy" in your archives. Those looking for just such information will appreciate your effort.
- If you have a friends group or a volunteer program, design a brochure about the group or program and place it where visitors sign in to your archives.

- Speak about the archives, or, if you are uncomfortable with public speaking, have a strong supporter or staff member speak.
- Ask some of your supporters to attend. It tells the media there are others who support the archives and the work you do.

Historic Photographs

In 2009 the *Wall Street Journal* ran a story about a group in El Paso, Texas, trying to identify historic photographs. This is an excellent way to showcase the value of publishing old photographs for which there is not much information. Newspaper readers love the challenge of identifying people, places, and events in these photos, and traffic increases in repositories as those readers try to help with identifications. You can place unidentified photographs on your website and ask for information. Once people in the community know about the photos, they will check your website frequently.

Another way to involve historical and genealogical groups in the identification of photographs is to invite them and other community members to come to the archives. Spread the photographs around the room on tables, providing plenty of white cotton gloves or some way to protect the photographs. Offer these visitors some method of identifying each photograph. A staff member might be there to write lightly in pencil on the backs. If you have the time and resources, copy the photographs and allow the guests to write on the photocopies. This type of event has been a great success at several archives. One invited the Experimental Aircraft Association to meet in the archives and help identify old photographs of aircraft. They came armed with books and worked until all were documented!

Through the years many historical societies have become the keepers of historical photographs. Some county historical societies, whose collections are housed in an archives, have made their photographs available to businesses for a reasonable price. One can find their photos throughout the community in banks, restaurants, and grocery stores. This is wonderful advertising for the archives and brings awareness of local history as well. In addition, the archives may reap a monetary benefit in the sales of photographic reproductions. See Chapter 7 for information on writing a statement of policy and procedures for providing photographic reproductions to outside parties.

Education

Genealogy Classes

A genealogy class is a wonderful way to combine your local or regional genealogical society and your archives. If you do not feel qualified to conduct the class, ask the society to have someone conduct it. Here are some tips for preparing such a class:

1. If possible, hold the class in your archives. This gives the attendees firsthand knowledge.

2. Prepare plenty of handouts for the class. Remind attendees to use these forms as originals and make copies from them.

3. The Internet is a great source of information for this type of class. There are a number of excellent websites, including:
   http://usgenweb.org/research/index/shtml
   http://www.genealogy.com/getting_started.htm#home (Learning Center)
   http://www.rootsweb.ancestry.com (Getting Started)
   http://www.ancestrylibrary.com/charts/ancchart.aspx (forms and charts)

4. Prepare a notebook for teaching the class. Include the main points you wish to tell attendees, along with copies of the sheets in their packet/notebook. This will keep you focused and in line with the material you give the attendees.

Genealogy Workshops

The genealogical society and your archives might consider collaborating on a genealogy workshop. The two most important things to consider are the selection of a speaker and publicity for the event. A genealogy workshop requires several months of preparation. For example, for a spring workshop, start planning in September. Follow these steps in the planning process:

- Select a committee or ask for volunteers. Make certain you have some energetic and organized individuals on the committee.

- Select a date and place.

- Next, select a speaker. Most genealogists will present two to three programs in one day.

- Check cost and expenses of the speaker, travel, lodging, and food. Also check the place of the workshop to find if there are any costs involved with renting the facility. Then set a price for the workshop. Consider giving members of the friends group or local genealogical society a reduced registration price.

- Many genealogy speakers have their own books to sell. Ask the facility if its policy allows speakers to sell books.

- Determine the cost of the event. Do you want to serve a catered lunch? If so, you must find a caterer and ask what they would charge. Usually, event attendees pay for lunch separately because some will wish to eat elsewhere. Divide the total catering cost by the number you expect. You want to make some profit but keep the cost within reason.

- Prepare a registration form with all pertinent information about the workshop, cost, and a deadline for replying (see Figure 10.6).

- Once you have firmed up the speaker, date, and location, begin advertising the event. Start with your local genealogical group(s).

Figure 10.6. Genealogy Workshop Registration Form

Genealogy Workshop Registration Form

[Your Organization]
[Name of Event/Agenda, including speaker(s)]

About the speaker(s):

_____

_____

Cost of workshop 40.00*
Includes a notebook of the lectures and
materials provided by the speakers.
Buffet Lunch 10.00
Registration at door *45.00*

Overnight Lodging
Reasonably priced overnight lodging is available close to
the university campus. [List hotels along with telephone numbers.]

Name: _____ **Phone:** _____

Address: _____

_____

_____

No. attending: Workshop @ 40.00 _____ **Lunch @ 10.00** _____

I am interested in the following lineages or data: _____

_____

_____

_____

Mail form and check by [Date].

- Put together a list of names of people to whom you will send information about the workshop. Send not only to individuals but also to genealogical societies in your area or region.
- If possible, allow individuals to register at the door. You can set this price a bit higher than that of pre-event registration.
- Publicize, publicize, publicize!
- Most genealogists will send you handouts to distribute at the event. Prepare a notebook with copies of this material for each attendee. If you do not provide a notebook, make certain everyone receives the handouts.
- Name tags are a must, along with a list of those who have registered. If you are catering the lunch, make different-colored name tags for those who have paid for lunch. Otherwise, at lunchtime you will not be able to differentiate easily between those who have paid and those who haven't.
- Prepare a list of jobs for the volunteers: working the registration table, setting up refreshments, selling books, and so on.

- If you are taking some registrations at the door or you are selling books, provide a cash box with change.
- Prepare an evaluation of the workshop with space for suggestions for next year.

You can send the registration form to anyone interested in attending a genealogical workshop. Include information you will need to set up the workshop as well as information for those who attend from out of town.

Educational Scholarships

Historical societies are especially interested in advancing history education among students. Many donate scholarship money for students wishing to study history. Some might be willing to furnish money to pay a student a stipend to work in your archives during a summer. Other groups sponsor writing contests in which students compete for scholarship money. If there is a college or university nearby, a society can endow a scholarship in its name to assist a young person with education expenses. This is especially helpful when the scholarship is designated for student workers in your archive.

Historical societies typically establish the scholarships in the history departments of colleges and universities. They should discuss any fund with the Development Office on campus. Usually, an endowed scholarship must start with $10,000. The fund can be named for the organization or in memory of an individual. Many universities will allow the scholarship to go to an individual who works in your archives. If desired, the societies or friends group may opt to pay for a scholarship each year or each semester.

An organization may wish to provide a scholarship directly to a graduating senior in the public schools or as a prize for a writing or speaking contest. The Daughters of the Republic of Texas frequently sponsor contests on a particular topic of interest to their organization.

Exhibits/Displays

Exhibits are a great way to celebrate a special occasion in the history of a society or organization. Use that group's special day or event to put together an exhibit about the organization, write an article for the local newspaper, and/or put the information on your website. Ask the members of the groups to participate in some way so that they support the event.

Displays and exhibits can benefit both your archives and your local historical and genealogical societies. First, such displays can entice individuals to your archives who might not normally visit. In addition, a display can bring attention to the societies and organizations that help you, such as the local historical society. You can create a display that celebrates an important date in a group's history, such as its founding, or some other important event that the group's members would like to promote.

Exhibits and Displays

Here are some things to think about when considering an exhibit or a display:

- If you do not have a display area, consider buying or having someone create one. Make certain it has a lock for security purposes.
- Work with your historical societies to develop topics for display. Make sure the archives has materials, objects, or photographs that relate to particular topics.
- Advertise, advertise, advertise!
- Send invitations to those whom you know would be interested.
- Provide light refreshments if you have a location outside the archives. The societies are usually willing to help do this.

Conclusion

As an archivist, you must plan ahead, and you must look for ways to market your archives and the collections held there. Historical, genealogical, and lineage societies plus friends organizations are vital to your public relations. Customer, or patron, service is your prime method of getting the word out that you hold something special and are willing to care for the collections entrusted to your archives and to assist the individual who walks through your doors in any way possible. It is your job to make certain you have finding aids or inventories to point the researcher in the correct path. Develop your volunteer base to assist you in your tasks. Marketing means much more than simply advertising; marketing for the archivist is your means of survival and gives you a future. If you are new to the field, visit archives within your vicinity and ask questions.

THE PLAN

1. Include in your marketing plan a list of the historical and genealogical societies with which you deal regularly.
2. Formulate guidelines for working with volunteers from historical and genealogical societies, and make these a part of your plan.
3. Copy the forms presented in this chapter, modify them to your needs, and include them in your plan.
4. Make sure someone in your archives has the authority to deal with historical and genealogical societies, and lay out their duties and responsibilities in your plan.

References

Finch, Elsie Freeman, and Paul Conway. 1994. "Talking to the Angel: Beginning Your Public Relations Program." In *Advocating Archives: An Introduction to Public Relations for Archivists*, edited by Elsie Freeman Finch, 5–22. Metuchen, NJ: Society of American Archivists and Scarecrow Press.

Herring, Mark Y. 1993. *Organizing Friends Groups: A How-To-Do-It Manual for Librarians*. New York: Neal-Schuman.

Thompson, Ronelle K.H., and Ann M. Smith. 1999. *Friends of College Libraries*. 2nd ed. Chicago: Association of College and Research Libraries.

Donors

Victoria Arel Lucas

Introduction

Donors are generous people who are inclined to share their wealth, even if they are not particularly wealthy. But don't expect them to beat a path to your door. For one thing, they need to know you exist. For another, they need to know why they should give their money, time, records, or other resources to your archives instead of to others. To convey the reasons why donors should choose your institution as the beneficiary of their generosity, it is necessary to both advertise your assets and to build a relationship with each prospective donor. This is called *relationship marketing*, and it requires you to get to know each donor and each prospect.

In her book *Effective Donor Relations*, Janet Hedrick (2008) tells how the fundraising profession had to change during the 1980s and 1990s to adapt not only to decreasing giving but also to decreasing loyalty by donors to groups to which they had given in the past. This trend played havoc with development programs. To meet the increased need for relationship management with regard to donors, Hedrick (2008: 20) says the new professional field of donor relations evolved to build "greater loyalty and satisfaction" among donors.

Effective Donor Relations is a handbook for a new profession represented by groups like the Association of Donor Relations Professionals (ADRP). Now, the same professionals who deal with donor relations primarily in financial terms may be the ones who also have ultimate authority over donations of records. As an archivist in an academic or nonprofit setting, you might now find your donor-relations work subsumed under the authority of the head of development or the director of donor relations.

Nevertheless, you, the archivist, are the key to encouraging loyalty and satisfaction among existing donors and marketing the archives to new prospects from a position of professional skills and personal knowledge of archives' contents and value, as well as personal relationships with donors. No matter who is in charge of institutional donor relations, you are in charge of working with donors to your archives, because "loyalty and satisfaction" are personal.

Your other marketing strategies will involve putting your archives' selling points out there. What is different about marketing to donors and prospective donors? The best answer is that you have to know a great deal more about them than you do about a random visitor to your website or library. Donors are not like researchers, who are primarily concerned with access and fee structures. Whether they give money, materials, time, and/or records, donors need understanding and communication on their own terms. It is up to you to find those terms, and in the process you have to examine your own resources and needs.

Setting Goals

Institutions often avoid going after records donations because they think that some types of collections will just naturally come to them (from alumni, community leaders, or people rumored to be planning donations). But in the meantime these "predestined" gifts may be lost to personal or natural disasters, sale, relatives, or friends (Kemp, 1978). This is true not only for records donations but also for gifts of money and other resources, which may be spent on other institutions as well as on personal assets. An archives may shine and be perfectly managed and organized, even well known to researchers, but prospective donors might not know it exists.

In other words, you should not procrastinate: there are things you can do now that will not only enhance your donor list but will also enhance your holdings. This does not mean you have to immediately call a donor or prospect and ask for something. Instead, spend some time planning your efforts to market your archives to current and prospective donors, and you will reap the rewards of that planning later.

Start by setting goals for your marketing efforts. Ask yourself and your staff these questions:

- Are you short on certain kinds of records that would be a draw to researchers or that would complete your collection in an area specified by your mission statement?

- What kinds of resources—and how much of each—do you need?

- Can your budget numbers be broken into manageable units—so much for supplies, so much for acquisitions, so much for utilities, and so on? Could you ask a donor to pay the electric bill? (In that case, would it be too cute to put a sign next to all the light switches, "Electricity courtesy of Mr. & Mrs. Smith"?)

- Do you have any needs that can be met by a donor whose name could be attached to the result—such as chairs, display cabinets, or (think big!) a new building—and publicized?

- What kinds of things will get in the way of marketing to donors—money, personnel, time? And how can these factors be mitigated or overcome?

- Which goals can be achieved realistically at this time?

Write your answers and discuss how your goals can be achieved with the resources you have.

What Do You Have to Offer?

What makes your archives so special that people would want to contribute records or resources to it? Perhaps you have already defined your selling points for other marketing campaigns; however, donors have different needs from those who use only the records and facilities of an archives. What are your selling points to donors? These are often very personal and could be idiosyncratic, but look at your archives carefully to see if you can really offer the following:

- Security
- Confidentiality
- Trustworthiness
- Recognition (to the desired degree, or anonymity)
- Permanence
- Preservation
- Reliability
- Organization
- Accessibility

One donor, who was not local to the archives in which I worked, was more concerned about security than any of the other selling points on my list. She flew out to visit the archives and questioned staff and management very closely about access to the "vault" or restricted storage area. What safeguards were there against stealing? How were records divided up and categorized? It was necessary to change some procedures to satisfy the donor—but she had a point, and her demands were reasonable. Her concerns strengthened the staff's case to management to put security measures in place that they already wanted.

Another donor was most concerned about permanence and accessibility, and he was so concerned about them that when the institution let the archivist go as a cost-cutting measure, he contacted the administration and offered to fund her position for a year on the condition that they work with him to find permanent resources to keep an archivist on staff. In this case, the donor's loyalty and general satisfaction saved a job.

In both of these cases, the archives' other assets on the checklist had been proven to the donor's satisfaction. That proof was given through marketing but on a level that many archivists did not realize as marketing. Tours, letters, e-mail, phone conversations, visits—every communication with a donor or prospective donor is marketing when it is personalized, positive, and constructive and emphasizes the assets on the checklist. (You can use much of the following information when creating the press kit discussed in Chapter 5.)

Getting Started: Collecting and Storing Donors' Personal Details

You already know your current donors, and you may have some idea of who in your community would most likely become a donor. Your main task will be to build loyalty and satisfaction (Hedrick, 2008). This means that working with donors and prospective donors is not so much sales as it is courtship. To court new donors, you need to know as much as possible about the people you will be contacting. The personal touch is very important here, and that is why you need to start with information. One way to do this is to know personal details about each donor—such as the names of their spouses and children, the nature of their gifts, and their personal preferences for privacy, communication, and inclusion—so you can converse with each one fluently.

However, knowing personal details about more than one donor would challenge the memory of an elephant, so it is important to keep complete records that are easy to access. You can keep computer records on a desktop and/or laptop computer, a USB-type or other external drive, and/or a personal-assistant application, such as an iPhone or Blackberry. Whichever device you use for your primary records, it is a great idea to back up your records on a second device.

The best place to start recording the information you already have and what you learn about prospective donors is a database. When you look for the right software to fit your needs, you will find everything from simple spreadsheets to expensive and complicated customer management software. Until you can make an informed decision about the kind of database you must customize or might have the budget to buy—or management or donors purchase for you—you can begin to enter your records into a simple spreadsheet like Microsoft Office Excel, which archives often use for initial inventories or to upload entries to databases.

When you can move to contact management software, you may want to shop for something that provides an expansible interface, with fields that can include web links, images of documents, maps, contact information, names, addresses, photographs, and other data not easily indexed in text documents or a simple spreadsheet such as Excel. You will want to make sure it is easily portable and exportable. Later in this chapter, you will find recommendations for features you can look for when choosing applications.

What Kinds of Information Should You Keep?

Begin by placing in the donor database information that is currently in your "contacts" list or Rolodex: donor or agency contact information with data about each person's family and frequent topics of conversation, such as pets, hobbies, or favorite foods. You can add notes about conver-

Why You Need a Computerized Donor List

- No one's memory is good enough to keep track of every important personal detail about your donors and prospective donors. You need to get this information out of your head and into a form that is usable by other people, not just in case of your own vacation or illness, but so that staff can help.
- You need a simple way to analyze your donor demographic; you can do this by storing the same kinds of information on each donor and making it easily accessible. You can then provide statistics at a moment's notice instead of after hours of going through paper files.
- When donors or prospective donors call, you can go to one place to look for information; you do not have to hop from Rolodex to control file to computer inventory.
- When you meet prospective donors, you can record information about them in your database and add research as you get to it.
- Most important, you need a detailed record (as scans or locations) of every control document, such as deeds of gift, inventories, and thank-you letters.

sations and meetings, addresses, maps, and other data about the donor or potential donor and likely or actual donations. Also record any surveys or personal visits.

Figure 11.1 shows some of the fields you will need in your spreadsheet, laid out in worksheet form and "wrapped" to fit on the page. The following list provides explanations for the fields shown, ending with other information you might want to include:

- **"Full" versus "preferred" name**: Chances are your donor or prospect has both a full name used for signing legal documents

Figure 11.1. Sample Worksheet for Donor Data

Full Name	Preferred Name	Cell #	Home #	Office #	Preferred #
John Paul Jones	Jordi	372-383-3829	380-283-2938	293-293-3928	home

E-mail address	Spouse's Name	Children (1)	Children (2)	Preferred comm.	Pets
jordi@nom.com	Tenille (f), see detail	Michael; see detail	Lorne; see detail	cell phone	Misty (dog) (1)
					Caroline (cat)

Car (1)	Car (2)	Lawyer's Name	Inventory	Deed of Gift	Copyright Restrictions
Dodge van, beetle green, lic. #DI2038	red Ferrari, lic. #XP3928	Quayle, Jones & Fill, LLP, 323-362-3829	26 boxes papers, videotapes; see detail	yes; see image; see control file for original	Yes, see Deed of Gift

Will?	Further Donations?	Spouse Detail			
See detail	Under discussion; see detail	2nd wife; widowed			

and a name he or she prefers in ordinary conversation. Use the full name when preparing deeds of gift, ceremonial papers, and so on. Use the preferred name when you and your staff are ready to make and accept phone calls and talk with relatives, friends, and institutional officials about your donor. Other suggestions: Make a note about your donor's preferences about being addressed by a title or nickname. For instance, some people with a doctorate prefer not to be addressed as "Doctor" while others treasure the title.

- **Phone numbers**: Gather as many as you can and note or high-light the preferred number. If that isn't the number you've had the best success with, note that as well. Include phone numbers of best contacts, family, and so on.

- **E-mail address**: Some people have more than one e-mail address. Note which one the donor most often uses and whether, in general, the donor is an e-mail communicator. Some people use but dislike e-mail or are infrequent e-mail writers.

- **Spouse's and children's names**: Enter these as soon as you can. You will be communicating with these family members as well, and you will want to ask after them as soon as you find out about them. Find out as much detail as you can about the donor's family without seeming to be merely nosy. This will help you sound concerned and interested (because you *are* concerned and interested).

- **Preferred communication method**: Always make a note of your donor's preferred means of communication as soon as you know it. You will acquire this knowledge over time unless you can get it from the donor's friends, family, acquaintances, or professional colleagues.

- **Pets**: If you're not an animal person, this might not seem important to you, but remember that pets may be important to your donor and/or his or her family. When you hear a pet's name, write it down and be sure it gets into your database. If it's a child's pet, note whose pet it is and what kind.

- **Vehicles**: Again, this might not seem important, but if Dr. So-and-So shows up at your institution's restricted gate with a box of records or a check, having a description of his or her car(s) and/or license number(s) may be of immense help. Depending on your circumstances, it also might be important to convey to staff so you get a heads-up if someone sees the donor coming and you're hip deep in another project.

- **Lawyers**: Never belittle, bypass, or ignore your donor's lawyer. Get information about that firm or person as soon as the subject comes up. This person can be an ally (or enemy!) when it comes to living wills, wills, deeds, copyright, and other legal matters, so find out the lawyer's or firm's name(s) and treat them with respect.

- **Inventory**: Having readily available information about what exactly your archives and/or library already has or what the donor has already donated is vital. When you get those "whatever became of" questions, you should be able to answer them without much research. Inventory should include all resources donated, and it should indicate whether some donations are confidential or there is restricted information available about them. You don't want to tell the local newspaper that Dr. So-and-So donated part of the money for the new building when he or she wanted that kept confidential.

- **Deed of gift and other documents**: What documents do you have in your control file? Until you can buy or customize a database that can contain entire documents, you should still scan your control file and keep a folder on your virtual desktop with filenames in your spreadsheet corresponding to those in the folder. That way you have everything—if not in one place, at least in a convenient spot when someone (your manager? your donor's lawyer? Donor Relations?) wants to know whether a deed of gift or some other document has been signed or received.

- **Copyright restrictions**: Copyright is a complicated subject beyond the scope of this chapter. Do note all documents relating to donor statements about copyright and be sure to document all conversational references to the topic.

- **Will**: This field relates to whether the topic of bequests has been discussed with the donor. All notes and correspondence about this subject should be carefully tracked.

- **Further donations**: Has the donor mentioned or promised further donations? Has an inventory or assessment been made of possible records donations? Have any actual amounts or kinds of resources been mentioned in relation to donations of money or other material goods? Carefully document that here, or refer to a file in your desktop folder.

- **Spouse detail**: It is important to know if your donor has been divorced or widowed and (possibly) whose children are whose. This is important information not only because you might want to avoid references to a divorced spouse (and other faux pas) but also because there might be legal ramifications of wills, deeds of gift, copyright, and other matters due to family complications.

- **Other possible information fields**: Obviously you want to keep track of physical addresses, mailing versus home addresses, vacation homes, and similar information. Harder to elicit would be information on how your donor feels about publicity. Some donors want to be anonymous; others like and expect public acknowledgment. People have varying degrees of comfort or discomfort with publicity. Some do not mind having their families included in publicity; others want their family life kept private and unmentioned. These matters are important to document.

Demographic information that will help you analyze your donor base and extrapolate to further prospects includes not just the physical address, but age, gender, schools attended, membership in community or professional organizations, and interests or hobbies. If you discover that half your donors are members of the historical society or graduated from a particular university, you might want to look into that further as a way to recruit other donors.

Recording Information and Finding Leads

The most important information you record with reference to a donor of records is the inventory of holdings. An initial inventory might be in any form, from a handwritten or laptop-recorded document to a spreadsheet. If you are using a spreadsheet to keep information about your donor, then be sure you make reference to every file, whether scanned or physical or born digital, that appraises or inventories your donor's records. If you are using a relational database application such as FileMaker Pro, you will be able to program the application such that you are able to jump easily from a database entry to your inventory or to link out using a URL to a webpage such as a wiki or shared web document (like Google Docs).

Incorporate or reference (at least as an electronic file in the same folder, if not in a relational database) any biographical material you can find about current or prospective donors. If prospects or donors are authors, incorporate links to or reference their works. Not only can these be conversationally useful and good material for a control file, but the topics addressed and language used by donors will help you to understand his or her interests, ethics, feelings, and preferred terms—all very important when addressing him or her. These might also be traits that cut across a donor community to be identified and exploited in marketing terms.

If you can manage it, set aside an hour a day (or even a half hour) to record information about current donors and prospects, research new prospects, and scan your control file. Do not lose any crumb of information from donors, prospects, and record keepers. If you are on the phone with Mrs. S. and she mentions that her dog Lollipop is barking and that's why she is having trouble hearing, immediately record the name of the dog. Ask her in a conversational manner for details about the dog, such as age, breed, and so forth. Record anything personal, no matter how trivial, because during the next conversation it may be a good idea to ask about Lollipop. As a conversation starter or stress reliever (talking about endowments or deaccession, for example, can be difficult and exhausting), drop in a comment about someone you know with the same breed of dog. In fact, you never know what might be useful as a demographic marker or personal identifier to help you communicate with donors, so ignore nothing.

Some of the information may be devoted to "leads" rather than existing donors—those people who are likely donors of money or records, either soon or as a bequest. For institutional records received via retention schedules and/or personal donation at retirement, prospective donors are leads as well. And probably every company has departments that drag their feet at releasing records to the archives when the time comes. Marketing your department to these recalcitrants should be one of your goals; gathering information about these department heads and staff and making contacts with them will serve you well in the future.

Making Entries with Care and Sensitivity

When recording donor information, do not betray prejudice or reveal potentially controversial attitudes. For instance, after discovering that one or more donors, prospects, or family members are LGBTQ (lesbian, gay, bisexual, transgender, or questioning), you can add a field called "gender preference" and record that fact. It is a demographic factor that could be important—particularly for an archives specializing in LGBTQ records. However, avoid at all costs using derogatory terms or comments. Even the discovery that a staff member does not get along with a donor's spouse or a sibling might be relevant to record in as tasteful a way as possible: should that staff member become unavailable to complete the negotiation, this information would explain to his or her successor why that particular family member is cold to the idea of donation.

Scout public databases and demographic surveys for fields to add to your spreadsheet. Look at local organizations, market surveys, local businesses, newsletters, and newspapers for factors that relate to the community of which the archives is a part. It is important to look out for materials and interests relevant to the mission and community of the archives, and your research should help identify these.

When gathering data, be careful to avoid the impression of nosiness or that your organization is recording information that will become public. If any donor suspects that data is being kept about him or her, you and your staff must be in a position to honestly assure the donor that the information is for staff use only and that the data will remain confidential except where the donor approves release. For instance, when writing a press release in which it is revealed that the donor is a graduate of Ole Miss and grew up in the community in which he or she currently lives, do not assume that this is public knowledge that the donor wants published. Always allow your donor to vet any information to be released in blogs, press releases, tweets, or other electronic or print media, unless the information comes from previously published sources known to be reliable and friendly (such as your institution's public relations department).

A good place to record discussions or results of the vetting process is in the donor spreadsheet or contact management application. One possibility for passing information among staff members or even to remind the recording staff member would be to include a code that indicates whether certain information has been approved by the donor to become public, or—on the other hand—revealed in confidence only. For instance, one symbol— < —could indicate that the information is confidential. A second— [—could mean that its confidentiality status has not been discussed. A third— > —could mean that the data point has been approved for public dissemination. Never betray a donor. The goal here is genuine loyalty on both sides.

Keeping Documents and Ticklers

Figure 11.2 shows the Donation Checklist from *Sample Forms for Archival & Records Management Programs* (ARMA International and Society of American Archivists, 2002) that you should use when setting up your spreadsheet or contact management software, including tickler functions.

Carefully track the progress of each of these processes (and any other relevant undertaking) so you can report to donors, archives management, and (if you have one) your donor relations department. Your database should reflect every stage of processing of your donor's records from appraisal through storage/digitization. This tracking will prove necessary for reports both to donors and management and (if you have one) to your donor relations group. Not only must you keep records of the records, but you will find it useful to note the who/what/where/when/why of contacts with your donors—as if your donor were part of his or her own record group. Otherwise, over the course of time, you may find it difficult to remember who contacted a donor when about important matters and what exactly was said.

If you receive institutional records in the course of its life cycles, regard the people from whom you collect records as donors and treat them accordingly. In this case, keep in mind that your database of contacts, inventories, acquisitions, and other processing may itself become an official record. Whatever the origin of your received records, your database will be part of your control files.

The Deed of Gift Is Paramount

One of the most important forms for an archives and one that requires continual reevaluation is the deed of gift. This form will differ according to the type and mission of a particular archives. The sample in Figure 11.3 is for a private archives receiving records from private donors. Two other sample forms are available in the *Sample Forms* workbook (ARMA International and Society of American Archivists, 2002), and other examples are listed on the website of the Archives Association of British Columbia (2009) under the heading of "Acquisition, Appraisal and Accessioning."

Calendar Pop-Ups Get in Your Face

It is very important to the relationship with donors and your institution that you follow through promptly on such things as thank-you letters, deeds of gift, and accessioning and cataloging, or at least planning these activities. If your software allows it, link out to your calendar or at the very least keep a "task" or "reminder" column that is checked every day for appointments, phone calls, a tickler e-mail, etc. Use a calendar that

Figure 11.2. Donation Checklist from *Sample Forms for Archival & Records Management Programs*

Manuscript Number/Name

Donor Name

❏ Initial Letter/E-mail/Call or Donation Received from Donor on _____

❏ Response Sent to Donor
   ❏ For Clarification of Letter
   ❏ Accepting Donation
   ❏ Declining Donation
   Notes:

❏ Further Correspondence
   ❏ Sample Deed of Gift Sent on _____
   ❏ Request for Further Information (i.e., Biographical Material)
   Notes:

❏ Waiting to Receive Items
❏ Items Received on _____

If Nonmanuscript Materials:
❏ Thank-You Letter Sent on _____
❏ Donor Added to Donor List
❏ Item Cataloged
❏ Item Shelved

If Manuscript Materials:
❏ Deed of Gift with Thank-You Letter Sent
❏ Accession Number Assigned #_____
❏ Manuscript Number Assigned #_____
❏ Waiting for Return of Deed of Gift
❏ Signed Deed of Gift Received
❏ Donor File Created
❏ Manuscript File Created, with Copies of Correspondence and Deed of Gift
❏ Collection Summary Completed
❏ Materials Rehoused/Put Into Folders
❏ Bibliographic Record Made
❏ Items Shelved
❏ Manuscript # and Name Added to Manuscript Shelf List
❏ Items Deaccessioned
Notes:

Source: From *Sample Forms for Archival & Records Management Programs* (2002) and reprinted by permission of the Society of American Archivists and ARMA International.

Figure 11.3. Aviation Safety and Security Archives Deed of Gift

EMBRY-RIDDLE
AERONAUTICAL UNIVERSITY

Aviation Safety and Security Archives
3700 Willow Creek Road
Prescott, AZ 86301

AVIATION SAFETY AND SECURITY ARCHIVES
DEED OF GIFT

Embry-Riddle Aeronautical University-Aviation Safety and Security Archives hereby accepts and acknowledges the donation of the collection of materials described below and subsequent additions to that collection.

Collection:
Description:
Restrictions:

The Aviation Safety and Security Archives accepts gifts with the understanding that the Archives makes all necessary decisions as to retention, use, display, loan, and discard.

Embry-Riddle Aeronautical University shall have and retain exclusive and absolute ownership of the material from the date the donor signs this receipt. The donor does hereby transfer any legal rights and interest in this property and subsequent additions upon their physical transfer, including copyright and literary property rights, as may be applicable, to Embry-Riddle Aeronautical University.

Material not retained by the Embry-Riddle Aeronautical University Aviation Safety & Security Archives is to be disposed of in the following manner:

Return to donor _____ Offer to donor _____ Disposition at Archives' discretion (discard or transfer) _____
                 Initial

Donor's or Agent's signature _____ Date _____

Name: _____

Address: _____

City, State, ZIP: _____

Telephone No.: _____

Email Address: _____

Accepted on behalf of the ERAU Aviation Safety & Security Archives _____ Date _____

Original retained in Aviation Safety & Security Archives.
Copy to Donor
Copy to Senior Director, Development
Copy to Library Director

_____

Conditions Governing Gifts

The Aviation Safety and Security Archives accepts gifts with the understanding that the Archives makes all necessary decisions as to retention, reformatting, use, display, loan, and discard.

The Archives will store, preserve, protect, and provide access to the gift in accordance with standard library and archives practices.

The Archives is not responsible to determine how the donor obtained the items.

The Archives is not permitted to furnish monetary appraisals of items donated.

Donated material will be made available to all researchers. Reasonable restrictions on access may be established for reasons of privacy or confidentiality. Any restrictions will be for a limited and clearly stated period after which the materials will be open for research use.

Rev. Oct. 2008

Source: Courtesy of Embry-Riddle Aeronautical University.

Figure 11.4. Example of a Pop-Up

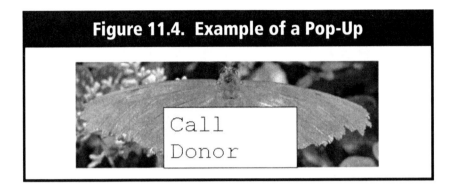

---

pops up a message on your personal computer or personal assistant device or cell phone (Figure 11.4).

If multiple staff members manage this process, use a group electronic calendar (in Microsoft Outlook or Gmail, for example). Even paper calendars can be useful, but everyone must remember to coordinate calendars. If a tickler file mentions that physical objects or papers need to be obtained, such as a deed of gift to be signed, be sure all relevant staff know where the tickler file is, and be sure that all calendar entries refer to the physical file.

Finding the Right Contact Management Application

At the same time that you are spending an hour a day transferring knowledge to and scanning control documents for your spreadsheet and related files, take a few minutes of that hour to evaluate software for contact management. These applications vary a great deal in size, portability, cost, and emphasis. Here are some suggestions for evaluation:

- Generalized databases may be used if you are willing and able to put in or buy the programming and/or setup work that it takes to modify standard database software such as FileMaker Pro, InMagic, Access, or even Excel.

- Some content management (or "asset management" or "digital asset management") software has built-in modules for information about donors or other interested parties. It could be that software already in use or under consideration has adequate space for your needs.

- Commercial sales database software—often characterized as contact management software (CMS) and customer/contact/client-relationship-management (CRM) software—might be attractive, if there is a budget for it.

- Portable applications for iPhone or similar handheld digital assistants such as Blackberrys cost a few dollars, and in some cases you can upload data from one of these devices to a desktop or laptop computer.

Beware of customizing software already in use unless you are an expert in that particular database application. It can be a time trap. Look carefully at using generic database applications before diving into these programs just because of familiarity with them. How many donors and potential donors, including contributing departments, do you anticipate? What are the storage limits of these applications? How much space is there in each field? Are website links needed and, if so, supported? Although content management software may initially have room for your data, three or four intense contacts alone can be quite a chore to maintain in terms of volume of information, and there is danger in growing out of the space available in the cataloging software.

The cost of commercial databases varies from $20 to many thousands of dollars, and most of the ones available are made for sales (*Salesforce*) or fundraising professionals (*The Raiser's Edge*), or other commercial uses. Before buying or modifying database software, you might want to familiarize yourself with these genres.

Chances are that unless you are an organization of the size and donation range of the California Academy of Arts and Sciences, you won't be in the market for *The Raiser's Edge*, the most expensive and complex software available for contact management. Its manufacturer, Blackbaud, does not list costs for *The Raiser's Edge* on its website, and most other websites where it can be purchased do not give figures either, instead referring to the "expense" involved. Michelle Murrain (2009), blogging at *Zen and the Art of Nonprofit Technology*, is specific: "There is a $10K license fee that you have to pay if you use the on premise or hosted versions. Expect a $35–45K price tag for development and integration. Their SaaS [user-hosted] offering, NC Grow has a $20K/year price tag."

If your archives is not in that class, but you have a budget for software, you may wish to look up "CMS" or "CRM" in your favorite search engine. CMS is generally slanted toward salespeople and costs around several hundred dollars. In many cases, the actual price of the software not only depends on which modules you purchase, but often a software company will withhold a price quote until you give your contact information. This typically includes your name, job title, address, work phone, and e-mail address. Many sites offering information will ask for this personal profile, so consider the consequences on your time management of giving out personal information before signing up.

If you are curious about some of the more top-of-the-line software (such as *Salesforce*), you may wish to set up an e-mail address that is different from your main one for these communications and give out only that e-mail address. When contacted by software company sales personnel, have in mind a budget figure beyond which you cannot go. In many cases, just as with digital asset management systems, contact management systems often have trial versions usable in exchange for your personal profile.

One site that compares contact management software—including side by side in a matrix—is http://salesmarks.com/, which is currently emphasizing the 2010 trend toward "cloud computing," or using online applications for information storage and manipulation. Searching for "CRM" or "customer/contact relationship management" turns up many similar sites that offer comparisons at the cost of your contact information. *CRM Magazine* covers the customer relationship management industry and can provide an idea of the size of the current market for this kind of software.

Oracle (2007), the software company whose programs are the backend for many other commercial database products, offers an online publication, "Choosing the Best CRM for Your Organization." You may find some software manuals in public or academic libraries.

Although personal phone or personal assistant applications cannot substitute for a database, they can allow you to make note of conversations, questions, and ideas while away from your personal computer. You can later transfer this information to your main files. Some portable and prospective computer applications are called "farley files," after President Franklin Delano Roosevelt's campaign manager and subsequent postmaster general, James Aloysius Farley. Farley was said to have both a prodigious memory and files for people whom Roosevelt had met, and he used those resources to brief FDR before meetings.

Evaluating Your Choices

How can you evaluate this welter of claims? One helpful product is free from the website of CRM Software Evaluation (2011). This company offers a decision matrix that can help you determine which software packages you might want to explore in depth. As described on the website, the matrix is a downloadable "software evaluation form for business software comparison." Among the types of software for which forms are offered are CRM and CMS. Although donations are encouraged to help support the site, and you can purchase copies of the spreadsheet on media, neither donation nor purchase is required, and the site does not require your personal information. This company does not appear to aggressively use contact information in the United States.

The matrix (with sample fields shown in Figure 11.5) has organized lists of criteria, such as the software's handling of call history, appointment scheduling, data import/export, document management, follow-up date callbacks, and contact management.

For instance, you probably will not care about mass mailing, but you may find the "workflow and request routing control" task necessary to keep donors in the loop about processing; with it archives staff can track what is happening to each donor's or department's requests and questions. You enter priorities for each of the suggested criteria, fill in the vendors under consideration, and score how a vendor supports each desired feature, and then the software calculates those scores and totals them so you can see how each vendor's wares support your chosen priorities.

Once you have at least two strong candidates in mind, you might find it useful to download (at no cost) and read CRM Software Evaluation's (2011) "10 Secrets to Negotiating a Better Software Deal." The authors of this guide emphasize the benefits of putting together a Request for

Figure 11.5. Sample Fields in a Software Evaluation Matrix

	A	B	C	D	E	F	G	H
1	**Section**	**Weighting Factor ()-4)**	**1st Vendor's Score**	**Running Total**	**2nd Vendor's Score**	**Running Total 2nd Vendor**	**3rd Vendor's Score**	**Running Total 3rd Vendor**
2	**Section One— Overall Software Requirements**							
3	Operating System	(You fill in) 4	(You fill in) 4	(Calculated) 4	0	0	3	3
4	Handling of Links	2	2	0	3	3	4	7
5	System Maintenance	4	2	8	3	6	1	8
6								
7	**Section Three— Reports**							
8								
9	Data export Capability	4	3	11	2	8	1	9
10	Format of reports	2	2	13	3	11	4	13
11	(Your Data) Who accesses	3	2	15	2	13	3	16
12								
13	**Section Seven—Cost Comparison**							
14								
15	Cost of software and associated costs	4	1	16	3	16	4	20
16	Training cost	4	2	18	3	19	4	24
17								
18	**0**	**0**	**0**	**0**	**0**	**0**	**0**	**0**
19	**(7 sections in all)**							
20								
21	**Section Eight—Final Score**			calculated		calculated		calculated
22	Section 1—Overall Software Requirements							
23	Section 2							
24	Section 3—Reports							
25	. . . . . .							
26	**Vendor's Total Score**			calculated		calculated		calculated

Source: Software Evaluation, http://www.software-evaluation.co.uk.

Proposal for the more expensive software and being ready to negotiate with software companies concerning the package you require and can afford, taking into consideration the common "bundling" of features, some of which you might not need or want.

Selling Your Budget to Management

These days, with performance-based evaluations and pressure to relate time management to performance goals, you might find it necessary to learn and use business terms to describe and justify the amount of time spent purchasing, setting up, and populating a contact management database—as well as the time and money spent stroking donors and keeping records on contributors. To learn the corporate jargon needed to make the "business case" for funding lunches and breakfasts with donors, long-distance calls, and travel to survey and perhaps retrieve materials, among other things, pick up some publications about performance results.

One publication available at this writing is a free e-book offered by Dow Jones on their website (Thieke, 2011). Once again, registration with personal and workplace information is required, but I have not experienced a lot of contact from this organization as a result.) Such concepts as "communications performance indicators," "balanced scorecard," and "six sigma" might be useful—although be warned that fashions change in business buzzwords, and next year these terms may be dated. Use the web and contacts and meetings with your institution-wide donor relations and PR professionals, local or online marketing courses, and/or contacts with community clubs and organizations to keep abreast of the current trends in evaluation of performance and justification of expenditures.

Drawbacks of Database Software

Because most archives already maintain at least one database software package, you may already be aware of some of the downside of the software. Following is a list of possible drawbacks to using database software:

1. Databases require painstaking setup and maintenance. As Susan Taylor and Mark Mitchell (1996: 22) write in their article "Building Donor Relations," database setup takes time and money: "Developing a database system may be expensive in terms of managerial and clerical time devoted to developing, organizing, and maintaining the database. Your initial development may require several months of work before yielding a usable database."

2. Databases require frequent backups. Considering that a donor database—whatever form it takes—must remain private, look carefully at backup media and storage options. Even maintaining a completely professional attitude when entering data—while it might save staff the embarrassment of having Dr. D. find out that they call him "Pookie" behind his back—will not make up

for the sense of betrayal any donor or record keeper will feel at discovering that his or her private information has been made public. This applies as much to Joe in Corporate Communications as it does to a university's multimillion-dollar donor. Consider using as backup USB or external mechanical drives that get locked up after use rather than keeping the redundant copies on a networked drive.

3. Attention-to-privacy issues entail careful consideration and work. You have to be in a position to assure donors and corporate partners of their privacy and the confidentiality of their information, so, first and foremost, password protect the donor database. Although it is necessary to back up the database, do not allow access to any copy of it by any unauthorized person.

4. Databases sometimes run out of room or cease to be supported by software companies. If either situation happens to your archives, it is urgent that you export data, so be sure that whatever database you choose can do so easily. Also, be sure that the exportation process is documented for staff use.

Now That You Have Your Database, What's Next?

You've chosen a database software package and it is now installed on your computer. You are ready to use it to build that loyalty and satisfaction that is so necessary to good donor relations. Following are some ideas for using the information in the database.

Prioritizing and Recording Your Tasks

Because an archivist's work is never done, prioritizing work and meeting self-imposed deadlines are important. A database coupled with a calendar and checklists helps fight procrastination. As J. Wesley Cochran (1992: 31–33) writes in *Time Management for Librarians*, the tenth "cause of procrastination" is "lack of information." Two other causes include "feeling overwhelmed" and lack of "personal control." Calendaring tasks lays aside that "old English proverb, 'One of these days is none of these days.'"

If donors do not feel that their gifts are appreciated and cherished and their intentions realized, they will not be back, and they will not recommend the archivist's institution or department to others. An archivist's effective management of time and tasks helps keep donors happy.

Using Your Database as a Marketing Asset to Local Donors

For local donors and prospects, the way your archives looks is an important marketing point. If the archives is a stereotypical dusty and disheveled alcove, prospective donors will run the other way with their papers, and even Bernie from the marketing department will put off bringing the records due on the first of the year if he fears he will never be able to find them again. Donors' events can also show you personally to your best advantage, and do not forget you are an asset too. Your professionalism, personal touch, and community standing are assets that can be leveraged to build trust and develop loyalty to the archives that can bear fruit in the form of continuing donations and specifications in wills.

This means using your database as a lever to open up your community to archives events. Got volunteers? Get hold of them by their preferred means (hopefully indicated in your database), whether e-mail, phone, snail mail, Facebook, instant messaging, or Yahoo Group, and start to get together about the next event to be held at your archives. This is where your details about the people in your database come in handy. Are your volunteers members of other groups who could be brought in to produce, work, plan, or clean up after the event? Are they musicians, cooks, storytellers, singers, or experts in subjects your community will enjoy?

If your donors are too busy to help plan, produce, or work your event, at least invite them—and do so in a special way. Use their preferred means of contact also, making phone calls and sending out special invitations to those who prefer paper mail. Use the database to make lists of donors and prospective donors who RSVP for volunteers and/or staff at the door who will greet these special guests and make them feel welcome. Use the same lists to check up on them during the event, to put them at the speakers' table, or make them comfortable in every way your database has recorded they like.

Are your donors, prospective donors, and/or volunteers Facebook, Twitter, or other social media users? Even if they aren't, other members of your local community are. Be sure you are using these means to advertise your events and that your database records who is working with these media. Do not forget to record your event not only for your archives' own archives, but also in your database—who helped, when and how—and use these records to prepare proper thank-yous that show your genuine appreciation, with checklists and calendar notations to help you and your staff and volunteers to follow through.

Approaching Donors with Openness and Inclusiveness

Inviting donors to share in project planning and participate in successful events demonstrates openness, trustworthiness, and caring. Tailoring those invitations to different stakeholders will pay back the time and effort it takes to create a detailed database of information about donors and prospective donors. Building donor relations is not a short-term project. Databases must be built for the life of an archives, so—as in all other aspects of the job—you should think about the future and how to preserve not just donor's materials, but good relationships with donors as well as the information accumulated about donors. This information documents provenance and strengthens the archives' case for continued processing and preservation. It is important to document the knowledge received about donors as carefully as the records and contributions received, so that there can be a continuity of loyalty and satisfaction—which rightfully accrue to the archives and not to the archivist personally, but which of course also create good feelings about a caring and loyal archivist and archives staff.

Because you care about the future, you are naturally attracted to other people who feel the same way—your donors. My experience is that once I get to know donors I get to like them as well. Even if that is not always the case with difficult and demanding donors, your professionalism will carry you through. Your database should soon be full of details that will help you understand and show concern for your donors.

Simply receiving a donation and thanking the donor are not enough if the donation then seems to disappear from the archives. Unless a donor prefers anonymity, both recognition and continued news about the gift and its uses must be a part of continued communication from the archives. And if a ceremony is appropriate, it is possible to make donors light up when they are recognized for the value they have brought to the institution, especially when you demonstrate heartfelt gratitude.

Using information about the donor or department representative and his or her preferences, types of donations, and potential gifts to publicize the gifts where appropriate not only enhances communication with prospective donors but also builds loyalty. Because you now have a way of tracking conversations and correspondence with donors, use that to anticipate and root out mistaken impressions on each donor's part. For instance, some donors think they will have special privileges with regard to their physical donations in terms of use or even borrowing. Openness about the terms of gifting, as well as continued emphasis on these terms, should help to keep this from becoming an issue down the road. Spell out exactly what special privileges go with donation, whether financial or physical. Does the donor become a member of the Million Thanks Club or get invited to special tours, banquets, buffets, or meet institutional officials? All of these are great rewards and should be used liberally, but they could also be spelled out—as both enticements and as limiting factors—not in the deed of gift but elsewhere as appropriate.

Despite the fact that many archives are attempting to implement the Greene and Meissner (2004) guidelines that suggest paths to "more product, less process" for making collections more quickly accessible, backlogs still exist. This means that not every donation will be processed immediately. There should be careful documentation of any discussion with donors and prospects about processing priorities, and—if you can find a way to do it—bringing up the subject of donating money for processing. In a corporate archives where access is expected immediately or soon after accession, you should broach the question of resources with the manager of the department needing access. Perhaps that department can help with staffing or lobby for more resources for the archives. It might not be helpful to have this conversation twice with the same person, so be sure to record it along with any follow-up.

Related conversations with private donors needing to be revisited but not broached more than once are those of endowments and deferred giving. These are important to document thoroughly and immediately after occurrence.

When recording leads and related goals, be sure to look into issues of competition and cooperation with other archives. If a prospective donor has expressed interest in your institution, but you know that records of this sort are being collected by another institution, it is your duty to point out the other collection. Then it is absolutely necessary to record the fact that X University's collection was mentioned by staff. The fact that ethical behavior prevailed can then be demonstrated should there be any questions later.

Managing Donor Expectations

Along the same lines, carefully recording disclosures, disclaimers, and discussions and agreements can be very valuable if future disagreements should arise. This is especially true where deaccession is concerned. It is extremely important for the loyalty and satisfaction of donors that they understand the archives' deaccession policy or—in the case of institutional record keepers—the terminal stage of the document life cycle. This is a delicate subject with most donors, who do not like to think that their materials may one day be discarded. It may be unthinkable by staff as well during accession. However, the donor must understand *up front* that the day may come when his or her collection of precious materials might no longer fit the mission of the archives or be supportable by its resources. See ARMA International and Society of American Archivists (2002) for good advice on deaccession (under "Archives II. Disposition/Accessioning"). Two deed of gift forms are included in this workbook, which features a sample "Deaccessioning Policy" on pages 10 and 11 (unnumbered) after the green "Archives II. Disposition/ Accessioning" tab. The deed of gift must include a section on what the donor wants done with his or her materials should deaccession become inevitable.

Guidelines for deaccession might change. The Society of American Archivists currently has an official Deaccessioning and Reappraisal Development and Review Team working on guidelines, with a proposal as submitted to the Standards Committee currently available at http://www.archivists.org/saagroups/acq-app/ReappraisalDeaccessioning GuidelinesProposal.pdf. Along with the brief discussion of the topic, the sources cited there can be useful to anyone struggling with deaccession and reappraisal policies. The *Sample Forms* workbook has what is probably the best advice, capital letters and all: "WHEN IN DOUBT, DO NOT THROW IT OUT!" (nineteenth page under "Archives II Disposition/ Accessioning").

Replevin is another sticky matter that proper documentation and expectation management might help. Along with the establishment of trust and loyalty through open communication, documentation of donor expectations is important to prevent disappointment. Use the donor database to document conversations in which each donor, prospective donor, or record keeper expresses expectations. In my experience both as a donor and as an archivist, there is often no time or too little time allotted to discussions of donor expectations. Keep in mind that, notwithstanding a deed of gift, the donor can always take back what he or she has given, and documentation of the donor's expectations and discussions about those expectations can ensure that, if replevin ever comes up, it will not be due to misunderstandings about archival policy and procedures.

If donor expectations—either in the present moment of discussion or later in perusal of notes or transcription—appear to be deviating from the archives' policy, mission, or resources, you must address the issue. For instance, if a donor expects immediate access to his or her records, you must point out that there may be an interval in which access will not be possible. If the donor feels—as many donors have—that continued use of his or her donated records and/or artifacts includes borrowing (not just scanning, photocopying, and/or photographing) and using without regard to archives staffing or the requests of other patrons, you must steer some conversation toward archival policy. You can use initial marketing materials in the form of brochures or webpages to broach the subject of what happens to records once donated.

Where repeated solicitation of money and/or records is concerned (always the case with continued accessions under retention schedules), continual communication between you and the donor is as important as precise documentation. With continuous records, personnel turnover becomes less important as a factor in data loss, and, with the precise information available through identifying demographics in a database, how to solicit which donor and when are clearer. The success of repeated solicitation will still be based on donor satisfaction.

Donor satisfaction is based on expectations being addressed, and it is your responsibility to manage expectation and practice openness with donors. Continued communication about what an archives is doing with a donor's gifts also contributes to satisfaction if the donor's expectations are met. In this way, effective communication contributes to the development of loyalty and satisfaction, but communication can be difficult.

Sometimes the hardest thing to do is say "no." A donor database will help in understanding donors and how best not to offend by saying "no" to one or one part of a gift, while saying "yes" to another or keeping your options open for the future. If you have kept notes and references on donors' values and pronouncements, you can use the donor's own opinions and knowledge in discussion with him or her about the reasons for turning down a gift. Your careful database documentation will also help prevent contradiction of what staff members have said and accepted before.

Marketing Media

Once you have entered all information on donors and the prospective donor community in a database, you will more easily see the best means of reaching them. If there are 50 people and/or institutions in the donor database, perhaps 25 of them will respond to e-mail, another 15 to telephone calls, nine to hardcopy newsletters and letters, and the other one only to a personal visit. It will be necessary to tailor activities—a blog attached to e-mail, a printed newsletter, telephone calls asking whether the recipient would like a report on specific activities or would be interested in an event—to the donors' and prospects' preferred communication media.

This does not mean you have to write a separate blog and newsletter, but you might have to print the blog or newsletter—perhaps with a few modifications—and mail it as well as post it. Some of the donor audience might respond to Twitter or social media such as Facebook, which might be a good place to connect with at least part of the target donor community.

Donors are not a wholly separate market from other groups in your target population, and some of what you produce for others may work for them as well as recruit from other groups. For instance, if your institution is educational, consider your alumni magazine or newsletter. The magazine covers in Figure 11.6 show how an alumni magazine—in this case from Embry-Riddle Aeronautical University (ERAU)—can do double duty to both thank and honor donors and also to recruit alumni by demonstrating how donors are treated.

The covers and cover stories of these issues are devoted to donors Harry Robertson, who has donated significant time, money, and records to ERAU, and Christine and Steven Udvar-Hazy, who donated the money for a new library. Their selected institution is showing appreciation for these valued donors, but the other side of that coin is the message to alumni that they can be placed in the same seat of honor if they too devote some of their wealth to supporting their alma mater. Inside one of these issues is a "philanthropic report," with pie charts breaking down "giving" by source, type, and purpose, as well as lists of names recognized for giving money and their affiliation with "Gift Societies and Clubs."

Some alumni and donors may respond to such appeals. This is a broadcast, not a narrowcast, and given your database you will be capable of narrowcasts with much more specificity. Surveys—formal or informal—may help you decide how to reach or attempt to reach your potential and actual donor population. Here are some ways of taking surveys that will return a better response than you would get through the mail:

- Hold a dinner, buffet, brunch, special exhibit, or tour for donors and potential donors. Before you let them leave, ask them to fill out a short survey about their preferences.

- When you contact your donors, or they contact you, ask them informal questions about their preferences.

- Pose questions in blogs, podcasts, on your website, or in your Twitter topics.

- Print surveys to be filled out at events or during open hours.

Figure 11.6. How Alumni Magazines Can Market to Donors: Two Covers from *Lift* Magazine Published by Embry-Riddle Aeronautical University

Source: Courtesy of Embry-Riddle Aeronautical University.

- Give prizes, special favors, tours, or other goodies to those who include their personal information so you can contact them further.

The preferences of most interest are your donors' most favored ways of listening to the world. The most important thing you want to know about them is the media they use. Do they read print magazines and newsletters? Do they blog or read blogs? Do they tweet, listen to podcasts, or go to events? If they like to attend events, what kinds do they like best? Extrapolate from the answers you get to a prospective population of donors who do the same things in the same proportions, and note the responses you get in your database where you know the identity of the person who filled out the survey.

What should also pop out of your demographic analysis is what else target donors have in common—what kind of music they prefer, whether they like being recognized in public, how often they like to hear from the archives. It will be possible to target groups and individuals according to their preferences and language. As the archives makes trial runs with different media, record responses in the database—or lack of responses—when using each medium. Keep in mind that narrowcasting using electronic media and postal mail is the least expensive way to reach a donor audience once enough is known about them to know how best to reach them.

What to Say

Now that you know how best to communicate with your donors, what do you say? Here is where your selling points come in. Use that checklist what you have to offer and feature points in your blog or tweet or podcast or newsletter or magazine article.

- How does your archives stay secure, and how are you monitoring security? Without revealing any secrets, what are the methods and mainstays and who are the people involved in your security? Tell personal stories.

- What makes your archives trustworthy? For a moment, put yourself in the place of someone who knows nothing about how archives are collected and organized, and perhaps describe a little of how papers and artifacts are authenticated, transported, organized, and preserved. How are they kept separate, one collection from another?

- How are your donors recognized? What are their privileges and honors? Are there societies, friends groups, clubs? Do you give banquets, buffets, or tours? Are donors recognized by signs, plaques, photographs, or in publications? Is it okay if someone is too modest for signs and bookplates? And if someone wanted anonymity, how would records be kept without revealing the identity of the donor?

- How do your donors know that their records or their investment will be there for their grandchildren or other heirs? Even the Eastman Company wound up selling its archives to pay off debt; how are you different? What sustains you and makes your archives permanent where others might be shaky? (Hint: your institution, your donors, your community.)

- How are your records and artifacts preserved? Here you can really hook your readers/viewers/listeners not only with juicy stories of how you have preserved things but also—where you do not mind giving away some knowledge—telling them how they can preserve their own stuff. This could actually be to your advantage if people are taking care of their papers and objects before they give them to your archives.

- What makes you reliable? Is it your personal integrity, the backing of your institution, the excellence of your staff, or all of the above and/or some other favorable factors?

- What is it about the organization of which your archives is a part that makes it a desirable affiliation? And in the other meaning of organization, you can market your organizational (cataloging) methods as up to date and effective.

- How have you made your records accessible, and to whom? Is it clear how and why some records are restricted? Why is accessibility a good thing? Why is restriction a good alternative to not receiving records at all? (For instance, at the archives where I worked last, there are thousands of photographs depicting scenes of aircraft accidents. After some staff deliberation, it was decided that when photographs showed human remains, they would not be placed online, and appropriate warnings would be placed on the photograph containers, because the photos would not be restricted from onsite uses. We felt it was not decent to expose the families and friends of accident victims to possible unpleasant surprises on the web nor to expose researchers to grisly scenes without warning. Nor did we want to encourage unhealthy curiosity.)

- Confidentiality is harder to describe and sell. Think of it as based on the word *confidence*. Why should donors have confidence in your ability to control information that should not be open to all? Here you cannot tell stories, but you may be able to relate how confidentiality of control files and records are accomplished in your archives.

As you communicate, keep in mind that managing and preserving a good relationship with each of your donors and potential donors is one of the most important functions of an archivist—now and for the future.

Conclusion

Marketing to donors is not a separate activity from communicating with donors. As we've seen throughout this chapter, good, personalized, open communication with donors is the path to donor loyalty and satisfaction, and these are the twin goals we are striving to reach. Communication is enhanced by good record keeping and good accessibility of data on your part. Once there is loyalty between you and each donor, on an individual basis for the donor but extending to staff and management for the archives, the donor will think first about giving to your archives before he or she thinks about giving to anyone else. If the donor is satisfied with the way he or she is being treated, with the degree of recognition or anonymity desired, he or she will keep coming back to give gifts and accept your esteem.

THE PLAN

1. Create a list of goals for dealing with your donors, and include this list in your marketing plan.
2. Include a listing of your donors as an addendum to your plan.
3. Make an evaluation checklist to help you evaluate your programs to donors and prospective donors, and include this as a part of your plan.

References

Archives Association of British Columbia. 2009. "Acquisition, Appraisal and Accessioning." Port Coquitlam, BC: Archives Association of British Columbia. http://aabc.ca/TK_03_acquisition_appraisal_accessioning.html.

ARMA International and Society of American Archivists. 2002. *Sample Forms for Archival & Records Management Programs.* 2nd ed. Lenexa, KS, and Chicago: ARMA International and Society of American Archivists.

Cochran, J. Wesley. 1992. *Time Management for Librarians.* Westport, CT: Greenwood Press.

CRM Software Evaluation. 2011. "10 Secrets to Negotiating a Better Software Deal." CRM Software Evaluation. http://www.crm-software-evaluation.com.

Greene, Mark A., and Dennis Meissner. 2004. *More Product, Less Process: Pragmatically Revamping Traditional Processing Approaches to Deal with Late 20th-Century Collections.* University of Wyoming. http://ahc.uwyo.edu/documents/faculty/greene/papers/Greene-Meissner.pdf.

Hedrick, Janet. 2008. *Effective Donor Relations.* Hoboken, NJ: John Wiley & Sons.

Kemp, Edward C. 1978. *Manuscript Solicitation for Libraries, Special Collections, Museums and Archives.* Littleton, CO: Libraries Unlimited.

Murrain, Michelle. 2009. "CRM & CMS Integration: Blackbaud Raiser's Edge and NetCommunity." *Zen and the Art of Nonprofit Technology* (blog), February 13. http://zenofnptech.org/2009/02/crmcms-integration-blackbaud-raisers-edge-and-netcommunity.html.

Oracle. 2007. "Choosing the Best CRM for Your Organization." Oracle. http://www.oracle.com/us/products/applications/siebel/051087.pdf.

Taylor, Sue Lee, and Mark A. Mitchell. 1996. "Building Donor Relations: Enter Database Marketing." *Nonprofit World* 14, no. 6: 22–24.

Thieke, Diane. 2011. "Talk to Me: 10 Tips for Translating PR Results into the Language of Business." *Dow Jones Insight.* http://www.dj.com/ebook/2008/talktome/index.asp?from=hptracking_talktome24feb2009&segment=Marketing.

Additional Resources

Bajaly, Stephen T. 1999. *The Community Networking Handbook.* Chicago: American Library Association.

Bybee, Howard C. 1999. "Reducing Gift Anxiety through Carefully Worded Gift Policies." In *Gifts and Exchanges: Problems, Frustrations, . . . and Triumphs*, edited by Catherine Denning, 15–31. Binghamton, NY: Haworth Press.

Daniels, Maygene F., and Timothy Walch. 1984. *A Modern Archives Reader: Basic Readings on Archival Theory and Practice*. Washington, DC: National Archives and Records Service.

Daubert, Madeline J. 1993. *Financial Management for Small and Medium-Sized Libraries*. Chicago: American Library Association.

Foss, Sam Walter. 1975. "Some Cardinal Principles of a Librarian's Work." In *American Library Philosophy: An Anthology*, edited Barbara McCrimmon, 31–38. Hamden, CT: The Shoe String Press.

Greer, Roger C., Robert J. Grover, and Susan G. Fowler. 2007. *Introduction to the Library and Information Professions*. Westport, CT: Libraries Unlimited.

Juarez, Miguel. 2005. "Donor Relations for Librarians." *Art Documentation* 24, no. 1: 38–41.

Lane, Alfred H. 1980. *Gifts and Exchange Manual*. Westport, CT: Greenwood Press.

McCook, Kathleen de la Peña. 2000. *A Place at the Table: Participating in Community Building*. Chicago: American Library Association.

Pearce-Moses, Richard. 2005. "A Glossary of Archival and Records Terminology." Chicago: Society of American Archivists. http://www.archivists.org/glossary/index.asp.

Varlejs, Jana, ed. 1992. *Agents of Change: Progress and Innovation in the Library/information Profession*. Jefferson, NC: McFarland & Company.

College Students

Gregory A. Jackson

Introduction

University students, especially those in graduate-level library programs, know that there is an archives or special collections repository on their campus, but undergraduate students are less likely to have use for such a mysterious trove of information. Only about 37 percent of archives users are undergraduates—despite there being higher numbers of users when total number of students is considered (Allison, 2005). The majority of undergraduate research materials are books from the library shelves or easily searchable electronic journals. Undergraduate students and graduate students in fields other than history or library science need to become comfortable with archives to further their research skills and reach their full scholarly potential.

Although students generally recognize college and university libraries as "the place to be" for research, the same is not necessarily true for archives or special collections repositories. Although undergraduate students may consider research papers to be mandatory and tedious, archivists can show these students how relevant special collections can be to their research. Cathy Johnson and Wendy Duff (2005) speak of researchers building social capital by making "deliberate efforts to establish a relationship" with the archivist, believing it will pay off later. Archivists should not delay in undertaking this deliberate building of social capital—though temporary due to the short time students are in school—with the college students within their reach. College and university students in archives programs are already members of professional associations. At the end of Fiscal Year 2008, the Society of American Archivists (2008a) noted that a whopping 21.5 percent of its membership were students.

The next generation of professional archivists will come from these ranks of young men and women. By ensuring that they understand the importance of special collections repositories and archives to further not just academic research, but pure and directed research in many fields, archivists just may fertilize a budding young archivist as well.

Connecting with college students cannot be accomplished through passive acts; it requires archivists and manuscript librarians to come out of the stacks and meet the students where they live and learn—in classrooms, coffee shops, internships, career days, school club meetings, social events, and even in the school paper. To properly build these relationships, it is not enough to think "out of the box"—the archivist must think "out of the office." In addition to getting out from behind the desk, it is important to extend an open invitation to students to visit, research, and even browse exhibits. Outreach implies actions that go beyond the normal audience or segment of the population. Archivists should:

- Take outreach literally as the act of reaching out—doing something or reaching people outside of the usual bounds of the archives user community.
- Extend outreach to help students become familiar with collections and how to use them.

This chapter will explore different programs and outreach efforts and exhort the archivist to come out of the stacks and meet the students on their own turf.

Archives Outreach to College Students

It is impossible to tell when outreach as an art or science became mainstream, but some organizations such as the Society of American Archivists and the Mid-Atlantic Regional Archives Conference have had outreach committees for more than a decade. A sampling of different organizations and institutions such as the Library of Congress, Smithsonian Institution, University of Pennsylvania, and the Mid-Atlantic Regional Archives Conference (MARAC) yielded, as one might expect, a variety of outreach efforts that ranged from a spiffy new website or brochure to fellowships and internships. Staff at some institutions have been doing outreach for years as a regular function of their duties, although more informally or in a less centralized way. For example, the Library of Congress has done K–12 outreach since the 1990s, but there are also junior fellowships and internships given to undergraduate students, graduate students, and young professionals by the various individual reading rooms (Library of Congress, 2009). The Mid-Atlantic Regional Archives Conference has also had an outreach committee for more than a decade (Lauren Brown, Mid-Atlantic Regional Archives Conference Archivist, e-mail message to the author, June 16, 2009).

Literature on the Topic

Although it appears that outreach, by that name, has been done for almost two decades, the amount of literature produced is small in contrast to other archival topics in general and college students in particular. Literature regarding archival outreach to college and university students is even harder to find. There are books written specifically about the operation and management of college and university archives, but often the chapter about outreach is located way in the back of the book, seeming to indicate a lack of importance. For example, *Managing Archives and Archival Institutions*, edited by James Gregory Bradsher (1989), contains two good chapters on public programs and exhibits, both near the back of the book. Jeanine Mazak and Frank Manista (2000) wrote an interesting chapter about their case study concerning archives and university freshmen, which focused more on reference, but the case study itself can certainly be seen as a form of outreach. Mary Jo Pugh's (2005) *Providing Reference Services for Archives & Manuscripts* contains a section addressing students as researchers, but, like Mazak and Manista's, it is a reference approach. More recently, literature regarding archival outreach and post-secondary school students has begun to appear. In 2008 the *American Archivist* published a pair of case studies on outreach toward college or university students: Xiaomu Zhou's (2008) study of student research activity and Wendy Duff and Joan Cherry's (2008) study examining the impact of archival orientation on undergraduate students. The publication of these two studies was a welcome addition, given the recent level of publication on the subject. Perhaps the most relevant work on the subject is Tamar Chute's (2008) chapter in *College and University Archives: Readings in Theory and Practice*. Chute's essay bears directly on the importance and types of outreach that can be utilized by a college or university archivist.

Why Is Outreach Important to Archivists?

Even though archives contain written records from which history is written and their importance is monumental, they are under-recognized by the majority of students. Often archives have no titles of their own. They are often an adjunct of another facility—usually a library, corporation, or historical society. Although experienced student researchers know that the university library holds more than books, the lack of a separate identity for the archives sometimes coincides with a lack of visibility to students.

It is unusual for an undergraduate student to conduct primary source research, except for students taking historiography or historical methods coursework. Graduate students are more likely to research thesis or dissertation topics in the archives. Only those already familiar with research (historians, journalists, genealogists) will head directly to the archives of their local government, university, or historical association.

But archives and manuscript libraries are not just about getting out information, they are also about putting in information. Countless college and university clubs and associations perform activities and even charitable works that often go unrecorded because students are not part of the "information in" process. Unless students are made aware of the purpose (or even just the existence) of the archives, much of the "history" of their institutions will go uncollected.

Without recognition, funding for archives will decline, and resources are needed to maintain and upgrade access to the collections. This could create a vicious downward spiral, wherein reduced funding makes archival collections less useable, and, being less useable, they will be considered a poor use of resources, resulting in further funding reductions. The inverse of this can be true, also. When archives are seen as a highly visible and active part of public life, they are more likely to attract funding as well as patrons. And the more patrons that a repository serves, the better the justification for increased funding that will allow for increased staffing and better access.

For archivists in colleges and universities, being on students' radar screens as early as possible enhances research experiences for both students and archivists. It helps students get the most relevant information for the research project and helps archivists when trying to elicit the proper information needed to best assist researchers. The more students know about how to use the archives, the easier and more productive their work will be. This positive experience will translate into a larger awareness of, and appreciation for, archives and manuscript repositories in general—and an archives in particular.

Options to Consider

You will likely find it impossible to use all of the approaches found in the following pages. In fact, some of these approaches are predicated on the assumption that not only are college and university archivists interested and able to reach out to college and university students, but local historical societies or corporate archivists are as well. Some of these ideas are hard to implement in a very large university and some may be difficult in a small college. Much outreach hinges on factors outside of the archives, so no matter which type of archives environment you work in, you should be realistic in your expectations. Before you write a plan, ask yourself the following questions and consider how your answers will affect your outreach efforts. A great idea may suffer in the execution stage if it is not supported by your institution.

- Are you a subsidiary of a larger organization, such as a library or museum?
- Does this organization allow you the freedom to initiate your own projects, or does it want to "control the message"?
- Have you already established relationships with the faculty and/or students?
- Would you have the support of senior school officials (deans, head of departments, etc.) to carry out your outreach project?

Organizational Relationships

Does your archives already have a good relationship with the students at your school or with the school in your area (if you are an independent entity, such as a local historical society)? Some things may be easy to accomplish if you are a part of a college or university library, but those same efforts may be more difficult for a local archives—although not impossible. Getting access to students is more difficult if you are outside the system rather than already a part of it. Related to this is the consideration of whether an independent repository holds collections that are useable by students in the area. This is almost always the case for local historical societies. Students at any college or university with a history program or local history courses will find the collections valuable. However, if yours is a corporate archives or a specialty institution, your holdings may not directly relate to college coursework at nearby colleges or universities.

Staff Resources

Another consideration is the size of your staff and the talent that is available to carry out your outreach programs. If you are the lone arranger in your institution, you may have to scale back your ambitions, given that time spent on outreach will reduce time available for other archives functions. Evaluate the time and resources that are available to you and make a reasonable plan for connecting to students in your area. Ask yourself the following questions before you commit to a plan that may overextend your resources:

- How much time do you devote to outreach activities now?

- Is any new outreach initiative going to replace an existing one, or will you have to find more time in the work schedule to support it?

- If you undertake this project, what will go undone?

- Can you collaborate with anyone on this project?

- Can you delegate portions of this project to others?

Not every act of outreach needs to bring students into your archives; sometimes it is enough to take your collections to them. See if you can provide a useful service to your target audience in a way that works for you and for them. If you take collections or pieces of collections to a classroom, make sure you have the approval of your supervisor and make sure you document each time you take an item outside the physical confines of the archives. Also, if your policies include special considerations for handling the materials, such as gloves, follow the guidelines outside the archives; for example, provide gloves for students in the classes you visit.

Connecting Students to Archives

Following are ideas that you may be able to use to connect to college students. Each idea has a brief explanation of how to carry out the plan and a sample document or checklist. There are no detailed instructions, as your institution or archives will be different and you will need to tailor programs to situations.

Targeting College Students for Archives

1. Where do the college students hang out? Place materials about your archives there.
2. What classes offered by the college include assignments for which students could use archives research?
3. Which professors need to be convinced to make archives a part of their curricula?
4. What materials in your archives can students use for research for these classes?

Assess Your Resources

Make use of any special talents that you or your staff may possess, such as experience in graphic arts, exhibitions, public speaking, or even just being friendly. (These should be part of your press kit, discussed in Chapter 5.) Also consider what physical resources you have or will need. Do you have computers, projectors, or software? Finally, consider collaborating with a department or group that might have the resources that you lack to produce a targeted outreach campaign.

Making Connections Using Institutional Resources

Sometimes the best way to connect to students is by using the institutional resources that are already available to you—usually at little or no cost. Perhaps one of the most obvious ways to reach students is through their professors and their classes. One prominent essay on outreach makes faculty a target of outreach (Chute, 2008), but, for the purposes of this chapter, our target is students.

Other human resources may be available to you as well. If you are a college or university archivist, you should also have a good working relationship with the library staff, including the cataloger. If special collections are made available through the online catalog, more students will be able to take advantage of the materials that your repository holds. The institution's administration may also be helpful to your outreach programs. Their understanding of the relationship between research and the archives might help secure you a spot in the new-student orientation program.

Finally, do not forget the physical resources that exist on the campus. These may be available to the local historical society archives as well as to the institutional repository, especially if it holds items relating to the school or the community. Space for exhibits (or even advertising for programs) may be available on the campus if the material can support the mission of the institution or one of its departments. Because resources are often scarce, taking advantage of the ones easily available will help you complete your outreach mission.

There are many forms of outreach, and, no doubt, you will think of many that are not discussed in this chapter. Following are suggestions for reaching college students.

Faculty Outreach

One way to reach out to college and university students is through the faculty. A little preliminary work in the college/university catalog will allow you to identify classes that will likely be able to make use of your collections. If you are not a part of the institution, you can send a letter or e-mail to faculty who teach in the subject areas of your collections. Ask for a course syllabus, and try to match materials from your collections to their courses. If you can find areas that the faculty member wants to use, see if you can do an in-class or, even better, on-site orientation relating to the applicable collections. Xiaomu Zhou (2008) notes that "archivists must customize the orientation and sample materials to meet the basic needs of each individual class." If time is available, it may be useful to meet with any students during their research to see if they have what they need. It also may be useful to compose a message that the faculty member can cut and paste into an e-mail or syllabus for his or her students.

MARC Cataloging of Special Collections

Undergraduate students use the library catalog (OPAC) to find research materials for their term papers and other classroom assignments. If archives materials are not included in the OPAC, then college students

---

SAMPLE OUTREACH MESSAGE TO FACULTY

Research materials and assistance on some topics covered in this course are available in the University Archives. The University Archives is located on the ground level of Building 322. To browse a list of collections and electronic finding aids, visit the University Archives website at http://www.biguniversity.edu/library/special collections/finding_aids.htm. For more complete information concerning the archival collections, contact the archives staff at 222.333.4444 or visit the archives in person. Regular operating hours are Monday through Friday, 8 a.m.–5 p.m.

cannot find the materials and may never know to visit the archives. Work with the catalogers in your institution to make sure that archives holdings are included in the catalog.

If it is possible, have collection-level bibliographic descriptions available in the library's catalog. If you use a content management system (CMS) in your repository, you may be able to export or print a MARC record directly from your program into the library OPAC. In this case, your cataloger will probably love you, because he or she can just edit the entry (which may be lengthy) to match the style used at your repository. Needless to say, it helps to have a good working relationship with your library staff, especially the cataloger.

If possible, work together to develop a system that will highlight collections in the various subject areas, linking collections information and finding aids (either analog or digital) to the library catalog. Becoming familiar with the basic entries required for a MARC record at your institution will help you understand how to make a simple but complete catalog entry that will explain your holdings in a given area. If possible, include any subject guides, digests, references, or objects related to the collections, possibly through hyperlinks in the MARC record to outside sources on the library or archives server. See the sidebar for an example of a CMS-generated MARC entry, which has been edited for size. The original (unedited) entry was two pages long. Some catalogers have neither the time nor inclination to create catalog entries of such depth. The MARC entry's purpose is to alert a researcher to the existence of archival or special collections material related to his or her topic.

Orientation

One of the best ways to get students acquainted with who and where you are is to get a spot on a sign-in sheet for new students. Many colleges or universities are large enough to use sign-in or check-in documents. Students get a stamp, signature, or initials when they visit the various departments required. This might include the library (to obtain a card), the health center, dormitory, student services (ID card), registrar, and so on. If your school uses this system, it is a great opportunity to give students a quick overview of when you are open, what is in your collections, and how to use the archives.

In other schools, orientation may be a day- or half-day-long program in which representatives from various departments will come and give a five-minute (or longer) orientation on need-to-know topics. This is an even better opportunity: your staff will be able to cover the most important topics with all new students at once, saving time for both. The only disadvantage is not having the student visit your location, which usually is off the beaten path, in the basement or some other spot that requires a little navigation. See the dean of students, the director of student services, or whoever puts together the orientation program and let them know that you

Sample MARC Entry for a Collection

LDR 00000npcaa a 4500

005 20091021085011.0

008 010101i18972008xxeng##

099 9 _a01/us-pba-Mss-05.003

100 3 _aJones, Thomas
_d1893-1973

245 00 _aThomas Jones Family Papers
_f1897-2008

300 _a1.50
_fLinear Feet

351 _aSee Finding Aid for specific descriptions attributes.

506 _aThere are no restrictions to this collection.

520 2 _aThe collection includes correspondence to/from Thomas, his wife and some of his children and some material relating to his interest in the fine arts. Family history material from two of his children are included.

541 _aThomas Jones Family
_cThe family information housed in the Swedenborg Library Archives was donated by Sally Jones.

545 0 _aThomas Jones 1893–1973. The second son of industrialist John Jones, he became a minister. Jones resigned from his church in the midst of a serious doctrinal disagreement and helped found another church. Jones is probably most remembered as a supporter of the fine arts. A collector himself, he became widely known for his sale of a Monet painting for over 1 million dollars.

561 _aThe materials in this collection were in family custody until their incorporation into this collection.

610 0 _aJones Church

650 0 _aCollectors

655 0 _aBusiness Letters

655 0 _aClippings (information artifacts)

856 42 _3Control Card
_uhttp://archives.giantschool.edu/index.php?p=fictitious_collections/controlcard&id=6

want to connect to the students so they are aware of how you can help them. Put your archives on the itinerary for the orientation tour.

It is important, whether they are coming to see you or the other way around, that you have something relevant to say. Do not just give them the "Hi, I'm Fred the archivist and I am in the library basement" line. Tell them about your most-used collections, and let them know not just that you have material relevant to their courses, but that you are interested in what their student organizations are doing. Tell about or show any special subject or topical guides that you maintain for their use. If relevant, tell them how to browse your finding aids on the web, explain how one works, and perhaps review call slips, if you use them. Give them contact information so that they know your hours, where you are located, and the numbers to call if they have questions. Consider putting this information on a bookmark or a card so they do not need to write it all down.

Career Day

If your college or university sponsors a career day, consider taking that opportunity to speak about archives work as a career. Career days often highlight what jobs or careers can be found in various academic disciplines. This is not to be confused with a job fair during which companies come on campus to recruit. (If you are actually hiring, a job fair would be a good bet too.) Arrange for a place or table, and make yourself visible. Do what it takes—within good taste, of course—to draw attention. You might want to make available some kind of interactive attention getter or interesting information. Consider allowing students to handle historic documents (have gloves available or use sleeved material). You can use that as an opportunity to talk about the necessity of proper care for material. Or you could do something fun like assembling document boxes for speed or have a surprising facts quiz backed by information in your collections. Silly photos from the past—especially those of current professors—are also likely to entertain.

One fun activity is to have students deacidify newspaper clippings themselves by providing them with tubs full of a combination of club soda and Maalox antacid that has stood overnight in the refrigerator. Each student submerges a clipping in the solution and then places it between the pages of an old, discarded book to dry.

Do not let your table be dreary or stuffy. Do not just bring a few old items and expect to catch the attention of the students. Dress up your space with items of interest, both new and old. Use the school colors to keep your display cheery—unless your school colors are black and gray! Here are some content ideas for your table:

- Information about the professional organizations on a local, regional, and/or national level

- Examples of current employment notices from a variety of government agencies, colleges or universities, and private corporations

- Examples of job descriptions from employment notices past and present

---

Pertinent Information for Orientation Presentations

- The purpose of your archives—what do you collect?
- When are you open?
- Can the student access information or finding aids online? What is the URL?
- Can the student make requests via e-mail or an online call system?
- What services do you provide, and how much do they cost?

- Information regarding graduate education (especially if your institution does not offer it)
- Examples of large companies and government agencies in your area that employ archivists
- Descriptions of your internships or part-time student positions, if you have any
- Interesting documents that the students can look at and perhaps handle, if encapsulated
- White cotton gloves to allow touching of documents or objects
- Cloth or other material used to shade collections material from light when not needed
- Entertaining or humorous photographs or images, including those from sporting events, famous alumni, funny student (or faculty) antics, and historical events
- An example or two of professional literature, whether books or professional journals
- A pad and paper to take down names and e-mail addresses of interested students
- Your business cards; if you don't have any, have some made

Most important, bring your best smile and a sunny disposition. These will always help make a positive impression on you audience.

Exhibits

All too often, archival exhibits are restricted to the library or, even worse, the archives reading room. Try to look beyond these traditional and somewhat limiting locations, and see what you can offer students at other campus locations. Try to use display space in common areas such as the student union, dining hall, field house, or other places that students have time to view them. An exhibit in a hallway is much more likely to be ignored by students hurrying to class than one in the field house lobby where they may be lingering before or after a sporting event.

Choose the occasion and timing to maximize the impact of your exhibit. An exhibit about the college ice hockey team is perhaps less interesting if it is held during baseball season than if it went up when it looked like the hockey team was going to have a chance of making the division tournament or playoffs. Consider placing the exhibit in the field house or some other place where it will be seen by those with an interest.

Exhibits present an opportunity to show students the type of material available to them, such as the professional papers of the professor who advocated for the construction of the new science building, the change to a coeducational format, or even just a change in the way students are recruited. See the sidebar for specific suggestions for campus exhibits.

Connect to Your Target

Although using faculty, staff, administration, and exhibits provides a path to your target, it is just as useful to go out and make contact with

---

OPPORTUNITIES FOR EXHIBITS

Most buildings on campus have some kind of display area, whether it is a wall-sized trophy case in the field house or a standalone glass display case in the lobby or hallway of an academic building. Use these when you can to exhibit relevant materials from your collection. Make sure that students and faculty who see the exhibit know that the materials came from the archives.

When/Why

- **Homecoming:** This is a good time to focus on ten-year reunions with associated photos, alumni, and events.
- **Big sports rivalry:** Florida–Georgia football? Duke–UNC basketball? Johns Hopkins–Maryland lacrosse? Need I say more?
- **Anniversary of major event:** The anniversary of a major change or addition at your college/university or even in your city or state can be the basis of an exhibit. Events like moving to a coeducational environment, opening the new law school, or even the memorializing of a tragic event are possible candidates.
- **Community- or government-sponsored awareness time:** Black History Month, Disability Awareness Month, Archives Month, and so on, can be targeted.

Where/What

- **Library:** Install a revolving display of interesting collections, new accessions, items of relevance to building, the library or monthly events like Archives Month in October or Black History Month in February.
- **Archives:** This is the place to exhibit things that might not go anywhere else. Most people don't "browse" in the archives, so make it short and sweet.
- **Academic buildings:** Do you have collections regarding science or a former science professor who made an impact or won an award? The building that hosts most classes of that department would be a good candidate for a small exhibit.
- **Field house:** Highlight a current rivalry, but celebrate a past one.

---

students directly. Whether you use an e-mail or a class visit, you can communicate directly with students who are likely to want or need the services that your archives provides. Presentations or lectures on topics of interest are another avenue of outreach. Perhaps the most rewarding—and challenging—way of reaching students is to work with them directly as interns, advisory panel members, or as an advisor to a student archives group or SAA student chapter. Sometimes the direct approach is best.

Make a Direct Connection

One way that you can connect with students is to give them a helping hand when it comes to research. Let them know that you have resources that may help them with their work. Some colleges have faculty or upperclassmen available in a help center to assist with framing projects and developing lines of research. If you are faculty or staff, send an e-mail at the beginning of the year targeted to those groups that you identified earlier. If you are a local history institution, send an e-mail to those faculty members you know can use your material. They can forward it to students if they feel it is helpful. Coordinate with faculty to arrange for archives "reminders" on projects coming due in areas where your collections are relevant.

Another way to get in there with student work is to coordinate with the school newspaper. Let the editors know about your collections and how they might be used. Offer to write an occasional or recurring article about collections or items that are relevant to current events at the school or in the world at large. If your collections hold some items of unusual interest, consider highlighting them in an "item of the month" type article. While everyone has heard about the letter with George Washington's signature, how about the newspaper report of UFOs landing on the football field or bones dug up during construction? Think about the items that will catch students' attention and their imagination. Although not every archives has skeletons in their collection closets, you are bound to find some unusual or entertaining material!

Getting Out There

It is important to get out of the office and be seen around campus. Even though you may be just one of hundreds of faculty (or staff) at a large university, this can be very helpful at a small institution. In addition to being a presence on campus yourself, the archives should have a presence of its own. Sponsor a coffee shop or formal presentation. Find and invite an interesting speaker to address students (either formally or informally, or both). Consider topics of contemporary interest that are also historical. Appearances of famous alumni are a good choice.

Presentations are a good way to introduce students to local historical repositories. If that is you, consider getting in touch with the proper department at your local college or university and offering a program for their students. You might even provide a "show and tell" of objects relevant to their studies. Take this contact opportunity to leverage later archives internships or student worker positions.

Many departments have a little money in their budget to provide coffee and refreshments for such events. Take advantage of this, if it is available. If you are targeting students, provide pizza or other food. Sometimes the offer of a bagel might just be the thing that makes it worthwhile for a busy student. This is a great place for tweets or other updates—"First five students to the coffee house get a free latte!"

Ensure your advertising of any event and any "perk" offered features the repository name prominently. When introducing the speaker, give the archives a plug. One of the worst things that you can do is provide incomplete or inaccurate information regarding your program. Be sure that you have all the correct information before creating your poster or advertisement. This helps ensure that you don't forget to add missing information that you may be waiting for—intending to add it when it becomes available. Offering incomplete information (as in "call for further info") only creates another obstacle to someone who might want to attend. Make it as easy for them as possible! You would be surprised what can get left out if proper attention is not given to the process. Make sure you include:

- A proper and descriptive title for the program, not something enigmatic or confusing.

- The speaker's name (spelled correctly) and title, if applicable.

- A brief description of the program, enough that people have a clear idea of what it contains and what to expect. Ensure you use proper descriptors—such as "speech," "interactive," "workshop," or "group discussion"—to accurately describe the program.

- The date and time that the program will begin. If there are to be refreshments before or after, make it clear at what time the

---

SAMPLE OUTREACH LETTER TO A FACULTY MEMBER

Dr. Smith,

I noticed that you will be teaching "Topics in Twentieth-Century Sociology" next term, with a focus on grassroots social movements in the United States. In the Big Gigantic University Archives, we house several collections that may be relevant to your course.

The Thomas Jones papers contain hundreds of notes and letters written to his friends and others active in the African American community during the late 1950s and early 1960s. It also contains the text of presentations that he gave throughout the city regarding civil and educational rights in the community.

We also hold the Robert Williams papers. Williams was a local antiwar protester and agitator who, through the group Youth Against War, organized more than a dozen small protests outside the local armed forces recruiting stations. The Williams papers contain letters, posters, and notes from planning meetings. The group ceased operations in March 1991.

If any of your students would like to use these collections for research papers, or if you would like them to get a chance to see these collections, I'd be happy to provide a presentation to your class or host you and your students in the archives. Please feel free to contact me by phone or e-mail if you have any questions. I'm happy to provide assistance wherever I can.

Amy Jones, Archivist
Big Gigantic University Archives

speaker will actually begin the presentation. If the program is to be especially long, more than 90 minutes, make sure you say so.

- The address or location of the program. Don't assume everyone knows where things are, especially if you are advertising to people outside of your campus or town.

- If necessary, provide directions or descriptions relating to the nearest large street. For example, "Brighton Auditorium, Big Gigantic University, 2400 Campus Dr., one block south of Main St."

- Cost. If the event is free, say that.

- A phone number and e-mail address that people can use to get further information, if needed.

Archives Student Advisory Panel

Although each repository has (or should have) a guiding policy that states what the archives or manuscript repository will collect, consider taking input from students about what they feel is important to collect. This might be particularly useful for a local history, historical methodology, or anthropology class. It could be a department-wide (or even school-wide) endeavor, depending on the size of the student body. Consider what student events/activities there are on campus. Do these events generate items of enduring historical value? Who should be responsible for collecting them? What about the materials from "outsiders" (groups that are generally considered, or consider themselves, outside the mainstream of society) or underrepresented population segments? Hearing the student perspective can be enlightening, especially for those of us who have been on the faculty side of the desk for many years.

Even though you may not have the authority to decide which collections will be accessioned, consider making a case to your administration for collecting some "unofficial" perspectives on campus life. At a large university, student organizations may number in the hundreds, so you obviously cannot collect (nor might you want to collect) material from every organization. Faculty advisors to these groups can often help decide whether there is useful documentation being generated that will help tell the story of the institution. An outing group that organizes recreational trips and produces little in the way of documentation might not be as good a choice as another group that regularly organizes presentations by local politicians or community members and advertises them heavily on campus. Consider major organizations, such as the student paper, student government, or discipline board (if there is one), but do not ignore smaller, active ones, either. When discussing the idea with students, consider these questions:

- Which student or campus activities do you think have the most impact on student life?

- How are these activities manifested? Formal organizations or informal groups? Both?

- Do they leave evidence of their activities—photos, posters, papers, letters, announcements?

- Are these materials completely ephemeral? Does someone save them or the original drafts?
- Does this group or organization have impact? Longevity?
- Is the group recognized or sanctioned by the college or university?
- Is there a point of contact from which materials can be collected?
- What volume of material might appraise as being useful to a collection?
- What might be the annual cost of processing and maintaining this collection?
- What future use would be made of this material? By whom?
- How would you justify to the administration the additional cost of maintaining this collection?

Internships

Although it is always nice to have an intern to help out, internships should not mean that you have a "copy-jockey" or a gopher at your beck and call. A good internship allows a student to exercise his or her growing skills while assisting the mission of the archives. There are many different roles that interns can play in your repository, and many of them have little to do with being an archivist, although most of your candidates will likely be looking for this type of experience.

A "regular" archives internship is designed so that the intern learns what it is really like to work in an archives. Of course, no two repositories are alike, but hopefully an intern can learn the basics of best practices in any archives. Some of the tasks that you can ask of an archives intern with include helping with reference requests, updating finding aids, and processing incoming material. While interns will not likely be experienced enough to perform higher level tasks, such as conducting reference interviews or appraisals or writing complete finding aids (although second-year interns might), accompanying you while you perform these functions enhances their experience.

Designing an archives internship need not be complicated, but you should do it with care. Be sure you follow these steps:

1. Verify which faculty or administration member is responsible for internships or experiential learning opportunities.
2. Determine the requirements for awarding credit. Be sure to program enough hours and check to see what type of evaluation is necessary for assigning a grade.
3. Check with the department under which the internship will be awarded credit. What are the requirements? Who will evaluate the student and assign a grade?
4. Design your internship so that it benefits the student, not just the archives. Remember, internships are to be learning experiences, not an opportunity to exploit the student body for free labor.
5. To guard against surprises later, submit your internship plan to the responsible faculty or administration member.
6. Get the word out!

There are other tasks that students outside the usual history or library science tracks can perform. Some interns may be prepared to perform more specialized tasks, such as digitization of materials, giving them a taste of metadata systems such as Encoded Archival Description or Dublin Core (or other) metadata schemes. Creative types might be able to prepare a small exhibit for an upcoming event, such as homecoming or a game between rivals. Public relations offers another area where students can help. English or journalism students can write newsletter articles; graphics design students can make brochures. Consider the following short list of possible specialized internships:

- **Archives Processing Intern**: This is the traditional internship for and about archives. The internship should include basic training in the philosophy and purpose of archives, as well as the hands-on skills necessary for processing or research.

- **Digital Services Intern**: Is your archives' website looking tired? Or is your scanning backlog growing larger every day? Maybe a tech-savvy college student is just what you need to get that digital project going. Make your message heard in the digital world, through websites, social networking, or information sharing.

- **Archives Communications Intern**: This internship might look good to a student in the field of English, journalism, or communications. The intern would assist in the development and production of printed outreach materials, a newsletter, or articles for the campus newspaper relating to your archives or your collection.

- **Graphics Design Intern**: How would you like some new pamphlets or posters to jazz up your outreach efforts? A graphics design student might be able to give you the fresh look that you need to draw attention.

Form an SAA Chapter or Interest Group

If your institution is large enough and has an archives track program that trains future archivists, you might find it useful to form a student chapter of the Society of American Archivists (SAA). The requirements to form an SAA-affiliated chapter are available on the SAA's website in Section XIII of the governance handbook (Society of American Archivists 2011). Only graduate-level students are eligible to form SAA chapters. For smaller institutions, you can always form an unaffiliated interest group. If you have a small institution, have no graduate program, or choose not to be affiliated with the SAA, your options are broader. You can certainly operate the same way and with the same purpose but not be required to meet the mandatory requirements of the SAA, although your institution may have its own guidelines. In an e-mail to the author dated June 4, 2009, Scott Zeigler, a graduate student at Drexel University, explained that even though his group missed the SAA deadline, they formed their own group titled DUAL (Drexel University Archivists League). This group was recognized by the university, which

Forming a Student Chapter of the SAA

A student chapter seeking recognition from the Society of American Archivists must submit the following information to the SAA Executive Office at least 30 days before the Council meeting at which the request will be considered:

- The organizing document
- The name(s) and address(es) of the chief officers(s)
- A copy of the letter of recognition from the academic institution in which the chapter is located, granting the student chapter official recognition as a student organization; some small colleges may not use any standard type of chartering document, so be sure that the letter clearly notes your status as a recognized group
- A letter from the faculty advisor—either an archivist or an archival educator in the parent institution—who must be an individual member of SAA and who has indicated his or her willingness to work with the student chapter
- A list of all SAA members enrolled as students at the institution who wish to form a student chapter

required them to submit a "constitution." Of course, students may always form their own groups, unsanctioned by their college or university, but may not get the "perks" that sanctioned groups do (free meeting space, ability to advertise through institutional bulletins, etc.). (See the sidebar for information about forming a student group.)

A third option, if you have the budget and student interest, is to support a student poster presentation at the annual SAA meeting. Graduate students have created posters and presentations regarding digital archives, SAA student chapters, outreach, and electronic records (Society of American Archivists, 2008b). Rules for submitting a poster for presentation are generally found on the SAA's website pages for the next annual meeting. See the sidebar for the 2009 rules. Check each year for requirements to ensure that you've got the latest information.

Conclusion

Outreach is at its best when the archivist is actually out in the community. Yes, someone must do the processing, provide reference services, and mind the store, but many of us do not have the staff to make outreach a primary activity anyway. Take what time that you do schedule for outreach (or time that you steal away from processing or other jobs) and spend some of it out of the office. Spend it in ways that maximize your connectivity to the students. While online exhibits and programs are a type of outreach, they rely on a certain "if you build it, they will come" mentality. However, if students are not willing to come see an exhibit, they're likely not interested in "surfing" for it either. Online exhibits are certainly useful, but it is not outreach in the truest sense of the word.

Keep in mind that you do not necessarily think about things the same way that a student does. Although most of us realize this on an intellectual level, we do not always remember it on a practical level. What we think of as enjoyable and useful from an educated and relatively complacent perspective may not be worthy of the attention of a student who is trying desperately to finish three or four final papers and preparing for an examination. Pay attention to academic schedules, contemporary topics of interest, or the issues that concern the student government or the university newspaper.

Observe the dynamics at your institution. Where do students go to relax and "hang out"? Where might they be receptive to a low-level plug for the archives, and where might they be receptive to a full-blown bid for attention? Balance your perception of their greatest need (for your services) with their perception of their greatest need for your services. Remember that you will have more impact if students perceive you as giving rather than wanting.

Finally, enjoy your relationship with the students. They are beginning the same path of life with which you are already familiar. If you support them well, they will be the next generation of advocates for archives and special collections.

2009 Requirements for Submitting an SAA Poster Presentation

Individual posters may describe applied or theoretical research that is completed or underway; discuss interesting collections with which students have worked; or report on archives and records projects in which students have participated (e.g., development of finding aids, public outreach, database construction, etc.). Submissions should focus on research or activity conducted within the previous academic year. (Society of American Archivists 2009)

THE PLAN
1. Make sure any handling policies (such as wearing gloves) are included as an addendum to your marketing plan.
2. Set forth guidelines to help you and your staff deal with college students. Examples include such things as how to transport archives materials to classrooms and how to deal with professors and who has the authority to do so.
3. If you will regularly contact certain professors or student groups for public relations purposes, include a list of these in your marketing plan for easy reference.

References

Allison, A. 2005. "Connecting Undergraduates with Primary Sources: A Study of Undergraduate Instruction in Archives, Manuscripts, and Special Collections." Master's thesis, University of North Carolina-Chapel Hill.

Bradsher, James Gregory, and Mary Lynn Ritzenthaler. 1989. "Archival Exhibits." In *Managing Archives and Archival Institutions*, edited by James Gregory Bradsher, 228–240. Chicago: University of Chicago Press.

Chute, Tamar. 2008. "Perspectives in Outreach at College and University Archives." In *College and University Archives: Readings in Theory and Practice*, edited by Christopher J. Prom and Ellen D. Swain, 137–154. Chicago: Society of American Archivists.

Duff, Wendy, and Joan Cherry. 2008. "Archival Orientation for Undergraduate Students: An Exploratory Study of Impact." *American Archivist* 71 (Fall/Winter): 499–529.

Johnson, Cathy A., and Wendy M. Duff. 2005. "Chatting Up the Archivist: Social Capital and the Archival Researcher." *American Archivist* 68 (Spring/Summer 2005): 113–129.

Library of Congress. 2009. "Fellows and Interns," *Manuscript Reading Room*. http://www.loc.gov/rr/mss/interns.html.

Mazak, Jeanine, and Frank Manista. 2000. "Collaborative Learning: University Archives and Freshman Composition." In *Library Outreach, Partnerships, and Distance Education: Reference Librarians at the Gateway*, edited by Wendy Arant and Pixie Anne Mosley, 225–242. Binghamton, NY: Haworth Press.

Pugh, Mary Jo. 2005. *Providing Reference Services for Archives & Manuscripts*. Chicago: Society of American Archivists.

Society of American Archivists. 2008a. "Fiscal Year 2008 Annual Report." Chicago: Society of American Archivists (June 30, 2008). http://www.archivists.org/governance/annualreports/2008AnnReport.pdf.

———. 2008b. "The Next Generation of Archivists." *Archival Outlook* (September/October): 20–22.

———. 2009. "Archives*Records/DC2010." Chicago: Society of American Archivists. http://www.archivists.org/conference/.

———. 2011. "Student Chapters." *Governance Manual*. Chicago: Society of American Archivists. http://www.archivists.org/governance/handbook/section13.

Zhou, Xiaomu. 2008. "Student Archival Research Activity: An Exploratory Study." *American Archivist* 71 (Fall/Winter): 476–498.

Sample Archives Marketing Plan

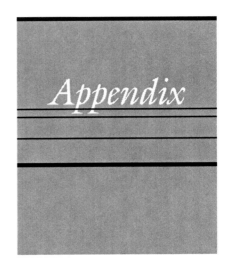
Mission Statement

The Blue Frog Archives exists as a constituent part of the University of the Peach Valley University Library System and strives to serve the public of the town Garnet Mesa, the larger population of Woody County, and the faculty, staff, and students of the university through the acquisition, preservation, and maintenance of primary source historical materials of the Quadrangle Region and making these materials available to the public for research purposes.

Target Markets/Audiences

1. Faculty, staff, and students of Peach Valley University
2. General population of Garnet Mesa
3. General population of Woody County
4. Members of the Woody County School District, including administrators, teachers, and students
5. Members of the Garnet Mesa Historical Society, the Woody County Historical Society, the Woody County Cemetery Preservation Association, the Quadrangle Genealogical Society, and the Beeswax Historical Preservation Society
6. Members of various lineage societies present in Woody County

Services Provided

1. Collection, preservation, and maintenance of historical materials
2. Preservation of community members' historical materials
3. Access to historical government records of Woody County, the City of Garnet Mesa, and the Village of Beeswax

4. Access to historical family and personal manuscripts related to the Quadrangle Region

5. Access to national and international historical genealogical and historical databases through institutional subscriptions

6. Classes on genealogical research topics

Marketing Tools and Policies

1. The archives will publish a monthly newsletter in paper and electronic format called *The Peach* and distribute it to all media agencies and all interested parties.

    a. A newsletter committee consisting of the director of the archives, the preservation archivist, and the senior secretary of the archives shall be responsible for putting together the newsletter, updating the newsletter mailing list, and editing the newsletter. The committee will put together a set of "Newsletter Guidelines" to be approved by the library director and placed as an addendum to this Marketing Plan.

    b. All electronic versions of the newsletter will conform to guidelines as set forth in Section 508 of the *Americans with Disabilities Act.*

2. A press kit containing information about the history of the archives, the extent of its holdings, special collections in its holdings, biographies of the staff of the archives, and statistics and demographics from the archives most recent annual report shall be created for distribution to the media and other interested parties.

3. A sample template for all press releases shall be created and placed as an addendum to this Marketing Plan.

4. A list of local, regional, and state media outlets shall be compiled by the senior secretary of the archives with assistance from the director of the archives and shall be annually updated. The list shall be attached as an addendum to this Marketing Plan.

5. The director of the archives shall be the official liaison from the archives to media outlets. The director shall put together a crisis management plan for dealing with the media when problems occur.

6. All photograph reproduction and sales shall be subject to the Photograph Policies developed by the archives staff and made an addendum to this Marketing Plan. These guidelines shall include procedures for publishing photographs in the archives on the web.

7. Materials and language agreed on by the archives staff that should be used in all presentations to outside groups shall be put in a written plan and placed as an addendum to this Marketing Plan.

8. All sample handouts given to outside groups during presentations shall be standardized and placed as addenda to this Marketing Plan.

9. All evaluation instruments created for assessing the success of archives programs, events, and presentations shall be placed as addenda to this Marketing Plan.

10. Policies for the proper handling of materials in the archives shall be developed and placed as addenda to this Marketing Plan.

11. All guidelines developed by the university, the library, and the archives in relation to dealing with volunteers shall be placed as addenda to this Marketing Plan.

12. A list of all groups the archives interacts with on a regular basis shall be drawn up and placed as an addendum to this Marketing Plan.

13. A list of all past donors and a second list of potential donors shall be created and placed as addenda to this Marketing Plan.

14. A website committee shall be formed and shall be responsible for the development of website guidelines and shall be responsible for updating the website, blog, and any podcasts created by the archives.
    a. The committee shall also be responsible for drafting a policy for social media use by the archives and its staff and shall attach this policy as an addendum to this Marketing Plan.

Marketing Strategies

1. Provide training and instruction in genealogical research through periodic classes offered by archives staff.

2. Market collections and services to university students by approaching faculty teaching courses relevant to the materials in the collections and to classes through onsite visits by archives staff.

3. Sponsor the Peach Valley University History Club.

4. Co-sponsor the Peach Valley University Archaeology Club.

5. Offer meeting space and guest lecturers to the various historical and genealogical societies of Woody County.

6. Create annual *Antiques Roadshow*–like event showcasing document preservation experts who appraise and evaluate historical documents brought to the event by persons attending the event.

7. Sponsor a semiannual speakers series on historical topics of interest to the archives' researchers.

Marketing Goals and Objectives

Note: Each goal and objectives set corresponds to numbers 1–7 of the previous strategies.

1A—Teach beginning genealogy courses to beginning genealogists in the community.

1AA   Teach an "Understanding the Census" and a "Using Genealogy Databases" course every two months.

1AB   Teach periodic courses on using vital records, immigration records, and other topics on a semiannual basis to beginning genealogists.

1B—Teach intermediate and advanced courses three to four times a year on topics of interest to intermediate and advanced genealogists.

1BA   Hold an annual one-day conference for genealogists, bringing in an expert to lead the workshop.

1BB   Teach intermediate and advanced courses in genealogy on a regular basis.

2A—Meet with department faculty in relevant departments at least each semester.

2AA   Meet with history, political science, and archaeology faculty whenever they request it, as well as on a semester basis.

2AB   Meet with faculty in other departments to assess the use of the collections for their coursework.

2B—Work with students in university courses to use the collections in the archives.

2BA   Offer a scholarship annually for the top research paper written using materials from the archives.

2BB   Give in-class presentations to classes.

3A—Provide space for monthly meetings of the Peach Valley University History Club.

3AA   Provide a meeting space and use of the archives bulletin board for advertisement of meetings and topics of presentations.

3AB   Provide other materials for the club as necessary.

4A—Provide space for the monthly meetings of the Peach Valley University Archaeology Club.

4AA   Provide a meeting space and use of the archives bulletin board for advertisement of meetings and topics of presentations.

4AB   Provide other materials for the club as necessary.

5A—Use the meetings of the various historical and genealogical societies of the county to advertise archives' program, activities, and collections.

5AA   Make sure a staff member is present at each meeting with some historical materials from the archives for viewing by the members.

5AB   Make sure archives' newsletters are distributed to all members via the mailing list and have copies on hand at all meetings.

6A—Hold the *Antiques Roadshow*–like event in the conference center of the library.

6AA   Provide staff from the archives and other area archives for appraisal and evaluation of the historical documents.

6AB   Make sure to include the local media in all news about events leading up to this event.

7A—Find speakers whose topics are relevant to the needs of the archives researchers.

7AA   Hold a focus group or do a survey through the archives newsletter and blog on possible topics for each speakers series.

7AB   Make sure the speakers series is heavily advertised.

About the Editors, Contributors, and the Society of American Archivists

About the Editors

Russell D. James is a professional e-book literary agent and freelance editor residing in Pensacola, Florida. As a literary agent, he specializes in working with records and information professionals. He was an archivist and records manager for more than a decade in public libraries, special libraries, and government records centers. He has written press releases for each of these. As a freelance editor, he specializes, in part, in writing press releases and has written them for small and large companies, Fortune 500 corporations, and nonprofit groups. He is the former managing editor of Cantadora Press of Pensacola, the former associate editor of the *Mexican War Journal*, is the founding editor of *Chapters and Loose Papers: A Newsletter of the SAA Student Chapters*, and has been the indexer for *Provenance: The Journal of the Society of Georgia Archivists* since 2003. He has published archives articles in *Provenance* and the *Journal of Archival Organization*. He is the author of more than a dozen books on history and genealogy and is a published novelist, poet, playwright, and short story writer, some published under various pseudonyms.

Peter J. Wosh directs the graduate program in Archives and Public History at New York University, where he has taught since 1994. His archival career has included positions at the American Bible Society in New York (1984–1994) and at Seton Hall University and the Roman Catholic Archdiocese of Newark in South Orange, New Jersey (1978–1984). His research and writing interests involve both archival topics and American religious history, and his books include *Waldo Gifford Leland and the Origins of the American Archival Profession* (Chicago: Society of American Archivists, 2011); *Covenant House: Journey of a Faith-Based Charity* (Philadelphia: University of Pennsylvania Press, 2005); with Menzi Behrnd-Klodt, *Privacy and Confidentiality Perspectives: Archivists and Archival Records* (Chicago: Society of American Archivists, 2005); and *Spreading the Word: The Bible Business in Nineteenth-Century America*

(Ithaca: Cornell University Press, 1994). Within the Society of American Archivists (SAA), he has served on the governing Council and as Editor of Print and Electronic Publications. He is a Fellow of SAA and a recipient of the Fellows' Ernst Posner Award for an outstanding essay in the *American Archivist* (2000).

About the Contributors

Suzanne Campbell is the special collections and programs librarian at Angelo State University (Texas). She teaches history courses at Angelo State and was previously a researcher at Fort Concho National Historic Landmark and a high school English teacher. She holds an MA in history from Angelo State University. She serves on the Texas Historical Records Advisory Board and the Advisory Board for Connecting to Collections for Texas and is a past member of the Texas Jewish Historical Society and the Texas Oral History Association. She has published historical articles in the *West Texas Historical Society Yearbook* and the *Journal of the Texas Jewish Historical Society*. She works closely with the historical and genealogical groups in west Texas and started her archives' Friends group.

Stephanie Gaub is collections manager and photo archivist at the Orange County Regional History Center in Orlando, Florida, where she assists museum store staff with the creation of specialized products that utilize images from the collections and actively oversees the photograph reproduction program. She previously served in archives and museum positions at the Erie Maritime Museum; the Erie County Historical Society, where she was responsible for the marketing program; and the Drake Well Museum. She holds an MA in historical administration from Eastern Illinois University and a certificate in museum collections management and care from The George Washington University. She is active in the American Association of Museums and the American Association for State and Local History. In addition, she has authored a book on the history of Orange County, Florida.

Lisa Grimm is a technology veteran, with experience working for Internet companies in the United Kingdom and United States since the mid-1990s. Her archives experience includes working at the Brooklyn Museum Libraries and Archives and as assistant archivist at Drexel University College of Medicine. She holds BA and MA degrees in archaeology from Boston University and University College London, respectively, and she obtained her MS-LIS at Long Island University's Palmer School of Library and Information Science. She is the owner and publisher of Superfectablog.com, a successful horse racing blog.

Gregory A. Jackson is the archivist at the Academy of New Church in Bryn Athyn, Pennsylvania. He oversees collections in both the Academy of the New Church Archives on the campus of Bryn Athyn College and the associated Glencairn Museum, located in the Bryn Athyn Historic Landmark District. Previously he held positions as educator and as historic site supervisor at Pottsgrove Manor Historic Site in Pottstown, Pennsylvania. He is a member of the board of directors for the Old York Road Historical Society and is the founding Chairman of the Alnwick Grove Historical Society. He holds an MA in museum studies from the University of Leicester (England) and is a certified archivist. He sponsors students as interns in his archives and works with historical methodology courses in using archives materials for their research, and he mentors undergraduate history students in their historical research and writing.

Michele M. Lavoie has been building websites for archives and special collections for more than 12 years. She is the archivist for the American Academy of Arts and Sciences in Cambridge, Massachusetts. Prior to her work with the Academy, she served as an archivist for History Associates Incorporated in Rockville, Maryland, and for The McGhee Foundation of Middleburg, Virginia. She is an active participant in the Mid-Atlantic Regional Archives Conference. She is also the author of "Caging Virtual Antelopes: Suzanne Briet's Definition of Documents in the Context of The Digital Age," published in *Archival Science* in 2003. She holds a Master of Library and Information Science with an archives concentration from the University of Pittsburgh and a BA in history from Dickinson College in Carlisle, Pennsylvania.

Victoria Arel Lucas is a senior specialist for the Electronic Technical Information Center at United Airlines. She was previously the archives/special collections librarian at Embry-Riddle Aeronautical University and project archivist in the Tobacco Control Archives at the University of California at San Francisco, and she has held positions at San Francisco State University and Stanford University. She received her Master of Library and Information Science from San Jose State University and is the author of the book *Rare Clips*. She is a certified archivist and consultant whose clients have included the Woods Hole Oceanographic Institution, the University of Waterloo, and hypertext inventor Ted Nelson.

Maria Mazzenga has served as education archivist at the American Catholic History Research Center and University Archives since 2005. After graduating with a PhD in history from Catholic University in 2000, she taught U.S. history at Virginia Commonwealth University, George Mason University, and Catholic University and worked as program manager of National History Day at the University of Maryland. She is the author of several articles on youth culture, the U.S. home front during World War II, education, and American Catholicism. She recently edited the volume *The Sound of Breaking Glass: U.S. Organized Religious Responses to the Nazis in the 1930s* (forthcoming) and is working on a book on the city of Baltimore during World War II. Her current research is on American Catholic responses to the Holocaust.

Elizabeth A. Myers is the director of the Women and Leadership Archives at Loyola University Chicago. She previously served in archives positions at the Evanston Historical Society in Evanston, Illinois, and The Newberry Library in Chicago. She holds a BA in history from Northern Illinois University and an MA and PhD in twentieth-century U.S. history, women's history, and public history from Loyola University Chicago. In addition to her work in archival education and outreach, she is active in the Chicago Area Archivists and Midwest Archives Conference. She also participates in the Women's Archives Roundtable and Women Archivists Roundtable of the Society of American Archivists.

Lauren Oostveen has spent more than half of her life online and has the blogs, tweets, videos, and "likes" to prove it. She graduated with a Bachelor of Public Relations from Mount Saint Vincent University (Canada) in 2007. She has worked in a variety of positions (communicator, social media wrangler, digitization coordinator, project lead) at the Nova Scotia Archives in Halifax, Nova Scotia, Canada, for more than three years. Lauren is also a freelance writer and has been published by newspapers, magazines, and industry papers, and she has a bi-weekly horror movie column in the *Chronicle Herald*. You can follow her on Twitter at @lauren oostveen.

William Jordan Patty is the processing archivist/librarian at George Mason University. He was previously a processing archivist at the Catholic University of America. He holds an MA in history from the University of Arkansas and a Master of Library Science from the University of Maryland. He has published archives articles in the *Journal of Archival Organization* and *Archivaria*.

About the Society of American Archivists

The **Society of American Archivists (SAA)** is North America's oldest and largest national archival professional association. Founded in 1936, SAA's mission is to serve the education and information needs of more than 6,000 individual and institutional members and to provide leadership to ensure the identification, preservation, and use of records of historical value.

Index

CPSIA information can be obtained at www.ICGtesting.com
Printed in the USA
BVOW051344051211

277601BV00004B/3/P